# A STUDY OF THE
# ETHICS OF SPINOZA

A STUDY OF THE
# ETHICS OF SPINOZA

(ETHICA ORDINE GEOMETRICO
DEMONSTRATA)

BY

HAROLD H. JOACHIM

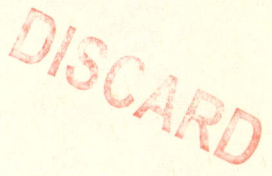

*NEW YORK*
RUSSELL & RUSSELL · INC
1964

Andrew S. Thomas Memorial Library
MORRIS HARVEY COLLEGE, CHARLESTON, W. VA.
51226

FIRST PUBLISHED IN 1901
REISSUED, 1964, BY RUSSELL & RUSSELL, INC.
L. C. CATALOG CARD NO: 64—11845

PRINTED IN THE UNITED STATES OF AMERICA

# PREFACE

THE Ethics is a work which presents many perplexities to the interpreter. Barren abstractions, tortured into the form of 'geometrical demonstrations' by a pedantic logic, appear to constitute the larger portion of it: and the remainder has been taken for poetry pure and simple. It has seemed easy to annihilate the first with a few catchwords of criticism, dismissing the second as the dreams of a mystic. In the following exposition I have tried to interpret the Ethics as a whole. I have assumed that the 'poetry' and 'imagination' which breathe through its pages are—as in a great thinker they must be—in the service of a mind, which is 'pedantic' only in its endeavour to think clearly and reason logically. The so-called 'mysticism' must, I am convinced, be read as part and parcel of Spinoza's metaphysical views; and the 'God' of the earlier parts of the Ethics must be interpreted in the light of the whole work. In the course of my exposition many difficulties and criticisms forced themselves upon me; but I have endeavoured so to arrange their discussion that it may interrupt the statement of Spinoza's views as little as possible.

Where it seemed important, I have traced the historical relation between the theories of Spinoza and those of Descartes; but I have made no attempt to give a general sketch of the latter's philosophy. It would have to be more than a sketch to be of value, and for a complete exposition I have no space.

In the desire to avoid needless obscurity I have sometimes passed over the views of well-known commentators in silence, and I hope this omission will not be attributed either to ignorance or to conceit. Wherever it was possible for me to trace a creditor I have acknowledged my debts, and in the appended list of 'References and Abbreviations' I have mentioned those commentaries which have helped me most.

In common with all English students of Spinoza, I am greatly indebted to the works of Sir Frederick Pollock, the late Principal Caird, and the late Dr. Martineau; and my obligation does not end where my interpretation differs from theirs. But, so far as I am aware, no English book appeals *only* to readers who wish to make a special study of Spinoza's philosophy; and I venture to publish this attempt at a critical exposition of the Ethics in the hope that, whatever its shortcomings, it may help to fill a gap.

I owe the interpretation of two of Spinoza's geometrical illustrations (below, p. 32 note 2 and p. 223 note 2) to the kind help of my colleague,

Mr. A. L. Dixon, Fellow and Tutor of Merton College : and I am glad to have this opportunity of thanking my friend, Dr. Robert Latta, Professor of Moral Philosophy in the University of Aberdeen, who read nearly the whole of this book before it was printed, and made many valuable suggestions and criticisms.

# TABLE OF CONTENTS

|  | PAGES |
|---|---|
| INTRODUCTION | 1–13 |

The *Tractatus de Intellectus Emendatione*. The Geometrical Method.

## BOOK I

**THE GENERAL NATURE OF REALITY** . . 14–97

### CHAPTER I

§ 1. MEANING OF THE ANTITHESES:

    (i) Substance and Mode . . . . . . 14–17
    (ii) Substance and Attribute . . . . 17–27

§ 2. INFINITE AND INDEFINITE . . . . . 27–35

### CHAPTER II

REALITY AS A WHOLE OR GOD . . . . . 36–64

§ 1. SUBSTANCE IS GOD . . . . . . . 36–38

§ 2. GOD IS THE 'ENS PERFECTISSIMUM' OR 'REALISSIMUM': INCLUDES ALL AFFIRMATIVE BEING: SUBSISTS OF INFINITE ATTRIBUTES . . . 38–41

§ 3. SOME OF GOD'S PROPERTIES. GOD IS ONE, UNIQUE, WHOLE, SIMPLE, INDETERMINATE, AND CONCRETE . . . . . . . . 41–45

# CONTENTS

| | PAGES |
|---|---|
| § 4. NATURE, VALIDITY, AND VALUE OF SPINOZA'S ARGUMENTS TO PROVE THAT GOD EXISTS OF NECESSITY | 45–58 |
| § 5. THE CAUSALITY OF GOD | 58–64 |

## CHAPTER III

### GOD AND HIS ATTRIBUTES (NATURA NATURANS)    65–72

§ 1. THE ATTRIBUTES AS 'LINES OF FORCE,' OR FORMS IN WHICH GOD'S OMNIPOTENCE MANIFESTS ITS FREE CAUSALITY TO AN INTELLIGENCE . . 65–67

§ 2. THE ATTRIBUTE OF EXTENSION. SPINOZA AND DESCARTES . . . . . . . . 67–69

§ 3. THE INFINITY OF ATTRIBUTES. THE ATTRIBUTE OF THOUGHT. GOD IS SELF-CONSCIOUS . . 69–72

## CHAPTER IV

### GOD AND HIS MODES (NATURA NATURATA)    73–97

§ 1. DEGREES OF PERFECTION OR REALITY . . 73–74

§ 2. FORMAL STATEMENT OF THE ORDER OF THE MODAL SEQUENCE . . . . . . 74–82
  (i) *Immediate* and *Mediate* infinite and eternal modes
  (ii) Particular things

§ 3. MODAL SYSTEM OF THE ATTRIBUTE OF EXTENSION. WHOLE AND PARTS . . . . 82–93

§ 4. MODAL SYSTEM OF THE ATTRIBUTE OF THOUGHT    93–97

## APPENDIX TO BOOK I

DIFFICULTIES AND CRITICISMS . . . . . 98–119
NOTE ON 'NATURA NATURATA' AND THE WORLD OF PRESENTATION . . . . . . . . 119–122

## BOOK II

### THE HUMAN MIND . . . . . . . . 123–219

#### CHAPTER I

**SOUL AND BODY** . . . . . . . . 123–145
- § 1. INTRODUCTION . . . . . . . 123–125
- § 2. THE HUMAN MIND AS THE IDEA OF THE BODY . 125–132
- § 3. CONSCIOUSNESS AND SELF-CONSCIOUSNESS . . 132–134
- § 4. SOME DIFFICULTIES . . . . . . 134–145

#### CHAPTER II

**THEORY OF KNOWLEDGE** . . . . . . 146–185
- § 1. 'IDEA' AND 'IDEATUM' . . . . . 146–152
- § 2. THE THREE STAGES OF HUMAN PROGRESS AS A DEVELOPMENT OF KNOWLEDGE . . . 152–185
  - (i) Imaginatio . . . . . . . 152–170
  - (ii) Ratio . . . . . . . . 170–180
  - (iii) Scientia Intuitiva . . . . . 180–185

#### CHAPTER III

**THE EMOTIONAL NATURE OF MAN** . . . . 186–219
- PREFATORY NOTE ON THE TRANSLATION OF THE TERM 'AFFECTUS' . . . . . . . 186
- § 1. METHOD OF TREATMENT . . . . . 187–190
- § 2. THE 'CONATUS' . . . . . . . 191–193
- § 3. WILL AND DESIRE . . . . . . 193–199
- § 4. ACTION AND PASSION . . . . . . 199–200
- § 5. 'AFFECTUS' AND 'IDEA.' THE THREE PRIMARY PASSIVE EMOTIONS . . . . . 201–208
- § 6. DERIVATIVE AND COMPLEX PASSIVE EMOTIONS . 208–218
- § 7. ACTIVE EMOTIONS . . . . . . 218–219

#### APPENDIX TO BOOK II

ESSENCE AND EXISTENCE—THE 'CONATUS'—'CUPIDITAS'—FREEDOM—TELEOLOGY—EMOTIONAL AND COGNITIVE IDEAS . . . . . . . . . 220–237

## BOOK III

**THE IDEAL LIFE FOR MAN** . . . . PAGES 238–309

### CHAPTER I
MEANING OF A STANDARD OF MORAL VALUE . . 238–254

### CHAPTER II
MAN AS A MEMBER OF THE 'COMMUNIS ORDO NATURAE': THE BONDAGE OF MAN . . . 255–263
§ 1. THE STRENGTH OF THE PASSIVE EMOTIONS, AND THE RELATIVE POWERLESSNESS OF THE ACTIVE EMOTIONS . . . . . . . . 255–261
§ 2. THE LIFE OF MAN AS INTELLECTUALLY AND MORALLY IN BONDAGE . . . . . 261–263

### CHAPTER III
THE MORAL LIFE AS THE LIFE OF REASON . . 264–291
§ 1. INDIVIDUALITY IN THE GRADE OF 'RATIO' . 264–268
§ 2. GENERAL PRINCIPLES OF THE LIFE OF 'REASON,' 'VIRTUE,' OR 'FREEDOM' . . . . . 268–273
§ 3. APPLICATION OF THE ABOVE PRINCIPLES . . 273–280
§ 4. THE POWER OF REASON . . . . 280–291

### CHAPTER IV
THE IDEAL LIFE AS CONSCIOUS UNION WITH GOD 292–309
§ 1. INTRODUCTION . . . . . . . 292–294
§ 2. THE CONCEPTION OF 'ETERNITY' . . . 294–298
§ 3. THE ETERNITY OF THE HUMAN MIND . . . 298–306
§ 4. REVIEW . . . . . . . . 306–309

# REFERENCES AND ABBREVIATIONS

## 1. DESCARTES.

Desc. Medit. = Renati Des Cartes Meditationes de Prima Philosophia.

Desc. Princ. = Renati Des Cartes Principia Philosophiae.

    Where the page is given, the reference is to the Latin edition of Descartes' works, published at Frankfort in 1692.

Desc. Epp. = Renati Des Cartes Epistulae.

## 2. SPINOZA.

VVlL = Van Vloten and Land's edition of Spinoza. Two volumes. The Hague, 1882.

TdIe = Tractatus de Intellectus Emendatione.

Tr. P. = Tractatus Politicus.

Tr. Th. = Tractatus Theologico-Politicus.

Ph. D. = Principia Philosophiae Cartesianae (Spinoza's version).

C. M. = Cogitata Metaphysica. The section-numbers referred to are those of Bruder's edition of Spinoza.

Epp. = Epistulae.

E. = Ethica ordine geometrico demonstrata.

K. V. = Korte Verhandeling van God, de Mensch, en deszelfs Welstand.

K. V. S. = Sigwart's German translation of the Korte Verhandeling.

## 3. COMMENTATORS ON SPINOZA.

Avenarius = Richard Avenarius, *Ueber die beiden ersten Phasen des Spinozischen Pantheismus*, &c. Leipzig, 1868.

Brunschvicg = Professor Léon Brunschvicg, *Spinoza*. Paris, 1894.

# REFERENCES AND ABBREVIATIONS

Busolt = Dr. Georg Busolt, *Die Grundzüge der Erkenntnisstheorie und Metaphysik Spinoza's*. Berlin, 1875.

Caird = Principal John Caird, LL.D., *Spinoza*. Edinburgh, 1888.

Camerer = Theodor Camerer, *Die Lehre Spinoza's*. Stuttgart, 1877.

Elbogen = Dr. Ismar Elbogen, *Der Tractatus de intellectus emendatione*, &c. Breslau, 1898.

Erdmann, ii = Dr. J. E. Erdmann, *Grundriss der Geschichte der Philosophie*. vol. ii. Berlin, 1878.

Erdmann, V. A. = Dr. J. E. Erdmann, *Vermischte Aufsätze*. Leipzig, 1846.

Grzymisch = Dr. Siegfried Grzymisch, *Spinoza's Lehren von der Ewigkeit und Unsterblichkeit*. Breslau, 1898.

Joël = Dr. M. Joël, *Zur Genesis der Lehre Spinoza's*. Breslau, 1871.

Loewe = Dr. Johann Heinrich Loewe, *Die Philosophie Fichte's*, &c. (with an appendix on Spinoza's conception of God). Stuttgart, 1862.

Martineau = Dr. James Martineau, *A Study of Spinoza*. Third edition. London, 1895.

Pollock = Sir Frederick Pollock, *Spinoza: his Life and Philosophy*. Second edition. London, 1899.

Sigwart, Tr. = Dr. Christoph Sigwart, *Spinoza's neuentdeckter Tractat von Gott*, &c. Gotha, 1866.

Sigwart, Sp. = Dr. H. C. W. Sigwart, *Der Spinozismus*, &c. Tübingen, 1839.

Thomas = Dr. Karl Thomas, *Spinoza als Metaphysiker*, &c. Königsberg, 1840.

Zulawski = Dr. Jerzy Zulawski, *Das Problem der Kausalität bei Spinoza*. Bern, 1899.

# INTRODUCTION

The early and unfinished *Tractatus de Intellectus Emendatione* is invaluable to students of the *Ethics*. As a fragment of a treatise on Method, it supplements Spinoza's theory of knowledge. But it has greater claims on our attention than this. For the treatise on Method is set in a framework, which exhibits the central ideas of Spinoza's philosophy with remarkable clearness. The writer of the *Ethics* comes before the world with a finished system: but the writer of the *Tractatus* allows us to see this system in the making, and shows us the motives which inspired it.

Philosophy is for Spinoza certain, demonstrable, and demonstrated knowledge. It is a system of necessary truth, whose consummation is the complete understanding of ourselves, and our place in the universe— the *most* that we are or can be. In other words, philosophy is for him the complete knowledge of human nature and life—'ethics scientifically demonstrated.' But it is also a great deal more. It is the ideal human life: for, in the complete understanding which is philosophy, we enjoy the only permanent satisfaction of our nature. This conception of philosophy—as the full knowledge, which is perfect life— is developed in the opening pages of the *Tractatus* as the outcome of Spinoza's personal experience [1].

Experience—he tells us—has taught him that none

[1] VVlL. i. pp. 3–5. The tone of the TdIe is that of a man who has passed through the stress of the struggle, and attained peace. Cf. Avenarius, p. 46.

of the objects which men usually set before themselves can yield complete satisfaction of desire. Pleasure, power, wealth—all fail to serve as a source of permanent, unbroken enjoyment. And they fail because of their nature. It is their nature to be perishable and finite; but permanent happiness can flow only from what is itself permanent and unchangeable. 'To set one's heart on something eternal and infinite—this feeds the mind with unmixed joy: an object of this kind can never be the source of sorrow and disappointment[1].'

So long as our mind is set on the pursuit of finite objects, it is impossible to fix our thoughts seriously on anything else. Yet, so far as they go, these objects satisfy desire and are 'good'—indeed the only 'goods' which experience affirms to us. Are we then to sacrifice a certain for a chimerical good? But further reflection shows that this is not the alternative that confronts us. We are in search of something completely good, as the sole remedy for the fatal disease[2] of unsatisfied desire: and this—the 'good' itself—is certain and real, and in no way chimerical. Our attainment of it is 'uncertain'— but this uncertainty diminishes with increased reflection. The end, then, is not chimerical, nor does its attainment necessarily involve the sacrifice of goods we already possess. The pursuit of power, riches, pleasure is not *in itself* incompatible with the pursuit of the supreme good: it becomes incompatible and a hindrance only if we make these objects 'ends' desirable for their own sake. But to surrender these as the ultimate ends of life is to surrender certain evils, and not to sacrifice goods. For pursue any of these objects as your ultimate end, and you will inevitably be led to despair and destruction. But it is not necessary

---

[1] 'Sed amor erga rem aeternam et infinitam sola laetitia pascit animum, ipsaque omnis tristitiae est expers.' VVIL. i. p. 5; cf. K. V. S. 2. 7, § 3.

[2] Cf. the simile, VVIL. i. p. 4.

(nor indeed feasible) to 'mortify all desires of the flesh,' in order to strive after complete happiness.

What, then, is in outline the nature of this supreme object of desire, attainment of which must afford perfect and permanent satisfaction?

To perfect knowledge, or in reality, there is no 'good' or 'bad,' no 'perfection' or 'imperfection.' Everything is what it is as a necessary consequence of the 'order of the universe' or the 'laws of nature.' But human knowledge knows only in part, sees things only from certain points of view and not in their unbroken and necessary coherence. And for that knowledge, 'good' and 'bad,' 'perfect' and 'imperfect,' express adaptation or non-adaptation to purpose. Since the purpose is not in the things, but in our view of them; and since our views are only partial and therefore many, 'good' 'bad,' 'perfect' 'imperfect,' are relative terms: and relative to such an extent that the same thing may rightly be called both 'good' and 'bad,' both 'perfect' and 'imperfect' in accordance with our varying points of view [1].

Now, in searching for the 'supreme good,' we are considering things as objects of human desire. 'Good' is that which satisfies the desires of human nature; absolutely good ('the supreme good'), that which completely satisfies those desires; relatively good (a 'true good') that which leads to this satisfaction.

But a 'good' of this kind is a state or condition of human nature itself. A 'good state' is one which we conceive to be far stronger [2], and more stable than our own, and which — for all we know to the contrary — is within our powers of attainment. A 'good,' in fact, is a *better state of ourselves*. The 'supreme good' for a man is to attain to such a development that he—if possible in common with his fellows — may enjoy

---

[1] See below, Bk. III. ch. 1; and cf. E. iv. praef., K.V.S. 1.6, §§ 7-9.

[2] Multo firmiorem—more self-sufficient or self-dependent.

a permanent realization (in his own person and in theirs) of ideal human nature, i.e. of that state which he conceives as the best human state. And—to anticipate[1]—we can say in general terms that this ideal state of human nature is 'that in which we know the union of man's mind with the whole of nature.' To know and understand *this*, would be to understand (and therefore to love) the eternal and necessary order of things. And full consciousness of this (and of our place in that order) would be perfect and permanent satisfaction of our desire[2].

This being the ultimate aim of all our efforts, we have next to consider the means. Of these the first and most important is to clear our intellect from error. Passing by, for the present, all other needs, we must turn our attention to the discovery of a method for removing the preliminary obstacles to the attainment of truth : a method to remedy the defects of our intellect, or to render it fit 'so to understand things that we may attain our supreme good.'

---

[1] VVlL. i. p. 6. 'Quaenam autem illa sit natura ostendemus suo loco, nimirum esse cognitionem unionis, quam mens cum tota Natura habet.' *Footnote of Spinoza's* 'Haec fusius suo loco explicantur.'

[2] This conception of the supreme good for man is the same as that elaborated in the Ethics (cf. E. v. praef., and Descartes, introductory letter to the *Principia*). Both in the Ethics and in the TdIe, the supreme good for man is the attainment (by oneself and others) of such development of our human nature as will enable us to 'know,' and therefore to 'love,' God, i.e. Nature. In both works this knowledge is conceived as freeing the mind from the external or alien compulsion of unreasonable passion — as 'mentis libertas seu beatitudo.'

If Spinoza's design had been completed, we should have in the TdIe the *Logica* to purge the mind of erroneous ways of thinking, that it may be fitted to attain the perfect state; and we should have in other treatises the *Medicina* for the body, the *Theory of Mechanics* for increasing the conveniences of life, the *Theories of Moral Philosophy* and *of the Education of the Young* for the formation of a suitable political society, and the *Theory of Physics* for an adequate knowledge of our corporeal selves and material things. (Cf. VVlL. i. p. 6, Descartes l.c., and E. ii. Lemma 7 S.)

At this point[1] the treatise on Method proper begins. Its details belong to Spinoza's theory of knowledge; and we need not treat of them here. But his conception of the general nature of the method is all-important for the understanding of the Ethics.

The aim of the method is to fit the intellect for the attainment of the 'best' knowledge of things. What then is the 'best' knowledge—in what form of apprehension do we most fully understand?

If the object to be known is self-dependent (and *in that sense* 'causa sui'[2]), we must, in order to understand it, grasp it solely by its own 'essential nature': if the object is dependent, we must grasp it by knowledge of its 'proximate' cause. For to understand a thing is to know why it is what it is—to see the necessity of its being. The method therefore must prepare the intellect for knowing under *this* form of apprehension—the form whereby we understand things 'per solam suam essentiam vel per cognitionem suae proximae causae.' And our task in this treatise is to lay down the method or way of thinking under this form of apprehension[3].

For let us be quite clear what a method is. The method of knowledge is that knowledge reflected on itself—the thinking of our thinking, 'cognitio reflexiva' or 'idea ideae.' If this were not so, we should never attain to any knowledge at all; we should be committed to the infinite process before we could begin to know. We should require a new method to test the truth of the first, and again a third to test the second, and so on. The case may be roughly illustrated from man's productive activities. To beat iron we require a hammer; to make a hammer we need another hammer—and so on (it might be thought) *ad infinitum*. And yet men, by the use of the simple tools with which nature provided them (e. g.

---

[1] VVlL. i. p. 7.   [2] VVlL. i. p. 30; see below, p. 53, note 1.
[3] Ib. pp. 10-16.

hands and raw material), have advanced step by step, through the perfecting of more complicated tools, to the most elaborate artistic products. So, the mind by the careful employing of its tools (the true thoughts which its inherited power has enabled it to fashion[1]) can advance step by step to a more perfect understanding.

We are not here concerned with the question as to 'how ideas arise in our mind at all.' It is enough for us at present that the mind has ideas, some of which are true: i. e. it thinks and can think truly. The aim of the treatise on Method is to trace reflectively the way in which we apprehend in true thinking: for the clear consciousness of the course of our thinking when we apprehend things through their essential nature or through their proximate cause—this itself is the method we are seeking.

We shall understand this more clearly, if we consider for a moment the nature of an 'idea.' An idea is an act of thought: to 'have an idea' is to think. Now an 'idea' must be distinguished from its 'ideatum.' The true idea of Peter, e. g., is not Peter himself: it is the 'objective essence' of Peter, i. e. *Peter as he is for thought*. And the idea of Peter, *quâ* an act of thought, has a distinctive being of its own which can in turn be the object of another thought—the 'ideatum' of another idea which presents the first idea 'objectively,' or is its *essentia obiectiva*. Every idea thus exhibits a double character. As presentative of an original, it is the 'objective essence' of its 'ideatum'; and, as an act of thought, it possesses

---

[1] 'So the intellect by its inborn power (by which I mean that which is not the effect in us of external causes) fashions for itself instruments of understanding: these give it strength for further works of understanding; from the latter it gains other instruments or the power of pushing its investigations yet further; and thus it advances step by step until it reaches the pinnacle of wisdom.' VVlL. i. p. 11.

In the footnote read 'non causatur.' VVlL. omit 'non': but it is a necessary emendation of Paulus, adopted by Saisset and Bruder; cf. Elbogen, p. 13, note 3.

# INTRODUCTION 7

a peculiar nature of its own (a 'real,' or 'formal' essence), which may in turn become the 'ideatum' of another idea[1]. This latter process may be repeated indefinitely, as is matter of common experience. Thus we all recognize that we 'know that we know,' and again 'know that we know that we know,' and so on *ad infinitum*. But we also recognize—and this is the important point—that knowledge has no need to wait for the completion of this infinite process. On the contrary: this indefinite regressive reflection itself postulates as its starting-point and condition the first idea or act of thought. In other words—applying this to our present purpose—all methods postulate the knowledge of which they are the methods; all reflection on the truth of an idea postulates the first idea or act of thinking. We cannot advance a step in knowledge, unless we can start with an idea which is itself true and the guarantee of its own truth. The test of truth must be given in the act of thinking: it cannot be applied externally by a separate act of thought. Our knowledge or certainty of truth *is* our knowing truly. If I think truly, I shall *eo ipso* be conscious that my thought is true: for to 'think truly' is to have *in idea* the real nature of the object of thought—to have *obiective* the *essentia formalis* of that which we are thinking. If I have a true idea, or think truly, I am, in the very act of thinking, convinced of the truth of my thought: and this conviction is but my way of feeling (being conscious of) the *essentia formalis* of the object of my thought[2].

A method, then, postulates as its starting-point true knowledge or a true thought of some kind. And the best method will be that which reflects upon the truest

---

[1] On this subject, and on an ambiguity in the expression 'esse obiectivum ideae,' see below, pp. 70 ff.

[2] 'Hinc patet quod certitudo nihil sit praeter ipsam essentiam obiectivam; id est, modus, quo sentimus essentiam formalem, est ipsa certitudo.' VVIL. i. p. 12.

idea—the most perfect knowledge. But there is only one idea, the grasp of which is absolute certainty: only one object of thought, the thinking of which is the complete guarantee of its own truth. For there is only one object of thought which is absolutely self-contained or self-dependent: only one object, therefore, which we can grasp fully and wholly in an act of thought. Everything except this is dependent for its being upon something other than itself: the thought therefore of everything except this calls for the thought of other things to guarantee its truth. Reality, God, Nature, the Most Perfect Being—however we name it—this alone is self-dependent and self-contained. This—and this alone—is an 'ideatum,' the clear thought of which gives complete certainty of truth. The true idea, which the method must use as a 'norm' to test the truth of all other knowledge, is the idea of the whole:—the ultimate test of all our knowledge and all reality is the complete system of experience. That alone is completely real, of which we can say 'If anything in any sense *is*, *this* must most assuredly *be* as the absolute prius of the being of everything.' And that alone is completely true of which we can say 'either *this* is true, or there is no truth.'

We can now shortly sum the principles of the most perfect method:—

(1) It must enable us to distinguish true from false, fictitious and dubious ideas, and (2) thus to keep our minds from the latter. (3) It must give us rules for apprehending things according to the norm or standard —i. e. for testing all our knowledge by the idea of the most perfect being, the source of all reality. (4) It must teach us to follow out our investigations and deductions from this idea in a due order:—i. e. so to arrange and connect our true ideas as to reduce them to dependence on the one idea which reflects the absolute prius of all being: for thus, and thus only, will our understanding

represent, as far as possible, *obiectivè* the nature of Reality, both as a whole and in all its parts [1].

It follows that a system of philosophy in its most finished expression must rest upon the idea of the 'Most Perfect Being'—that Being which is 'unique and infinite, i.e. which is all reality, beside which there is no reality[2].' The only true understanding of things is that which begins and ends with the idea of God or Reality. Hence, the Ethics begins with the idea of substance, or self-dependent being—that which is *in se* and therefore is conceived *per se*. It shows that the whole Reality (and only the whole) 'is' in this sense: and it 'explains' the world by showing how it is the inevitable consequence of this idea:—how if you develop or think out the character of the self-dependent being, the full nature of things will reveal itself to you as an intelligible system: a system as necessarily coherent as the space which you learn to know in its essential features by geometrical thinking.

*The Ethics as an example of 'the most perfect method.'*

The last illustration is not chosen at haphazard. The title of Spinoza's work is 'Ethica ordine geometrico demonstrata,' and the method of demonstration is not, for Spinoza, merely an external form into which the matter is forced. In adopting this method of exposition he is following, no doubt, in the footsteps of Descartes—at least he is carrying out a half-formed project of the latter—but he had very good grounds on his own theory of things for this proceeding. Descartes in the *Principia* professes to treat physics as geometry. Corporeal matter is simply that matter 'which is divisible, figurable, and movable in all ways—that which geometers call "quantity."' It is only with the divisions, figures, and motions of this matter that he is concerned; and he will admit nothing as true of these, unless it can be deduced from 'those common notions (Axioms), about whose truth we cannot doubt,' with the evident certainty

*The ordo geometricus.*

[1] VVlL. i. p. 16 and p. 30.  [2] VVlL. i. p. 26.

of mathematical demonstration. All the phenomena of nature, he maintains, can be explained in this way [1].

The next step is obviously to put the 'Principles of Philosophy' into geometrical form — and Spinoza, in his textbook of Descartes [2], has done so. But Descartes himself was prepared to treat metaphysics — with certain reservations — in this method, and has actually left us a fragmentary (and rather imperfect) specimen. In the second set of Objections to the *Meditations*, the objector urges Descartes to treat the subject 'more geometrico'—a method in which he is so great a master—for the better convincing of his readers. Descartes' reply is very instructive [3]. In the geometrical method, he says, the *order* and the *mode* of demonstration should be distinguished. As regards the *order*, the essential characteristic of all geometrical exposition is that nothing should be put forward which rests upon what follows. The earlier propositions must be intelligible without the later, the later must not be advanced until their grounds have been stated. This is obviously a requisite of all satisfactory exposition, and Descartes points out that he has observed this 'order' in his *Meditations*. But as regards the *mode* of geometrical proof; this is of two kinds, analytical and synthetical. The *analytical method* works back to the elements from the starting-point of the ordinary mind, and thus, if the reader will but attend, carries him to the truth over the road by which it was (or might have been) first discovered; but it does not compel an inattentive or hostile reader to accept its conclusions. This is the method of the *Meditations*— 'the best method for teaching'—and the method of Spinoza's *Tractatus*. But the ancient geometers make no open use of it; 'not,' Descartes says, 'that they were ignorant of it, but because (as I take

---

[1] Desc. *Princ.* ii. 64.    [2] Ph.D.; see Meyer's Preface.
[3] Desc. *Medit.* Resp. ad sec. obiect.

it) they valued it so highly that they wished to keep it to themselves as a professional secret.'

Hence, when mention is made of the 'geometrical method,' people are thinking of the *synthetical* mode of demonstration: that which starts from the elements (definitions, axioms, postulates), and builds up its conclusions out of them in a growing series of more and more complex propositions. It compels the reader's assent to its conclusions, by showing that they are involved in its premises—the elements, which he has admitted. And in geometry this method is very powerful; for the 'first notions' on which it depends are in accordance with our sensible experience, and therefore readily admitted by all. But in metaphysics, the clear and distinct apprehension of the 'first notions' is the most troublesome work of the whole science; for it involves a complete liberation from the prejudices of the senses. Still, to satisfy his objector, Descartes subjoins a specimen of the synthetic geometrical treatment of metaphysical subject-matter; a specimen, which is—as he admits—tentative and fragmentary.

Spinoza's use of the geometrical method may, no doubt, be regarded as a development of these hints of Descartes. The cogency and certainty of the synthetic form of geometrical demonstration must have appealed to him: its complete disregard of all teleological explanation we know strongly attracted him[1]. If the success of this method was so well established in geometry and in physics, why should it not prove equally powerful in metaphysics? To Spinoza there could be no doubt of success. Since for him the corporeal *is* the spiritual universe—since the series of physical causes and effects is the same (as an 'order') as the series of ideas—a method, which attained such brilliant results in the first, must succeed, if properly

[1] Cf. E. i. App.

applied, in the other systems of Reality. If the geometrical method explains the universe *quâ* extended, it must explain it also *quâ* 'thinking' or *quâ* conceived under any other Attribute [1].

No doubt the actual order of demonstration, the actual series of propositions in the Ethics, does not represent the order of discovery: that is perhaps exhibited rather in the *Tractatus*. Nor does it give us the only possible method of exposition. Nor again is it, simply as geometrical demonstration, a guarantee of the truth of the system [2].

Still, the method is, in Spinoza's view, adequate to the subject-matter; and, however it may appear to us, Spinoza never for one moment imagined himself to be torturing his material into an alien mould. Throughout, he makes it clear that—in his opinion—the most adequate scientific way of conceiving Reality is an extension of the geometer's method of conceiving space. It is under the categories of geometry that Reality must be thought. 'Cause' and 'effect,' e.g., to Spinoza, mean 'ground' and 'consequent'; efficient and formal cause are one and the same. To say 'God is the efficient cause of all things' is to say 'all things flow from the nature of God with the same timeless necessity as that with which the properties of a triangle eternally flow from its nature [3].' So, if we are to understand human passions and emotions, we must study them as they really are, not as we, with our human prejudices, estimate them to be. But 'as they really are' they flow from the nature of things with the same necessity with which all other consequents result. 'Accordingly,'

---

[1] See below, ch. 3. Science for Descartes and Spinoza was practically equivalent to mathematics. To treat philosophy in the geometrical method is therefore the natural result of their determination to regard philosophy as science—a demonstrable body of truth.

[2] For the Ph.D., which we know Spinoza did not wholly accept, is also in geometrical form, as Pollock well points out. (Pollock, p. 29.)   [3] E. i. 17 S. and often.

# INTRODUCTION

Spinoza says[1], 'I shall treat of the nature and strength of the passions, and of the mind's mastery over them, by the same method which I have hitherto adopted in this work: i. e. I shall consider the actions and emotions of man precisely as if I were studying the nature of lines, planes, and solids[2].'

It would be premature to enter into the problems to which Spinoza's use of the geometrical method gives rise. The consequences of his geometrical view of things are to a large extent the main features of his philosophy, and must be considered in their proper place, as parts of his system. His conception, e. g., of 'eternity' and of 'necessity': his rejection of all teleological explanation; these are at once dominant characters of his philosophy, and, if not the direct outcome of his geometrical view, at least largely coloured by it. Neither shall I attempt to criticize the method, or to point out its disadvantages—which lie, indeed, mostly on the surface, plain to view; our first task is to try to understand, and criticism at this stage would be worse than premature. But it is important to emphasize what I have already laid down: the form of Spinoza's exposition is essential to its matter. He casts his system in a geometrical mould, because the subject-matter, as he conceives it, demands such treatment. If, and in so far as, the method breaks down, we shall expect to find the inadequacy of the form revealing a corresponding defect in the matter: i. e. the geometrical method will fail, because Reality is more than the subject-matter of geometry, and therefore cannot be apprehended under geometrical categories[3].

[1] E. iii. praef.; cf. E. iv. 57 S.
[2] It is not necessary to multiply illustrations of that which every student of Spinoza can see for himself. But, in this connexion, notice how Spinoza throughout his writings chooses his examples from geometry; cf. e.g. Ep. 56, Ep. 73.
[3] Cf. below, pp. 115 ff.

# BOOK I

## THE GENERAL NATURE OF REALITY

## CHAPTER I

### § 1. MEANING OF THE ANTITHESES—SUBSTANCE AND MODE *and* SUBSTANCE AND ATTRIBUTE.

Book I. THE first part of the Ethics is concerned with the general nature of Reality[1]. Spinoza starts with the conception of Substance; proves that Reality in its absolute completeness (Deus sive Natura[2]) is the only Substance; and thence deduces his fundamental metaphysical positions.

*Substance and Mode.*

We have learnt from the *Tractatus* that a philosophical interpretation of things must begin with the idea of self-dependent or self-subsistent Reality. The subject-matter of philosophy, the Real, falls apart into two great divisions:—that which is in itself, and that which is in something else[3]. 'That, which is in itself,' i. e. that, the reality of which is self-dependent, is what Spinoza calls 'Substance[4]': 'that, which is in something else,' i. e.

---

[1] Cf. its title (de Deo) and E. i. App. sub init., ii. Praef.
[2] For the actual expression cf. E. iv. Praef.
[3] Cf. E. i. Ax. 1. 'Omnia quae sunt vel in se vel in alio sunt.'
[4] E. i. def. 3.

## SUBSTANCE AND MODE

that, whose reality is dependent, is called a 'mode,' or state of Substance[1]. We begin therefore with the antithesis of Substance and its states or modifications[2]— a more precise formulation of the popular antithesis of thing and properties, the metaphysical (though not the co-extensive[3]) correlate of the logical antithesis of subject and predicates[4].

It is important to bear in mind from the outset, that the division is within, or of, the real[5]: the modes or states of substance are not 'illusions'; they are real, though their reality is dependent on the reality of Substance in which they are[6].

Further, it is to be noticed that the antithesis between Substance and modes does not correspond to the later distinction between the thing-in-itself and its appearances. 'Modes' to Spinoza are not 'that which we know of Substance,' and 'Substance' that 'which we may think but cannot know.' There is, in Spinoza, no divorce between 'what is' and 'what is known[7],' though there is a constant distinction between complete and partial knowledge. For the present (if we are content with a rough and partly inaccurate statement of his position) we may say that, to Spinoza, *the completely real is the object of complete knowledge, and knowledge is of the real.* This is the general conception, which underlies the definitions of Substance and mode, and links the second half of each definition with the first. The second half[8]

---

[1] E. i. def. 5.
[2] Spinoza discards the form of the antithesis 'Substance and accidents' (which he had used, e.g. Ep. 4), as likely to mislead, cf. C. M. i. 1, § 11.
[3] Cf. Lotze, *Logik*, ch. 1, §§ 4 ff.
[4] Cf. e.g. Ph.D. i. def. 5, and K. V. S. i. ch. 1, note to § 7.
[5] Cf. E. i. Ax. 1 quoted in note 3, p. 14.

[6] This statement will be considerably modified below, cf. pp. 107 ff. It is, I think, true of Spinoza's *intention*, as revealed in the definitions.
[7] The difficulties, in this respect, to which Spinoza's conception of the infinite attributes gives rise, will be considered below.
[8] E. i. deff. 3 and 5.

Book I. asserts: if anything is real in the sense of being self-dependent, then knowledge of it means the conceiving it in its self-dependence or 'through itself.' And: if anything is real in its dependence on something else, then knowledge of it means the conceiving it 'through the conception of that on which it depends.' Substance, therefore, is 'that which is in itself and is conceived through itself'; Mode, 'that which is a state of Substance and therefore is in something else and is conceived through that other.' Hence it is one and the same thing for Spinoza to say that all Reality ultimately rests upon what is self-dependent; and that all true knowledge must depend upon a conception which is not itself dependent on any other [1].

From these definitions of the two sides of the antithesis it follows immediately [2] that Substance is naturally prior to its states. For the being and conception of Substance is independent of the being and conception of modes. To think Substance in its self-dependence is the only way to think it truly [3]. Not that modes are unreal, or that Substance exists in no state of itself. The more we understand the modes, the more we understand Substance; for modes are ways in which Substance is expressed [4]. The understanding of modes will teach us the understanding of Substance; for to 'understand' modes is to know them in their being, i.e. in their dependence on Substance. But the idea of Substance cannot be put together out of the ideas of its modes: the idea of a mode

---

[1] Cf. above, p. 5. *Substance* is that which we must—in the most perfect form of apprehension—grasp 'per solam suam essentiam.' *Modes* must be grasped 'per cognitionem suae proximae causae,' i.e. (as we shall see presently) through the knowledge of Substance.

[2] E. i. 1.

[3] E. i. 5 dem. ... 'depositis ergo affectionibus, *et in se considerata*, hoc est (per def. 3 et axiom. 6) *vere considerata*' ... (The italics are my own.)

[4] Cf. E. v. 24 (with i. 25 C, to which it refers for its proof).

## SUBSTANCE AND ATTRIBUTE

involves the idea of Substance, because the reality of a mode involves the reality of Substance. The general character of Substance is not altered by the particular forms which it assumes in its modes, but the general nature of modes is through and through determined by Substance. To conceive Substance through the conception of its modes, would be to conceive it as dependent for its being on their being. And this would be a misconception, for we should be endeavouring to grasp the whole through the grasp of its parts or partial expressions, forgetting that these parts are themselves unintelligible except in the light of the whole [1].

If you ask 'What is that, the reality of which is self-dependent?' you will find yourself forced to the conclusion of Spinoza. Nothing short of the complete Reality is self-dependent, i. e. 'God' or 'Nature' or the 'absolutely complete Reality' alone is 'in se,' or has 'substantial' being; everything else is 'adjectival' in its nature or has a reality dependent on that of the one Substance. But before following Spinoza to this conclusion, it is necessary to examine his conception of Attribute.

### Substance and Attribute.

At first sight it would seem as if Substance and its modes together exhausted Reality; and this is *in a sense* true. 'In the nature of things there is nothing given besides Substances and their states, as is clear from Ax. 1 and deff. 3 and 5.' (E. i. 6. C.) 'All things which are, are either in themselves or in something else (by Ax. 1); that is (by deff. 3 and 5), outside the intellect there is given nothing besides Substances and their states.' (i. 4 dem.) But the same demonstration proceeds: 'nothing therefore, which could serve as a ground of

[1] Cf. below, p. 65, note 1.

Book I. distinction between two or more things, is given outside the intellect besides Substances, or—what (by def. 4) is the same thing—besides the Attributes, and states of Substances.'

It seems clear, then, that *in some sense* Attributes and Substances are the same thing. Turning to the definition of Attribute, we find: 'By "Attribute" I mean that which intellect perceives as constituting the essential nature of Substance[1].' *The Attributes of a Substance, therefore, are the essential nature of that Substance so far as it is understood.*

A slight historical digression will confirm this statement, and at the same time prepare us for a more accurate examination of Spinoza's conception of Attribute. In the letters [2], and in an early draft of the beginning of the Ethics [3], Spinoza had actually defined Attribute in the same terms as Substance. 'By "Attribute" I mean everything which is conceived through itself and in itself, in such a way that its conception does not involve the conception of anything else. E. g. *Extension* is conceived *per se et in se*. But *motion* is conceived *in alio*, and its conception involves Extension[4].' This apparent identification of Substance and Attribute seems to have given some difficulty to certain students of Spinoza, and we find him returning to the subject in Ep. 9 [5].

---

[1] E. i. def. 4. 'Per attributum intelligo id quod intellectus de substantia percipit tanquam eiusdem essentiam constituens.' 'Constituens' is accusative neuter agreeing with 'quod'—as we learn from ii. 7 S. Intellectus, which I have translated 'intellect,' means *any* act of intelligence or understanding :—see below. Cf. i. 5. 'In rerum natura non possunt dari duae aut plures substantiae eiusdem naturae *sive* attributi.'

[2] Cf. e. g. Epp. 2, 4 and 9.

[3] So we gather from Epp. 1, 2, 3, 4, 8 and 9.

[4] Ep. 2, Sept. 1661.

[5] Simon de Vries (Ep. 8) had written (on behalf of a society of students who met to study Spinoza's manuscript writings)

After giving the definition of Substance, as we have it in E. i. def. 3, Spinoza proceeds (quoting from the MS. draft which he had sent to these friends), 'By "Attribute" I mean the same, except that it is called "Attribute" in respect to the intellect—the intellect as "attributing" to Substance the distinct nature in question. This definition, I assert, explains quite clearly what I mean by Substance or (*sive*) Attribute. Since, however, you desire it, I will add two examples to show how one and the same thing can be stamped with two names. (1) "Israel" means the third patriarch; so does "Jacob," but he was called Jacob because he had "taken hold on his brother's heel." (2) A "plane surface" means that which reflects all the rays of light without deviation; so does a "white surface," but it is called "white" in respect to the man who is looking at the surface.'

It follows, I think, from these and other passages in the same letters, that Spinoza, in his original draft of the Ethics, had retained the terminology of Descartes more closely than is sometimes supposed. Descartes, whilst admitting that God alone—the absolutely self-dependent Being—was in strictness entitled to be called 'Substance,' yet does not hesitate to call extended and thinking things (bodies and minds) 'Substances,' so far as they are independent of everything created and dependent only on God. Originally, I think, Spinoza was prepared to speak of the extended and thinking worlds indifferently as 'the *Attributes* of Extension and Thought,' or as '*Substantia* extensa' and '*Substantia*

to formulate certain difficulties—amongst them, *this* of Substance and Attribute. Spinoza answers in February, 1663 (Ep. 9). For a reconstruction of the definitions, axioms, and propositions originally sent by Spinoza to Oldenburg, see Sigwart, Tr. pp. 137 ff. Simon de Vries (in Ep. 8) is referring to a modified form of this Oldenburg draft: a form which approaches more nearly to the text of E. i, as we have it.

Book I. cogitans': and to define God as 'ens absolute infinitum constans infinitis substantiis sive attributis.' It was only to avoid misunderstanding[1] that he adopted the stricter terminology of the Ethics, according to which 'God' is the '*Substantia* constans infinitis *attributis*.' Traces of the older inaccurate terminology survive in the early letters: and E. i. 15 S. contains a direct reference to it—'Hence we have inferred that the ⟨so-called⟩ "extended Substance" is ⟨really⟩ one of the infinite Attributes of God.'

But the change of terminology marks a real change in point of view—an advance on Descartes. However much Descartes might insist that God alone was strictly self-dependent, strictly Substance; yet the bodies and minds, the 'things' which supported Extension and Thought as their adjectives, acquired in his Philosophy an independence of each other which amounted to a self-dependence of their own, and therefore required to be re-united externally. Spinoza, on the contrary, never for one moment allows himself to regard the particular bodies and minds as Substances[2]: and from the first grasps firmly the dependent nature of all being—even the extended and thinking worlds as wholes—on the one self-dependent being. Everything except the one Substance is for him adjectival in its nature. The *res extensa* and the *res cogitans* are (not two Substances with different Attributes, but) the one self-dependent Substance under two of its Attributes[3]. In framing the stricter terminology of the Ethics, Spinoza gets rid, once for all, of a twofold misinterpretation. His students can no longer suppose *either* that he agrees with Descartes in attributing a quasi-independence to the particular bodies and minds: *or* that he regards the worlds of Extension and Thought

---

[1] Such misunderstanding, e. g., as Oldenburg betrays (Ep. 3).
[2] Cf. e.g. Ep. 4.
[3] Cf. E. ii. 1 and 2.

# SUBSTANCE AND ATTRIBUTE

as in any sense self-dependent because mutually independent[1].

To return to Spinoza's definition of Attribute. For the present, for the sake of clearness, we will confine our attention to the two Attributes which the *human* intellect perceives as constituting the essential nature of the one[2] Substance:—'Extension' and 'Thought[3],' two of the fundamental characters of the ultimate Reality. So far as we can grasp the essential nature of Reality at all, we must conceive it under these Attributes. What is ultimately real manifests for our intelligence an 'extended' and a 'thinking' character. Now with regard to these two Attributes, there are four chief points to be observed:—

---

[1] Descartes (*Princ.* i. 51 ff.) explains that 'Substance' means 'a thing which exists without requiring the support or help of anything else.' Strictly, God and God alone is absolutely independent, and therefore 'Substance.' But besides God (the 'Substantia cogitans increata atque independens') there are the created works of God, which—so far as they are independent for their existence of everything except God—may be called 'Substances.' Thus the mind, or that of which all modes of thought (e.g. *imaginatio, sensus, voluntas*) are the properties, is 'Substantia cogitans creata': the body, or that of which all modes of extension (e.g. *figura, motus*) are the properties, is 'Substantia extensa creata.' They are both entitled to the name 'Substance'—in a sense *not univocal* with that in which it is applied to God—because they both are 'res quae solo Dei concursu egent ad existendum.'

[2] Strictly speaking, Substance is not 'one,' because that would imply that it was distinguished from *other* Substances, or could be counted as one amongst several realities (see below).

[3] *Extensio* and *Cogitatio*. What Spinoza understands by these will become clearer as we proceed. There is no single antithesis which can adequately represent his meaning. 'Ideal' and 'real' is in some ways satisfactory: but it suggests that 'Cogitatio' is not 'real,' and is therefore misleading.

Book I.   (1) *Each Attribute is a real character of what is.*

It is no arbitrary characterization of ours which asserts these Attributes of the Real. We do not fancy or imagine that the real exhibits these features. Reality *is* an 'extended' Reality—a corporeal, material, figured universe, a universe whose parts are 'solid,' are in motion and at rest, and so forth; and it *is* a 'thinking' Reality, a universe in which there is life, feeling, volition, thought. These characters, in whatever terms we express them, are the characters of Reality, which we find in it, but do not invent or make for it.

(2) *Each Attribute is an ultimate character of the Real.*

They are ultimate characters of Reality, in the sense that neither can be reduced to terms of the other. 'Extension' *is* not 'Thought,' nor 'Thought' 'Extension.' However we may regard the relation between them, it is undeniable that neither *is* the other; no acts of thinking or feeling, e.g., *are* the modification of the cerebral matter or the tremor of the nerves which inevitably accompany them[1]. Each attribute is thus 'complete' in itself: it 'is' and must be 'conceived' independently of any other Attribute of Reality. It is impossible to understand Extension in terms of Thought, or Thought in terms of Extension. Extension and Thought are mutually exclusive; but each is internally complete, or all-inclusive in its own kind. Whatever is in any sense 'extended' contains no positive characteristic which is not comprised in the Attribute of Extension: and all that is in any sense 'thought,' or exhibits any of the positive characteristics of 'thinking,' is wholly comprehended under the Attribute of Thought.

[1] Cf. especially Ep. 4.

(3) *Each Attribute includes the whole character which it expresses, and excludes all other characters.*

In this sense each Attribute is 'infinite' *in suo genere*: it is in itself the full, all-inclusive, expression of that character of Reality which it is. So far as 'extension' means anything or is anything real, that significance and that being are the significance and being expressed in the Attribute of Extension; and so, *mutatis mutandis*, with the Attribute of Thought. A single 'extended' thing—a particular body e. g.—is finite and dependent: a fragment torn from its context, in which alone it has its being and significance. Neither in its existence nor in its nature has it any independence. It owes its *existence* to an indefinite chain of causes, each of which is itself a finite body and the effect of another finite body: it owes its *nature* to its place in the whole system of bodies which together constitute the corporeal universe. Any attempt to explain it—to understand its essential nature—would carry you at once outside 'it,' or would force you to take 'it' as having in itself no essential nature or individuality: for 'it' is through and through constituted by its relations, and if you include these in 'its' nature, 'it' will have become merged in the whole Attribute of Extension which comprises within itself the system of extended 'relata' and 'relations.' A body, as Spinoza expresses it[1], is finite or limited in its own kind. It is not all that it professes to be—we can, e. g., always conceive a bigger body—and thus it is finite in a sense in which the Attribute of Extension is not limited. A body is, as it were, a 'part'—a limited fragment—of the Attribute of Extension. It is a 'mode' of Extension, or of Substance conceived under the Attribute of Extension; for it can neither be nor be conceived except in and through Exten-

---

[1] E. i. def. 2.

sion. On the other hand, no body is 'finite' in the sense that it is 'limited' by a thought, that it might be expanded so as to include thinking in its corporeal nature. In the chain of causes to which it owes its existence all are bodies, not one is a thought: and in the system of relations and relata which form its context, the relata are always bodies and not thoughts, the relations ways of corporeal interaction and not 'connexions of ideas.' Its incompleteness or limitations as a body are due (not to its exclusion of thoughts, but) to its exclusion of what is implied in the character which it professes—the character of Extension. The Attribute of Extension is 'infinite,' because it involves all the characters of extension: it exhausts the whole of Reality so far as it is an *extended* Reality. To conceive Reality under the Attribute of Extension, would be to conceive completely whatever positive character Reality possesses *quâ* extended. The Attribute of Extension is 'infinite' (not, of course, as the sum of the indefinite number of extended things, but) as the complete exhaustive expression of the essence, or positive character, of the Real *quâ* extended.

And the same applies, *mutatis mutandis*, to the Attribute of Thought.

A thought—e.g. an idea which is an act of my thinking, or again the complex 'idea' which constitutes my mind [1]—owes its *existence* to a chain of prior thoughts (a chain which unrolls itself indefinitely backward), its *being*, or essential nature, to its coherence with the whole Thought-Universe. Any single thought is 'terminated' by other thoughts in a twofold sense. Its *genesis* depends upon a series of thoughts, which can never be completed in regress and yet demands completion: and its '*being*'—i.e. its content, 'what,' or meaning—is but a fragment of the complete whole of Thought, and is

[1] See below, Bk. II. ch. I.

through and through constituted by that which, as a fragment, it attempts to exclude.

A single thought, or a complex of single thoughts, is but a mode of Reality *quâ* Thinking Reality—a mode of the one Substance conceived under the Attribute of Thought. That Attribute is 'infinite' in its own kind: it is the complete, exhaustive, expression of a certain positive character of the Real—its character *quâ* 'spiritual' or 'thinking.' The Attribute of Thought is everything that Thought is: all consciousness, all living, willing, feeling, &c., is comprehended in it.

(4) *Each Attribute is coextensive with Substance; or Substance is whole in all its Attributes, though different in each.*

Each Attribute then—Extension and Thought—as complete, exhaustive, or infinite in its kind, is coextensive [1] with the Reality under that Attribute. There is no 'body' which is not a mode of Substance under the Attribute of Extension; no 'thought' which is not a mode of Substance under the Attribute of Thought. And, conversely, Thought and Extension are essential to the being of Substance; i.e. Reality is through and through an 'extended' and a 'thinking' Reality. It is one and the same Reality which manifests both characters, and there is nothing real which is not both 'extended' and 'ideal.' There is no 'lifeless matter,' no 'immaterial spirit [2].'

---

[1] 'Coextensive' implies a spatial metaphor, and becomes misleading if its meaning is pressed. All that is said here as regards the 'coextensiveness' of the Attributes with one another (their so-called 'parallelism') and with God, is to be taken as provisional and subject to correction. See below, pp. 134 ff.

[2] Any two terms inadequately represent the antithesis of Extensio and Cogitatio. Perhaps it is best to say simply 'everything extended is at once also thinking' and 'everything thinking is at once also extended.' For further developments, see below.

Book I. What has been said of the Attributes of Extension and Thought applies in principle to any and every Attribute. We can therefore sum up our results as follows:—By 'Attribute' Spinoza means any character which is comprehended by intellect as (i) *essential to Reality*, i.e. as coextensive with it and necessary to its being [1]; and as (ii) *complete in itself*, or incapable of being reduced to terms of any other character.

It is, therefore, essential to Spinoza's conception of Attribute that it should be 'that *which intellect perceives* ...' Attribute is not 'extra intellectum,' but is essentially Substance as known or apprehended. On the other hand, it is no less essential that, while intellect apprehends, it should not be inventing. Attribute is not merely 'in intellectu'—not a mere way in which we happen to fancy Reality. It is no 'ens rationis' or 'imaginationis': for it constitutes the essential nature of Substance. When, in fact, Spinoza says, 'there is nothing given " realiter sive extra intellectum [2] " besides Substances and their modes';—*Attribute, as the 'what' of Substance, is not excluded from Reality.*

It is no mere creation of our minds, no arbitrary fancy, and in that sense it *is* 'extra intellectum.' But it is the Reality as known, and therefore—if 'intellectus' is taken strictly [3]—it is *not* 'extra intellectum.'

The conception of Attribute is Spinoza's way of expressing that the Real is what is known. Commentators have simply stepped outside this attempt to identify 'what is' and 'what is known,' and have said brutally '*Either* Reality *or* what is known or knowable.' There are difficulties enough in Spinoza's conception: but it is

---

[1] The 'essence' of a thing is that, the presence of which posits, the absence of which removes, the thing. E. ii. def. 2. Each Attribute is 'coextensive' with Reality in this sense.
[2] Ep. 4. Cf. E. i. 4 dem.; i. 6 C.
[3] See below (Bk. II. ch. 2) for the distinction between Intellectus and Imaginatio.

no use to begin by postulating dogmatically the ultimate severance of that which he conceives as fundamentally one. 'Attribute' is neither the Reality apart from knowledge, nor knowledge apart from Reality; but that which is known or knowable of Reality. And, for Spinoza, Reality *is* what is known or knowable—the content or 'what' of Substance is its Attributes; and it is a false abstraction which gives isolated being to either side of the antithesis. There is no Attribute which is not an Attribute of a Substance; no Substance which has not some Attribute. The more real a thing is, the more positive character it comprises—i. e. the more content it has for knowledge[1]. And, on the other hand, the more positive character a thing has (the more content it reveals to knowledge), the more self-dependent, the more 'substantial,' or fully real, it is[2].

### § 2. INFINITE AND INDEFINITE.

The antithesis between infinite and finite plays so large a part in Spinoza's philosophy, that it is necessary to understand clearly what meaning he gives to it, and in what sense every Substance is 'necessarily infinite[3],' every Attribute 'infinite in its own kind.'

The problem of the Infinite—so Spinoza writes to Meyer[4]—appears insoluble, because certain distinctions are apt to be confounded. People do not commonly distinguish between:—

(1) That, the infinity of which follows from its own nature, i. e. from the implications of its definition: and

---

[1] Cf. E. i. 9.
[2] Cf. Ep. 9, 'the more Attributes I attribute to a thing, the more I am compelled to attribute existence to it; i.e. the more I conceive it *sub ratione veri* ....'
[3] E. i. 8.
[4] Ep. 12 (April, 1663). E. i. 15 S. is virtually a restatement of the 'thoughts on the infinite' expressed in this letter, so far as they affect the question of the indivisibility of 'Substantia extensa.'

that which has no limits (not owing to the inherent quality of its self, but) in virtue of its cause;

(2) That which is called 'infinite,' because it has no limits: and that which, although contained within known limits, cannot have its parts expressed commensurately by any number;

(3) That which we can only think, not picture: and that of which we can also form an image.

Now, the existence of Substance is self-dependent, i.e. follows from its essential nature or definition[1]. A consequence of this is that Substance is unique, i.e. there cannot be more than one Substance of the same essential nature[2]. And it results from these two propositions that Substance must be conceived as infinite[3].

Substance, therefore, is 'infinite,' because existence follows necessarily from its nature, and because that nature is all-inclusive or self-contained. Substance is not limited either in essence or in existence: and this its completeness or infinity follows from its self, and not from the infinity of an external cause. The existence of Substance follows from the nature of Substance; or Substance is, in this sense, 'causa sui,' and its infinity depends upon itself as the cause of itself. Further, since Substance must exist, and since the 'must' indicates an immanent (and not an external or contingent) necessity: it follows that the existence of Substance cannot be conceived as the lasting for a time, even for an indefinitely long time. For its existence is the necessary consequence of its nature or definition, i.e. (E. i. def. 8) is 'eternal.' We can conceive its existence only as an

---

[1] Cf. E. i. 7, and below.
[2] Cf. Ep. 34, E. i. 5, and below.
[3] Cf. E. i. 8, Ep. 34, and below. E. i. 8 argues: Substance is unique of its kind and must exist. But if it must exist, it must exist either as finite or as infinite. But it cannot be finite, for that would destroy its uniqueness: for the finite (E. i. def. 2) is that which is limited by another thing of the same nature.

# INFINITE AND INDEFINITE

'infinite fruition of existing, or rather of being.' Its being is the being, which e.g. attaches to an 'eternal truth.'

An 'eternal' truth is one which must be true by its own internal necessity: its 'being' is its truth, and its truth is its self. Similarly Substance must exist, because its existence and its essential nature are one: its existence is its essence and its essence is its self [1]. But the case is different with modes. They are states of Substance, and their definition—so far as it is not simply the definition of Substance—cannot involve existence; for otherwise they would be self-dependent, i.e. Substances, not modes. It follows that, even though they exist, we can conceive them as not existing. No doubt, if we conceive modes as states of Substance, in their dependence on that which gives them their reality, we grasp them in their eternal necessity. We cannot *then* 'conceive them as not existing, even though they exist,' because we are moving in the region of scientific truth, for which 'must' and 'can not' have taken the place of 'may or may not.' We have substituted a systematic knowledge of the precise conditions of the change and contingency of the modes, for the fragmentary experience which viewed their existence here and now as an isolated and arbitrary fact. But so far as this is the case, we are not apprehending the modes *as such*: we are apprehending the order of the whole of Nature, grasping the essential being or definition of Substance. But so long as we attend to the modes themselves, or try to grasp their own essential nature, their isolated being, we cannot infer from the fact of their existence now that they will or will not exist in the future, nor that they have or have not existed in the past. The existence of a mode is therefore the lasting for a period, and is conceived in a manner *toto genere* different from that

[1] Cf. E. i. 20.

in which the existence of Substance must be conceived. The infinity of modes—when they *are* infinite—is the infinity of the cause on which they depend, and that cause is (not themselves, but) Substance.

It follows that—so long as we confine our attention to the nature of the modes in isolation from the order of the whole Nature in which they are—we can *determine* their existence and duration: i.e. we can conceive their existence (the period of their lasting) as greater or smaller, and divide it into parts. But to do this in the case of Substance and eternity—to conceive the nature and being or existence of Substance as admitting of more and less, as divisible into parts—is impossible, unless we totally alter our conception of 'parts,' 'greater and less duration,' &c. Hence the absurdity of supposing that extended Substance is made up of parts, that Substance under the Attribute of Extension is an aggregate of bodies really distinct from one another[1]. It would be no more ridiculous to suppose that the mere addition or aggregation of many circles could produce a square or a triangle, or anything else of totally distinct essential nature. All the so-called proofs that 'Substantia extensa' is finite rest upon a misconception of this kind[2].

And yet the error is natural to us; we are naturally inclined to divide 'Substantia extensa.' Why? Because it is easier to use our imagination than our thought; and so we confuse the infinite of imagination with the infinite of thought[3], the indefinite (or false infinite) with the complete (or true infinite). Taking the general term 'quantity' to express the characteristic of 'Substantia extensa'—its continuous magnitude—we must distinguish between a true and a false method of conceiving it. Quantity, if we conceive it by thought,

---

[1] Spinoza is attacking Descartes: cf. Desc. *Princ.* i. 23. And see below for the object of this polemic.
[2] Cf. E. i. 12, 13, and 15 S.
[3] Cf. above (3), p. 28.

# INFINITE AND INDEFINITE

as it really is—as Substance (i.e. Substance under the attribute of Extension)[1]—is infinite, unique, indivisible. But if we conceive it abstractly, superficially—as we have it in our imagination, as we picture it by the help of the senses—it shows itself finite, divisible, made up of parts, and of many kinds. Hence, if we conceive quantity in abstraction from Substance, we can, so to say, cut it up into any lengths we please—make portions of it: and thus we get *measure*, which is simply a device to enable us so to determine 'quantity,' that we may 'picture' or 'image' it as easily as possible. Similarly, if we take duration as the general term to express existence or being, we may form a corresponding imperfect or imaginative notion of it. For, if we conceive duration in abstraction from Substance; if we consider the existence of modes in abstraction from their necessary interdependence in the order of the whole of Nature; if we neglect their necessary sequence from the essential nature of Substance, which necessary sequence constitutes their 'eternity'—then we are conceiving their duration abstractly, or superficially. We can then cut up their duration or lasting into lengths: and so we get *time*— a device to enable us so to determine 'duration,' that we may 'picture' it as easily as possible[2]. Lastly, if we take the states of Substance in abstraction from Substance itself, and bring them under classes, so that we may picture them as easily as possible—we regard each state as a separate thing, and as 'one' amongst 'many' forming a class: and so we get the notion of

---

[1] Cf. Desc. *Princ.* ii. 8. 'Quantitas a substantia extensa in re non differt, sed tantum ex parte nostri conceptus. . . .' For the meaning of the term 'quantitas' cf. Ib. ii. 64. 'Nam plane profiteor, me nullam aliam rerum corporearum materiam agnoscere, quam illam omnimode divisibilem, figurabilem et mobilem, quam geometrae quantitatem vocant, et pro obiecto suarum demonstrationum assumunt; . . . .'

[2] On Spinoza's conception of 'duration' and 'eternity,' see below, Bk. III. ch. 4, § 2.

BOOK I. *number.* Measure, Time, and Number are thus nothing but ways of thinking, or rather picturing, things[1]. And since they are but 'helps to the imagination' they cannot be infinite: for if they were, they would cease to be Number, Measure, Time. Hence those, who have confused these 'aids to picture things' with the real things, have denied that there can be an *infinitum actu.* You never can have an infinite number, an infinite measure, an infinite period: though you can always go on adding, go on extending, go on imagining a greater and indefinitely greater lapse of time. But all this proves nothing as to the things. It is a fallacy to suppose that all things admit of 'imaginative' expression: and again a fallacy to suppose that all things which can be expressed in terms of Number, Measure, and Time, can be *adequately* or *commensurably* so expressed. This is clear even to geometricians. They are aware that many things do not admit of numerical expression at all; and further, that many which do, exceed any number which can be given. You can have in geometry an 'actually infinite distance'—i.e. one which, though given and real, is yet incapable of being adequately expressed by any measure or number of parts—an infinite, therefore, which does not depend for its infinity upon the multitude of its parts, but upon its nature: for such a distance would cease to be itself if it became measurable, i.e. if it could be expressed as a finite number of parts[2].

[1] 'Cogitandi, seu potius imaginandi, modi':—

'Entia rationis, seu imaginationis auxilia.' Ep. 12.

Cf. Desc. *Princ.* i. 57, 58.

[2] The people, against whom Spinoza is arguing, urged 'Since you can never have an infinite number or an infinite measure—for then you would not have a number or a measure at all—there is no such thing as an actual infinite. The infinite means the indefinite—that to which you can always add, beyond

# INFINITE AND INDEFINITE

Similarly with 'Substantia extensa': to attempt to 'determine' all the motions of matter which have hitherto which you can always go: but which, wherever you take it, is finite though not exhausted.' To this he answers: (i) Number and Measure are not things, but ways of thinking or picturing things. No inference can be drawn from them to the nature of things. There are many things which cannot be expressed in terms of number or measure at all. (ii) Further, mathematicians are familiar with many things which are not commensurate with any number, but exceed any number which can be given. Yet they infer this property of these things not because of the multitude of their parts (i.e. not from an attempt and a failure to sum their parts); but from the fact that the nature of the thing does not admit of being numbered

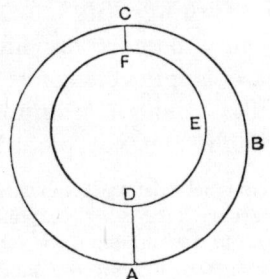

without a manifest contradiction. E. g., describe two circles with different centres one inside the other, ABC, DEF: join AD, FC so that AD represents the greatest, FC the least, perpendicular linear distance between the circumferences of the two circles. Then *the nature of the space* included between the circumferences *is such, that,* unless it were to cease to be itself (or a circle to be a circle), *no number* can ever commensurately express the divergences of distance within it— no unit, e.g., of which AD is a multiple, can be used as a measure to express by addition of itself any other distance between the circumferences, e.g. EB or FC. Or if we suppose some material —e.g. a fluid—starting at AD, to flow round the space, no number could adequately express all the varying expansions and contractions which it would have to adopt in order that it might always fill the space. And this (the infinity or indefiniteness of the inequalities of the space interposed between the two circumferences, or the infinity of the variations of expansion or contraction which a material flowing through it would have to undergo) is demonstrated mathematically from the *nature* of the space in question. It does not depend on the excessive size of the space: nor upon the fact that we have no minimum or maximum, no measurable starting or ending point. For the property belongs to any the least portion of the space (e.g. to that included between EB and FC); and we have a minimum and a maximum, viz. FC and AD.

For 'the fluid' in Spinoza's illustration, cf. Ph.D. ii. 9, 10, 11.

occurred—i.e. to express them by a definite number, their duration by a definite time—would be to attempt to make corporeal Substance cease to possess its own nature [1].

Putting results together, we can state Spinoza's view of the infinite thus:—It is not true, as Descartes had seemed to say [2], that the human mind, since it is finite, is incapable of comprehending what is infinite. But it is true that we cannot comprehend the infinite under those categories which enable us to picture the finite. The infinite cannot be regarded as merely a bigger, or a more lasting, or a numerically greater finite: its nature is in no sense made up of finite parts. It must be conceived in a manner *toto genere* different from that in which we conceive the finite. A continuous length is not made up of discrete points, nor a period of moments: in the same way, Substance under the attribute of Extension can never be comprehended if we regard it as 'made up' of bodies, finite extended things. Infinite magnitude ('Substantia extensa') cannot be measured, infinite duration (eternity) cannot be expressed in years and days, infinite Reality ('Substantia') cannot be explained as a sum of things (its modes). Every measure, every time, and every number are finite —measure, time, and number are applicable only to what can be 'pictured' as well as 'thought': infinity belongs only to what can be thought and not pictured.

---

[1] Spinoza's words are these: 'to attempt to reduce all the motions of matter which have hitherto taken place, and their duration, to a definite number and a definite period of time, is simply to attempt to deprive corporeal Substance—which we cannot conceive except as existing—of its states, and to make it cease to have the nature which it has:'—i.e. since 'Substantia corporea' must exist and its existence is eternal; if its states are reduced to a finite number and their existence to a limited time, its eternal existence is, as it were, left in parts bare of modes or states. The limited supply of actual changes or corporeal events would not suffice to fill out the eternal being of corporeal Substance.

[2] Cf. e.g. *Princ.* i. 41.

## INFINITE AND INDEFINITE

The infinite is that which has no limits: and Substance alone is 'infinite' in this sense: for it alone is 'absolutè indeterminatum[1]'—i.e. includes within itself everything that is; or is that on which all being depends. Every Attribute of Substance is 'infinite' *in its own kind*: for, though it excludes every other Attribute, and therefore is *not* them or 'is limited' in that respect, yet within its own kind of being it is all-inclusive and complete. The modes of Substance are 'infinite' so far as they are conceived as inherent in Substance; for in that inherence in their infinite cause they are complete. But it is possible to conceive modes 'abstractly'—i.e. apart from the Substance of which they are the states; as if they were independent things. And when we do this, they become fragments torn from their context, isolated, mutilated, incomplete portions separated from the order which gave them a borrowed completeness. They claim an independence without the right: and their spurious independence reveals its contingency, its limitations and shortcomings on every side. In fact, they show themselves as 'finite.'

The true infinite cannot have its nature expressed in number or measure at all. But there is a kind of infinite —the indefinite—which gets its name because it cannot be *commensurately* expressed in any number. Thus, the space between the circumferences of two circles with different centres belongs to the sphere of the measurable: and yet it is infinite (i.e. indefinite) because by its very nature it excludes all possibility of complete numerical expression. There is no number which can serve as a least common measure for any two of the different perpendicular linear distances from circumference to circumference: nor is it possible to complete the sum of all the 'inequalities' of such a space, to express them in a finite number.

[1] Cf. (for the phrase) Ep. 36.

# CHAPTER II

## REALITY AS A WHOLE OR GOD

### § 1. SUBSTANCE IS GOD.

Book I.   Hitherto we have made a preliminary examination of some of Spinoza's fundamental technical terms—Substance, Mode, Attribute, Infinite. We have now to study the use he makes of them in his attempt to understand the universe. Like Descartes, Spinoza finds that God[1], and God alone, is absolutely self-dependent, or has substantial reality. But there the agreement ceases. The 'God' of Spinoza's philosophy is something very different from the 'God' of Descartes.

The Ethics starts with the conception of God already formed[2], although Spinoza does not explicitly identify 'Substance' and 'God' in the definitions.

---

[1] As a rule I shall translate Spinoza's 'Deus' as 'God': but the reader must not understand by it the God of any religious sect whatever. 'The Universe,' 'Reality,' 'The Uniformity of Nature' (which various commentators have suggested as alternative renderings), are all of them sometimes useful: but much of Spinoza's language becomes meaningless or fantastic, if referred to them. 'The Uniformity of Nature,' e.g., can hardly be said to 'love itself.' 'The Absolute' would be by far the best translation, if it were not for its later associations.

[2] Spinoza seems to have reached this conception quite as much from the side of a philosophy of nature, as from the side of a theology. Cf. K. V. S. i. 2, § 12, 'From all this it follows that all-in-all is predicated of Nature, and therefore that Nature consists of infinite Attributes, each of which is perfect in its kind: which completely coincides with the definition usually given of God.' Cf. also K. V. S. i. 2, § 17. 2.

## THE CONCEPTION OF GOD

It is not till E. i. 14 that we have the express proposition, 'praeter Deum nulla dari neque concipi potest substantia.' 'God' is defined[1] as one Substance amongst others: a view which no doubt reflected popular opinion. The first fourteen propositions develop the definitions of God and Substance, and thus show that the popular view is untenable[2]. 'God and Substance' —so the argument really runs—'are, if you think out their definitions, coextensive or identical. Think out the conception of Substance, and you will find that in the nature of things there can be no Substance but God; think out the conception of God, and you will find that God alone exhibits the characteristics of Substance.' Put into modern terminology, the argument would be: The conception of self-dependent Reality forces us to the conclusion that there is nothing self-dependently real except the Absolute, the whole system; and the conception of the Absolute forces us to conclude that it alone is self-dependently real. The line of thought in these propositions merely brings together explicitly two conceptions which from the first were not two, but one. The progress, therefore, is an advance only in clearness, in bringing out the writer's meaning; it consists in the removal of misunderstandings. Hence the argument is in one sense no advance at all. It is, in fact, simply the development of what Spinoza stated at the beginning: its application to the nature of things.

Starting with the conception of Substance, as defined in def. 3, we get (E. i. 5): 'In the nature of things there

---

[1] E. i. def. 6. 'By "God" I mean a Being absolutely infinite, i.e. a Substance consisting of infinite Attributes, each of which expresses an eternal and infinite essential nature.'

[2] Cf. Sigwart, Sp., note (in the Appendix) 85. 'The first seven or eight propositions . . . . can only be explained if we assume that Spinoza is attacking the ordinary conception of Substance. To any one who has Spinoza's own conception of Substance in his mind, they cannot but appear almost ridiculous.'

cannot be two or more Substances of the same nature or Attribute.' *This really depends on the relation between Substance and Attribute.* The proof runs thus: 'For, if the Substances are distinct, they must differ; and, if they differ, they must differ either in their modes or states, or in their nature or Attributes (E. i. 4, i. 5 dem.). But a difference in Attributes is excluded *ex hypothesi.* And if they differ only in their modes, then they are really the same—i. e. the same in their permanent nature, the same *quâ* Substances.' *For a difference in Substance with identity of nature is meaningless: a Substance apart from its nature or Attributes is nothing.*

In E. i. 11, starting from the conception of God, we get: ' God, or a Substance consisting of infinite Attributes, each of which expresses an eternal and infinite essential nature, exists of necessity.' Putting these two propositions together, it follows that there can be no Substance other than God. For a Substance including in itself all forms of reality, all Attributes, exists and must exist: and (since there can be no duplicate of any form of substantial reality) whatever substantial reality there is must be God, or be included in the substantial reality of God.

§ 2. GOD IS THE ENS PERFECTISSIMUM OR REALISSIMUM: INCLUDES ALL AFFIRMATIVE BEING: SUBSISTS OF INFINITE ATTRIBUTES.

The conception of God is the conception of complete Reality. God is the 'ens perfectissimum' or 'realissimum,' that which includes in itself all reality or positive being. In the *Tractatus*[1] God is said to be 'All being; that besides which there is no being.' The definition of the Ethics gives the essential nature of God, and thus, in place of this somewhat vague expres-

[1] TdIe, VVlL. i. 26.

sion, attributes to God 'everything which expresses essential nature, and involves no negation[1].'

Everything, then, of which we can say 'it is,' is to be taken as real—as possessing some degree of perfection or real being—and therefore as belonging in some sense to God. Wherever we introduce negation—wherever we predicate limitation or finiteness—we are so far denying reality: and God is in no sense 'unreal,' or nothing unreal belongs to God[2]. God therefore includes everything real or everything so far as it is real: and the *essential nature* of God includes everything ' which expresses essential nature, and involves no negation.' In other words, God is 'a substance consisting[3] of *infinite* Attributes, each of which expresses an eternal and infinite essential nature.'

In E. i. 14 C. 2, we learn that 'the extended Thing' and 'the thinking Thing' are either Attributes or modifications of the Attributes of God: and later we hear definitely that Extension and Thought are Attributes of God[4]. But Extension and Thought, though Attributes of God, do not exhaust God's nature. The Absolute is more than Thought and Extension, though our intelligence apprehends only them[5].

---

[1] E. i. def. 6 Expl.
[2] 'Negation' does not of course mean merely grammatical negation: grammatically e. g. 'finite' is an affirmative, 'infinite' a negative term. But really infinite is affirmative, finite a limitation and therefore a negation of it. (Cf. TdIe, VVlL. i. p. 32.) The importance of Spinoza's sharp antithesis between affirmation and negation—which yet, as we shall see, does not exclude degrees of affirmative being, degrees of perfection or reality—will become apparent when we consider his treatment of the problems of sin, error, and individuality.
[3] 'Constans' — perhaps 'subsisting' would be a better translation, but the Latin expression is unsatisfactory, and needs further explanation.
[4] E. ii. 1 and 2.
[5] The K. V. is very instructive on this point, cf. K. V. S. p. 9. *Zusatz* 3 (evidently of later date than the text) '... *Hitherto* we have been able to find in nature no more than two Attributes

BOOK I. For the more real a thing is, the more Attributes it has :—i. e. the richer or more concrete its essential nature [1].

which belong to this most perfect Being. And these give us no satisfactory assurance that they are all the Attributes of which it consists: on the contrary, we find in ourselves something which obviously announces to us (not only more, but) infinite perfect Attributes, which must be proper to this perfect Being before it can be called "perfect." And whence is this idea of perfection? It cannot come from these two Attributes:—for two give only (the idea of) two and not (of) infinite Attributes. Whence, then? Certainly not from myself: otherwise I should have to be able to furnish of myself that which I have not got. Whence then, unless from the infinite Attributes themselves, which tell us that they are there, without also telling us what they are: for we only know "what they are" in the case of two.' K. V. S. i. 7, note 1: 'As regards the Attributes of which God consists, these are nothing but infinite Substances, each of which must itself be infinitely perfect.... It is true however that, *as yet*, of all these infinite Attributes only two are known to us through their own nature, viz. Thought and Extension.' These passages alone seem to me to establish beyond reasonable doubt (1) that 'infinita attributa' means an infinite number of Attributes—though we shall see presently how this expression must be understood: (2) that it still seemed possible to Spinoza (*at least when he wrote the late note to the K. V.*) to discover other Attributes of God besides Thought and Extension.

Ep. 56 shows in what sense Spinoza conceived it possible to have a clear idea of God, even though we know only two of God's Attributes.

'I have,' he there writes to Hugo Boxel, 'as clear an idea of God, as I have of a triangle. But this does not mean that I have as clear an *image* of God as of a triangle: for we cannot form a picture of God (imaginari). And I do not mean to say that I know the whole nature of God; but only some of his Attributes—not all, nor the greatest part. Ignorance of most does not prevent my having knowledge of some. When I began to learn the Elements of Euclid, I had a "clear perception" (knowledge) of that property of a triangle in virtue of which its three angles are equal to two right angles, although I was still ignorant of many of the other properties of a triangle.'

[1] E. i. 9. Cf. especially K. V. S. p. 12, note 1. '"Nothing" cannot have any Attributes, the universe ('de Al,' das All) must have all Attributes. "Nothing" has no Attributes because it is "nothing"; and so "something" has Attributes because it is "something":

Though we cannot comprehend, or even name, all the essential forms of God's being, yet we cannot conceive them as in any way limited. We must say therefore, God subsists 'of *all* Attributes,' or (since 'all' seems to imply a sum and therefore finiteness) 'of *infinite* Attributes.'

But we know that there is no such thing as an infinite number. Every actual number is always finite. We cannot therefore strictly mean that God's Attributes form an infinite number: we mean simply that no number can express them. Nor does this force us to admit that God's nature is 'indefinite': 'indefinite' is that which, whilst belonging to the sphere of number or measure, is yet not capable of exact numerical expression[1]. All that we really mean to assert of God, when we attribute infinite Attributes to him, is therefore that his nature is absolutely complete, includes all essential positive forms of being, and cannot be conceived as in any way limited or finite. If we *will* endeavour to enumerate God's Attributes, we shall find that no number can exhaust them: but this indicates no indefiniteness in God, but simply the absurdity of conceiving him under 'modes of imagination.'

### § 3. SOME OF GOD'S PROPERTIES.

We must leave for the present the problem as to in what sense God '*constat* infinitis attributis,' and consider certain general properties of God[2].

---

and therefore, the more a thing is something the more Attributes it must have. God therefore, who is the most perfect, the infinite, the all "something," must have infinite, perfect, and all Attributes.'

[1] Above, p. 35.
[2] Cf. K. V. S. i. 1, § 9.
'It is clear that man has the idea of God, because he knows God's Attributes.' Then, in a footnote, 'Better:—because he knows what is proper (proprium)

## 1. *God is one, unique and whole.*

God, as the only Substance, is 'one' or 'unique' (E. i. 14 C. 1); and, as comprehending all being in himself, is the Whole of which all things are parts.

Yet it is only with much hesitation, and after careful discussion, that Spinoza calls God 'unique,' and regards him as a 'whole.' For a 'whole' implies parts, and parts would seem to admit of existence in some sense independent of the whole. A 'whole of parts' appears capable of division. And what is 'one' or 'unique' must come, it would seem, under a real or possible class. But God is absolutely indivisible, and has no parts: for, if the parts retained the character of the whole and were themselves infinite substances, then there would be more than one God; but, if not, then God's substantial nature would vanish into non-substantial components, and he would cease to be. To 'destroy' a thing is, in fact, to resolve it into parts of such a kind, that none of them expresses the nature of the whole[1]. Indeed, a 'part' of a Substance can mean nothing but a finite Substance—but in God (or indeed in any Substance) there is no limitation or finiteness[2]. And it is only by a very improper use of the terms that God can be called 'one' or 'unique.' We call a thing 'one' only in respect to its existence, not to its essence: it is only when we have grouped things of a similar nature under a common class that we conceive them as numerable, instances of a type.

to God: for such things (e. g. infinity, perfection, immutability) are not Attributes of God. God, no doubt, is not God without them: but it is not through them that he is God; for they reveal nothing substantial. They are only adjectives, which require substantives in order to be explained.' Spinoza seems to have derived his distinction between Attributes and Propria from Chasdai Creskas (Rab Chasdai): cf. Joel, pp. 19 ff.

[1] E. i. 13 dem. and C., and cf. Ep. 36 to Huyghens.
[2] E. i. 13 S.

## SOME OF GOD'S PROPERTIES

But God's essence and existence are identical, and we Chap. II. cannot form a universal conception of his essence: it is not an instance of a type [1].

Yet in a sense God is one and unique—' one,' so far as we regard him as distinct from other things: 'unique' so far as we reflect that there are no other things; none, at least, 'real' in the same sense as God. God therefore is unique as comprehending in himself all reality, or as being the only Substance [2]. And, however Spinoza may hesitate, God is conceived by him as a whole, the totality of all being; though the 'parts' are not independent, in fact not *as parts* real. Between the finite and the infinite 'nulla est ratio': and yet, again and again, the infinite shows itself as the system in which the finite is—though *as in the system* it is no longer finite. Thus, our minds are parts or fragments of the infinite intelligence of God [3]. The Attribute of Thought is a complete whole or system which sustains in itself all 'ideae' or modes of Thought, which apart from the system are finite. The corporeal universe is a complete whole or system, of which all 'bodies' or modes of Extension are 'parts,' in which they have their being, abstracted from which their being is partly negated or finite. We shall meet with this conception (of 'whole and parts' as applied to each Attribute and its modes) again: and shall then consider Ep. 32, in which Spinoza gives full expression to his views.

### 2. *God is simple, indeterminate and concrete.*

'Of God's essence we can form no universal idea' [4]— i.e. God is no abstraction, but the most concrete reality. We do not reach the conception of God by abstracting,

---

[1] C. M. i. 6, § 2. Ep. 50 (to Jarigh Jelles).
[2] C. M. l. c., E. i. 10 S., i. 14 C. 1.
[3] Cf. E. ii. 11 C., v. 40 S., and below.
[4] Ep. 50.

leaving out, characteristics peculiar to the different forms of being (Extension and Thought, e. g.), and so postulating a 'being as such' which is nothing in particular. We start with the conception of the most concrete being, the fullest and richest nature. The Attributes, or forms of being, are limitations of this, or (if you like) its parts. They are coextensive with it, and yet coextensive only with, as it were, a layer of it. 'Thought' e.g. is all thinking, or is coextensive with Substance *quâ* thinking, and so far is 'infinite' or not determinate: but it is *not* Extension, and so far it is determined; though the determination does not affect its nature *quâ* Thought, but leaves it 'infinite in its own kind[1].' But God, though 'simple' (i.e. not put together of parts) is absolutely infinite or all-inclusive, and therefore no determination applies to him. For 'determinate' signifies nothing positive: it denotes only a privation of existence in that nature which is conceived as determinate. The nature, e. g., of Extension involves duration, position, quantity. 'Imperfection' therefore or 'determination' of Extension, must mean that the imperfect or determinate extension *might* last longer, *might* keep its place, or *might* be larger. But God's nature is not confined to any department of Reality: and therefore it requires—if it is to be perfectly 'indeterminate,' as its conception demands—everything that expresses being[2].

So far therefore is Spinoza from regarding God as the widest and emptiest abstraction of being—as that which is absolutely indeterminate in the sense of absolutely characterless—that he insists on the exact opposite. God is absolutely indeterminate, because he excludes nothing real, or comprises in himself all character. Hence to conceive God (or Substance) as he really is ('in se') is to conceive him in the fullness of his being: and this

---

[1] Cf. above, pp. 22 ff.        [2] Cf. Ep. 36 (to Huyghens).

involves the setting aside all limitations, and therefore all 'modes' as such[1].

### § 4. NATURE, VALIDITY, AND VALUE OF SPINOZA'S ARGUMENTS TO PROVE THAT GOD EXISTS OF NECESSITY.

1. *The four proofs all exhibit the same fundamental type of inference.*

'That there can be no Substance except God' followed —it will be remembered—from the two propositions (i) that in the nature of things there cannot be two or more Substances of the same Attribute, and (ii) that God, i. e. a Substance including within itself all Attributes— all forms of positive reality—necessarily exists[2]. Of this latter proposition Spinoza gives four alternative proofs[3], which we must now examine. The proofs appear to differ considerably: thus e. g. proofs 1, 2, and 4 are '*à priori*,' proof 3 '*à posteriori*': proofs 3 and 4 rest upon the non-Spinozistic supposition that there are or may be more Substances than one, or that God is the most real amongst other real (self-dependent) beings[4]— a supposition which, if maintained, would destroy the validity of the arguments: and yet in the main the thought at the bottom of them all is one and the same. It is this: *once grant that anything is actual, and you must grant that God necessarily is actual*. The argument is in fact transcendental in form, and shows that if anything in any sense real be admitted to be actual, its existence involves the necessary existence of the Spinozistic God. The validity of this reasoning depends upon what Spinoza means by God: its value depends upon what is understood by the necessary existence of God.

---

[1] E. i. 5 dem.   [2] Cf. above, p. 33.   [3] E. i. 11 and S.
[4] Cf. Spinoza's own words in E. i. 11 S.

Both these questions—the validity and the value of the argument—will occupy us presently. In the meantime we have to show that this is the nature of the inference involved in all four proofs.

Proof 4 [1] argues *à priori*, from the conception of God's absolute reality as identical with absolute power. It says that if anything draws its existence from its own intrinsic force, *à fortiori* must God—the being who has absolutely unlimited reality and therefore absolutely unlimited intrinsic force—do so. The argument therefore is: 'admit that anything exists necessarily, i.e. as the consequence of its being what it is, and you must admit that God (the being which *is* most and therefore has most ground for self-dependent existence) exists necessarily.'

Proof 3 [2] argues *à posteriori*, from the same fundamental conception as proof 4. It points to the facts. We exist at this moment, and our existence is either the necessary result of our own intrinsic nature (in which case we are Substances), or the necessary result of something else which exists because it is itself (in which case

---

[1] E. i. 11 S.

[2] As the third proof is somewhat obscure in the Latin, I give a full paraphrase of it: 'To be able to exist is a power, to be capable of not existing is a want of power. So far, therefore, as anything must exist, it shows power. But at the present moment many finite beings exist and must exist: if, then, nothing besides them were now existing of necessity, they—the finite beings—would be more powerful than God, the absolutely infinite being. Which is absurd. Either, therefore, nothing now exists of necessity: or God too exists of necessity.' ('Ergo vel nihil existit, vel ens absolute infinitum necessario etiam existit': the argument and the 'etiam' require us to understand 'Ergo vel nihil *necessario* existit.') 'But the first is false: for we exist, and exist of necessity. For we exist either as Substances or as modes (Ax. 1). If as Substances, then we are self-determined: if as modes, then we are dependent on something else which is self-determined. In either case, *some* existence is necessary. And, therefore, God too must necessarily exist.'

we are modes and imply a Substance). In either case, our existence as a fact shows that *something* is now necessarily existing. But if so, then that which is infinite in being, viz. God, cannot be able not to exist—for that would mean that the infinite being had less power than things (or a thing) which are finite. (If the 'something' on which our existence depends is infinite, then *cadit quaestio*—for it is God.)

In other words, the argument runs :—'admit, as you must, that some thing or things exist necessarily, and you must admit that God too exists necessarily.'

Proof 2 argues *à priori*, from the conception of self-conditioned, as distinguished from contingent, being. There is no such thing (so the line of thought runs) as chance, or absolute contingency. There must be an assignable cause or reason for the present existence or non-existence of everything. But if the existing or non-existing thing is contingent, then the reason or cause of its existence or non-existence will lie outside it—in something else. If, on the contrary, it be self-conditioned, then the reason or cause will lie within it. A substance, e. g., is 'in se,' self-conditioned; and therefore the reason or cause for its existence or non-existence must lie within its own nature. But a circle or a triangle is 'in alio,' contingent: and therefore the reason or cause why this or that circle or triangle now exists or does not exist will lie without it—in the nature of space, in the order of extended nature as a whole. If, for example, there is here and now a triangle, that factual existence must be the necessary consequence of that on which the triangle is contingent—e. g. the nature of space. If there is here and now no triangle, that must be because, owing to the nature of space, it is impossible that a triangle should exist here and now. If therefore there *is* no reason or cause why God should not exist now, then God *does and must exist now*. And if it is *impossible* that any such cause should be given, then it is *impossible* that God should not exist—i.e. he exists of necessity absolutely. But this is the case: it is impossible that there should ever be given any cause or reason to hinder God from existing. For such a cause would have to be (i) either in God's nature, or (ii) outside his nature. The first alternative is impossible, for it would make God self-contradictory—i.e. defective in reality or perfection. But the second is equally impossible. For where could the cause be? Not in another Substance of the *same* nature as God: for then, *cadit quaestio*: the other Substance would be God and would exist of necessity. Nor in another Substance of *different* nature from God: for then it could have no possible effect upon God (cf. E. i. 2).

In other words: All contingent being is but the necessary consequence of self-conditioned being. Admit contingent being, and you must admit the existence of self-conditioned being. But if the self-conditioned being is all-inclusive and perfect, then its existence is absolutely necessary. For no self-conditioned being can be destroyed from within, unless it is imperfect. And an all-inclusive self-conditioned being is all 'within.'

Lastly, proof 1 argues *à priori* from the conception of modal as distinguished from substantial being. It is in fact a more formal statement of the same thought as that expressed in proof 2, and runs thus:—

'God is a Substance, and not a mode. But the essential nature of a Substance involves its existence, and therefore God cannot be conceived except as existing, or God exists of inherent necessity.'

The proposition to which this proof refers (E. i. 7), and the Scholium (E. i. 8 S. 2) which explains its significance, together express the thought of proof 2 in a somewhat different form. We see from them that the real line of argument implied in proof 1 is as follows:—

Mode was distinguished from Substance, as that which is 'in alio' from that which is 'in se.' That which is 'in alio' is also conceived through that other on which it is dependent: and we can therefore form a clear and distinct (i. e. a true) idea of the essential nature of a mode, even though the mode itself has no actual existence at the moment[1].

The truth e. g. of our conception of triangle is in no way affected by the actual existence or non-existence of a triangle here and now. But the truth of that conception would be destroyed, if our conception of space were untrue: for it is as a modification of space, as a figure capable of construction according to the laws of space, that we conceive triangle[2]. And our conception of space, again, would be untrue if it did not ultimately rest upon a conception of substantial Reality—i. e. a Reality which is not possibly a fiction, but necessarily and permanently actual. It is possible, then, to conceive a mode truly, without implying its actual existence:—the 'ideatum' of an idea of a mode is not necessarily an actually-existent thing, but is *that of which the mode is a modification* conceived under the conditions of its modification. Hence the possibility of such a conception of a mode rests upon the fact that it is a mode, i.e. that its real being is to be 'in alio.' The conception of this 'aliud' ultimately depends upon the conception of substantial Reality, and *this*—the true conception of anything substantial—implies the existence of its 'ideatum.'

---

[1] We shall meet with most important developments of this conception in E. ii.

[2] Cf. the conception of the Universal in modern Logic. To have a true universal conception of triangle would mean to be able to formulate the exact conditions of spatial construction under which a triangle would result; cf. e.g. Lotze, *Logik*, §§ 30 ff.

BOOK I. The truth of our conception of a mode (where the mode is not actually existent) is guaranteed only by the actual existence of the 'ideatum,' the ultimate 'aliud,' which we conceive as that of which the mode is a modification. Substance is 'in se' and can therefore only be conceived 'per se': hence, if it does not actually exist it cannot be conceived truly. For, if it does not actually exist, there is nothing else in which it is involved, nothing from the conception of which its conception can be derived, nothing the reality of which guarantees its reality. To think therefore of Substance, if there *is* no Substance, is to think of something self-dependently real which yet *is* not—to have an idea to which no 'ideatum' corresponds, an idea which is the idea of nothing, or false. It is, in fact (not to think of Substance, but) to create a self-contradictory and fictitious idea [1].

In other words: it belongs to the nature of Substance to exist [2]: a Substance which *is* not, is not Substance at all. An unreal, non-existent, Substance is a *contradictio in adiecto*. Either, then, you must give up the idea of Substance, or you must admit that Substance (i.e. as we learn in the sequel, the one Substance, God) necessarily exists. But, if you give up the idea of Substance, you must give up the idea of mode as well. Either, therefore, nothing exists, or God exists of necessity.

## 2. *Validity of Spinoza's arguments* [3].

There is thus a common thought running through all four proofs, and it is simply this:—' If anything in any sense is, then God is and is of necessity: his existence

---

[1] E. i. 8 S. 2.
[2] E. i. 7.
[3] I have to express a special obligation to Bradley, *Appearance and Reality*, pp. 394 ff., McTaggart, *Studies in Hegelian Dialectic*, especially p. 72, and R. L. Nettleship, *Philosophical Lectures and Remains*, vol. i, though these writers must not be held responsible for what I say.

# GOD EXISTS OF NECESSITY

is necessary as th        ble implication of his nature.' CHAP. II.
We have an indication that this was Spinoza's meaning
in Ep. 12[1]: and it is most clearly shown in proof 3.
But indeed tl. first two proofs leave no room for doubt
as to Spinoza's line of thought. Because modal being
implies substantial, because the contingent involves the
self-conditioned, *therefore* the substantial, self-conditioned must be; and the 'must' expresses an inherent
necessity and not a necessity which depends on temporary conditions. And since for Spinoza substantial
or self-conditioned being is one and one only—since God
is the only and all self-conditioned Reality—it follows
that the existence of modal or contingent being involves
the necessary existence of God. The *necessary* existence
—i.e. not the necessity which is contingency, not God's
existence now as the consequence of some present set of
conditions, but his existence as the inevitable consequence of what is immutably the same, his own essential
nature. The necessary existence of God is his 'eternity[2]';
for he is incapable of contingent necessity, since there is
nothing real beside him on which he could be contingent.

Except in the third proof, Spinoza has not expressly

---

[1] Ep. 12. 'The modern Peripatetics have, I think, misunderstood the demonstration by which the ancients endeavoured to prove the existence of God. For that demonstration (as I find it in the writings of a certain Jew, Rab Chasdai) runs thus:—

'"If there is a regress of causes *in infinitum*, all things which are will be effects. But no effect can exist necessarily of its own nature: therefore there is nothing in nature whose 'essentia' is such that it must of necessity exist. But this is absurd: therefore also the former supposition."

'Hence the force of the argument lies (not in the impossibility of an actual infinite, but) in the absurdity of supposing that things which exist, but not by the necessity of their own nature, are not determined to exist by something which does exist necessarily of its own nature;' i.e. *the nerve of the proof lies in the absurdity of supposing that there can be contingent without self-dependent reality.*

[2] See E. i. def. 8; and below, Bk. III. ch. 4, § 2.

supplied the minor premiss for this reasoning, and hence he has been misunderstood. The first proof, as expressly stated, says simply 'God is Substance and therefore, since his existence is self-determined, he must exist': but the cogency of the argument depends upon the unexpressed postulate 'something—at any rate some contingent or modal being, some being therefore which implies self-determined or substantial being—does exist.' But this is a postulate—if indeed it can be called a postulate at all—which assuredly did not require explicit statement. For deny that anything in any sense is, and in your denial you assert at least your own existence. And this was a turn of the argument which Spinoza could assume to be familiar to the contemporaries of Descartes.

It will perhaps make the matter somewhat clearer, if I put Spinoza's reasoning—as I conceive its general purport to be—in a different form. He is really insisting upon the continuity of all experience: and he assumes, as he is most certainly entitled to do, that every one admits that something is in some sense real, that some experience is actual. Once grant that—and to deny it, you must *be* and so stultify your denial—and it follows that God eternally is, that God has necessary existence, or an existence which is the consequence of his nature and of it alone. For the reality and the contingency of a thing are precisely in inverse ratio. The more real a thing is or the more content or essence its self contains—then the more it depends upon itself, or can and does stand in its own right; and therefore the less it is dependent upon external causes, things other than itself—the less contingent its existence. On the other hand, so far as anything is contingent, so far its nature is dispersed into the other things upon which its existence depends; and thus the less there is of it in its 'self,' or the less real content its self includes. Now take any thing which is—start from any existent fact you please—from any piece of experience, however trivial and thin its content: and think out all that its being involves. If you do so, the 'thing's' reality will expand in your hands: more and more will force itself into its being. Or, indeed, the 'thing' and 'its' being will dissolve, until you find yourself ultimately forced to conceive (as that which you are really experiencing) the whole nature of things; until you are compelled to realize that the experience with which you started was a fragment—and a fragment which involved as its context the whole. The contingency and the finiteness (or defective reality) with which you started must (in the attempt fully to experience it) vanish: and in its place you will have the self-conditioned necessity and the complete or infinite reality, which Spinoza calls God. And it is because the Spinozistic God is (not merely one amongst other self-conditioned Reals, but) the only and all substantial Reality, that his proof of the necessary existence of God is valid. Experience as a Whole must be, because it is a whole—because it is through and through of one texture, because therefore every piece of it continuously implies the whole fabric: and therefore unless the Whole is and must be, nothing can in any sense either be or be conceived.

We can understand in what sense such a God is 'causa sui,'[1] or in what sense his 'essentia' involves (or is iden-

---

[1] On the development of Spinoza's use of the expression 'causa sui,' see Avenarius, p. 67, note 109.

But Avenarius is wrong when he says (l.c.) that Spinoza in the K. V. 'rejects the expression—though not the thought—of "causa sui"'; cf. K.V. S. i. 1, § 10.

God is 'causa sui' in the same sense in which he is the 'cause of all things' (E. i. 25 S.). But God is the cause of all things only as the conception of a triangle is the cause of its properties. (Spinoza, it is true, frequently speaks of God as the *efficient* cause of all things; but *efficient* is little more than another expression for *not-final*.) So God is the cause of himself only in this 'geometrical' sense. 'Substance,' Spinoza reasons, E. i. 7 dem., 'cannot be produced by anything

tical with) his 'existentia.' He is 'causa sui,' because there is nothing real except himself on which his being could depend. He is therefore not contingent, and—if he *is* at all—his existence must be conditioned by himself or identical with his 'essentia.' But to deny that he is at all, is to deny that anything is; and such a denial stultifies itself.

So understood, the ontological argument is valid, and does not come under Kant's criticism. And its validity depends upon the unique nature of the idea of God. If you apply the ontological argument to anything except the whole and unique system of experience, Kant's criticism is unanswerable. If existence is necessarily included in the idea of God, then 'God must exist' is an analytical judgement. It is contradictory to think the subject without the predicate: but—as Kant pointed out—it is not in the least contradictory to think neither subject nor predicate. You cannot conceive God without conceiving him to exist, if existence is included in the content of his idea: but you need not conceive God at all. But the cogency of this reasoning disappears the

else: therefore it is the cause of itself.' But, as he goes on to point out, this—the negative conception of not being produced by anything other than itself—becomes, if given a positive expression, simply the conception of God as himself the sole condition of his own reality.

As, with Spinoza, 'Deus agit' is equivalent to 'ex Dei natura sequitur,' so 'causa' is identical with 'ratio' (cf. E. i. 11 dem., *aliter*, and iv. praef., 'Ratio seu causa, cur Deus seu Natura agit et cur existit, una eademque est'); and the term 'causa,' in its more ordinary meaning, has no place in Spinoza's Philosophy (cf. Erdmann, ii. § 272, paragraph 3), nor does he intend it to be understood in a sense implying temporal sequence. Cf. TdIe (VVlL. i. p. 30), 'si res sit in se, sive, *ut vulgo dicitur*, causa sui' ... and in the Ethics, where he uses the phrase without express qualification, he yet carefully explains his meaning. By the conception of God, as the cause of himself and of all things, he means really to conceive God not as the *causa fiendi*, but as the *causa essendi*, to employ a distinction which Schopenhauer has made familiar.

moment that God stands for the whole Reality. Then CHAP. II. you cannot get rid of the subject of your analytical judgement without removing that which all and any experience involves: you cannot refuse to conceive God without ceasing to think or doubt or feel, in short, without ceasing to be. Hence, there is obviously a fundamental connexion between the uniqueness and the self-determined existence of God. In Epp. 34, 35, 36 (to Huyghens)—and the substance of these letters is repeated in a more compressed form in E. i. 8 S. 2—Spinoza proves God's uniqueness from his self-conditioned or necessary existence: but, as we have seen, the latter really follows from the former. The two properties are, in fact, convertible. Only the whole and unique Reality is self-conditioned in its being: and only the self-conditioned is the whole and unique Reality. God as the only individual is alone at once self-dependent and completely real. Self-dependence and all-inclusiveness imply one another, and attach only to the completely individual—the Whole. Contingency and finiteness go together, and stamp that of which they are the predicates as fragmentary—as only partially real.

### 3. *Value of Spinoza's proof.*

But the question still remains—*What* has Spinoza proved of God? For indeed we seem to have justified the validity of the inference at the cost of its value. What do we mean by 'existence,' when we predicate it of the Spinozistic God? Presence in the spatial and temporal series—possible or actual presentation to sense—this is no doubt *in some way* predicable of God. For we have the fact of 'actual existence' in this sense of the words, and if this were not at least an appearance of God, it would be in no sense 'fact.' God does show himself in an existence of this kind: but this showing himself is

Book I. but a fragmentary, a miserably inadequate, self-revelation. Facts of perception are 'real,' but they are not the whole nor the highest degree of reality.

It would be ludicrous to maintain that God's 'existence' was exhausted in this appearance of a portion of himself in space and time. This is not the existence which is involved in God's essential nature; God's essential nature is not the being of a fact or a series of facts. God's existence is—as we learn [1]—identical with his 'essentia': 'follows from it' therefore (not as a weakened and remote effect, not as a partial property which God has amongst other properties, but) as an equivalent expression for, as another side of, the same reality. God, that is, has and must have that existence, that actuality, of which his being is capable. Everything is as real (i.e. as actual) as its self can be; and God's self can be absolutely real—real with all or the fullest degrees of actuality—because it is absolutely complete. The actuality of a finite thing is as much or as little as its essential nature. Existence in space and time, and no higher degree of actuality, is the full and adequate expression only of things whose self is poor and limited: things, indeed, whose 'self' is for the most part a pin-point centre for the attachment of relations to other things. We shall find Spinoza showing that so-called 'things' (things which 'exist,' i.e. which we can see, hear, handle, or which are born, grow, and die: or again perceptions, emotions, ideas which 'occur' as events in an individual's consciousness) are what they are, and therefore exist as they exist, simply as links in an indefinitely extending chain of other things or links. But as a thing becomes more, as its self becomes fuller, its content more immanent, so its actuality (or its existence) ceases to be exhausted in occurrence in the temporal and spatial series. The actuality, for example, of an ideal of conduct, or a law of

[1] E. i. 20.

## GOD EXISTS OF NECESSITY

physics, is not confined to the sensible presence of this or that example of its working, nor to its occurrence as an event in an individual thinker's mind. Nor is its existence fully expressed in the institutions or systems which embody it. And when we come to the being which has absolute or complete reality in its self, whose self is all immanent, then the actuality or existence which is adequate to it, or which its essential nature carries with it, cannot be identified with any limited form of actuality—any limited power of working, or influencing, or manifesting its self. God's nature and his existence are one and the same; and God's power—omnipotence—is but another name for this union, for his 'essentia' in its actuality [1].

Hence the value which attaches to Spinoza's demonstration that God necessarily exists, depends upon the development of his conception of the 'essentia,' and therefore of the 'existentia' and 'potentia,' of God. The whole of his system is the explication of the conceptions which he is here establishing. To learn in what sense God necessarily exists, we must learn what God is; i.e. we must try to understand how Spinoza conceived the fundamental nature of the universe. Then, and not till then, we shall be able to see in retrospect the significance of the terms in which he now expresses God's being and existence. Already, it is true, he tells us that the existence of God, since it is the inevitable implication of his 'essentia' or indeed convertible with it, shares with God's nature the character of eternity. God's existence and God's nature are 'eternal truths [2].' But we can draw

---

[1] Cf. E. i. 20; i. 34; and ii. 3 S. 'Deinde, prop. 34, part. 1, ostendimus, Dei potentiam nihil esse praeterquam Dei actuosam essentiam.'

[2] E. i. 19; i. 20 C. 1. An 'eternal' truth is one which can never cease to be true. Thus, e.g., 'The interior angles of a triangle are together equal to two right angles' is an eternal truth because it can never cease to be

BOOK I. no further significance from this statement at present: it means—at the point we have reached—simply that God's nature is self-determined, and of its own inherent necessity *is* God's actuality.

### § 5. THE CAUSALITY OF GOD.

'God is the cause of himself and of all things: the cause not only of their coming to be, but also of their persistence in being: the cause of their "essentia" as well as of their "existentia[1]."' But Spinoza has to guard his conception of God's causality against certain misinterpretations.

A 'cause,' in the ordinary sense of the word, is itself an effect; its agency at least is caused, determined, elicited by something else. But there *is* nothing else beside God[2]: and God is in no sense determined or forced *ab extra* to be or to act[3]. Yet 'all things which are, are in God, and can neither be nor be conceived except in and through God': God therefore is the efficient, the essential (and not the accidental), the immanent (and not the transient), the first (and not the remote) cause of all things[4]. And since there is no cause within or without God (save only the perfection or reality of his own nature) which stimulates him to action, he is the 'free' cause of all things[5]. God therefore is

true; and it can never cease to be true because its truth is immanent, i.e. if the predicate ceased to attach the subject would cease to be. 'Eternity' therefore and immanent necessity, or self-dependence, would seem to be coextensive conceptions. We shall have to consider Spinoza's conception of eternity more fully below (cf. Bk. III. ch. 4, § 2).

[1] Cf. e.g. E. i. 15; i. 16 C. 1, 2 and 3; i. 18; i. 24 C.; i. 25.
[2] E. i. 15.
[3] E. i. 17 C. 1.
[4] E. i. 16 C. 1, 2, 3; i. 18.
[5] E. i. 17 C. 1 and 2. The various epithets which Spinoza gives to God as a 'cause' refer to a classification of the various kinds of cause, which we find in the K. V., part 1, ch. 3. This has been traced by Trendelenburg to Heereboord's *Collegium Logicum*,

## THE CAUSALITY OF GOD

not subjected to Fate; for there is no external order which controls his action or incites it to begin[1]. The activity of God is entirely his own: it is absolutely spontaneous or free. But, just because it is free, God's causality is absolutely necessary. The necessary is not opposed to the free: and the 'free' does not mean the lawless. The free is the self-determined or fully necessary. It is constraint *ab extra*—necessity in the sense of external compulsion—which is opposed to freedom or necessity in the sense of self-determination[2].

We must therefore, in conceiving God's causality, guard against several errors. All things follow inevitably from the nature of God, but they follow from it alone. There is no inscrutable 'Fate,' which binds even God to follow its laws. God is governed by nothing save his own nature, not even by the conception of an ideal to be attained by his activity. It is a perversion of the divine nature to represent it as acting 'sub ratione boni,' as striving to realize an aim or pattern. If God's activity were determined by an ideal—if he were working for the realization of a better or a best— that would mean that his nature is now defective, imperfect, worse than the ideal. But God's nature is always

---

cf. K. V. S., p. 171 (Sigwart's notes on K. V. i. ch. 3).—Zulawski gives a careful account of the various senses of 'causa' to which Spinoza refers; but his interpretation of 'causa transiens' (pp. 49 ff.) is very doubtful.

[1] Spinoza protests vehemently against the misinterpretation which treats him as a Fatalist. 'There can be nothing more absurd than to subject God to Fate' (E. i. 33 S. 2). 'I in no sense subject God to Fate: but I conceive that all things follow from God's nature with an inevitable necessity, just as everybody conceives it to follow from God's nature that he thinks himself. Nobody denies that this is a necessary consequence of God's nature; and yet nobody conceives that God is compelled to think himself by some Fate. On the contrary, everybody conceives that God thinks himself absolutely freely although necessarily' (Ep. 75).

[2] E. i. def. 7; Tr. P. ch. 2.

in every way absolutely complete[1]. God's causality must be conceived on the analogy of geometrical ground and consequent. 'From the supreme power of God— that is, from his infinite nature—an infinite number of things have necessarily flowed in an infinite number of ways. All things, i.e., have flowed (or rather always are flowing with the same · necessity) from the divine nature; in the same way as it follows from eternity and to eternity from the nature of the triangle that its three internal angles are equal to two right angles. God's omnipotence has been actual from eternity, and to eternity will persist in the same actuality[2].' And the same necessity or self-determination, which makes God's causality 'free,' destroys all contingency in the essential nature and in the existence of things[3]. There is no chance, no possibility of anything having been (or being) otherwise; and there is no arbitrariness, no irrational fiat in the 'decrees' of God. The existent order of the universe, and the existent nature of its component elements, not only *is* but *must be* what it is: and not only *must be* granting certain starting-points, but *must have been*—could not possibly have been otherwise. The laws of nature are the 'decrees' of God, and the 'decrees' are the expression of his nature, are coeval and coextensive with it, necessary and immutable as it[4]. 'Contingent'—taking the word in a wide sense as including 'possible[5]'—is a term expressing only our

---

[1] Cf. E. i. 33 S. 2, and Appendix ... 'si Deus propter finem agit, aliquid necessario appetit, quo caret.'
[2] E. i. 17 S.
[3] E. i. 29.
[4] Cf. e.g. E. i. 33 S. 2. Spinoza is arguing against views like those Descartes urges, e.g. Ep. I. 110, 115 (Cousin, vi. p. 305; ix. p. 162).
[5] E. i. 33 S. 1. A thing is called 'contingent' simply so far as our knowledge is defective. For if we do not know that its essential nature is self-contradictory, or if, though we know its essential nature to be free from self-contradiction, yet (because we are ignorant of the order of

## THE CAUSALITY OF GOD

defective knowledge. To take refuge in the 'will'—
the inexplicable and irrational 'good pleasure' of God—
for the explanation of anything, is to fly to the 'Asylum
of Ignorance.' 'Necessary' and 'impossible' alone express what is and what is not[1].

We must, then, cast into the lumber-room of theological prejudice the notions that God acts from final
causes, or from a will which is 'free' in the sense of
undetermined, incalculable, irrational. The latter view
is perhaps less mischievous than the former[2]: but both
are false. Either view argues a total misconception of
the divine nature; for both postulate defect, imperfection
in God[3].

---

causes) we cannot make any certain assertion with regard to its existence—then we cannot regard that thing either as necessary or as impossible, and so we call it either 'contingent' or 'possible.'

In E. iv. deff. 3 and 4, Spinoza distinguishes between 'contingent' and 'possible.' 'In E. i. 33 S. 1,' he says, 'I made no distinction between the "possible" and the "contingent," because there was then no necessity for that distinction.' But now he explains that (1) 'Contingent' things are those which, so long as we attend exclusively to their essential nature, show us nothing which forces us either to posit or to negate their existence; and that (2) the same things are said to be 'possible' in so far as, when we attend to the causes which must produce them, we are left unaware as to whether those causes are or are not *determined* to produce them;

cf. below, p. 259, note 7.

[1] Cf. E. i. 33 and S. 1 and 2; also Appendix. For the connexion of Spinoza's views (as to the causality of God, &c.) with those of Maimonides and other Jewish writers, cf. Joël, op. cit. And for Spinoza's conception of God's causality, cf. K. V. S. i. ch. 4; Tr. Th. ch. 6.

[2] E. i. 33 S. 2.

[3] Ib. Spinoza is partly arguing against Descartes, cf. e. g. Desc. Ep. 1, 110, and 115; *Princ.* and *Medit.* passim, where he constantly insists that God is infinite and therefore incomprehensible; and often has recourse to 'the ways of God which pass understanding,' in order to explain away manifest difficulties. Whether the orthodoxy of Descartes is any more sincere than Hume's pious horror of Spinoza's 'hideous hypothesis,' is a question to be determined by writers on the Cartesian Philosophy.

BOOK I.    In fact, these errors have both sprung from the anthropomorphism of theology. Though most people reject the coarser view, which conceives God as a larger man—with body and mind, with human passions, intellect, and will—yet they retain part of this misconception. They deny, indeed, that God has a body; and they carry their denial so far as to fall into a gross error. They do not see that Extension is an Attribute of God, that though God has not a finite body, yet God is 'extended' as well as thinking—that the corporeal extended universe is real and so belongs to God's nature[1].

And with this limited conception of the divine nature, there goes the fatal error which conceives intellect and will as somehow more essential to God than the other modes. They suppose that God has a will and an intellect; and that by his intellect he conceives and plans, by his will he chooses to realize, a divine work of art—the World. And though they suppose that God's will and intellect are perfect—that he is omnipotent and omniscient—yet their human conceptions cling to them in their theology. They conceive God's will and intellect, and his action, under the same ignorant misconceptions which have vitiated their understanding of human action. For they suppose—and their supposition is due solely to ignorance of the real causes of human action[2]—that man acts from final causes, and that his actions are 'free' because proceeding from an indeterminate 'will': and in like manner they attribute to God a similar—though an enlarged—causality and a similar 'freedom.' But the truth is that their whole conception of final causes and of freedom is erroneous. Man never acts 'freely' in this sense of the word: and

[1] E. i. 15 S. Again a polemic against Descartes' conception of matter; see below.

[2] On Spinoza's polemic against the Freedom of the Will and Final Causes, see below, Bk. II. ch. 3, § 3, and Appendix.

God does not act from final causes, for it would imply defect in his nature. Nor is God a 'person,' if that term be used to express a being in whose nature are united and yet distinguished two powers only, intellect and will [1]. For God is much more than a thinking and a willing being. And if we keep the names 'will' and 'intellect,' yet God's will and intellect differ *toto caelo* from man's. As applied to man and to God they are homonymous terms [2]. Nor again does God first conceive, then will, and then create. 'Will' and 'intellect' are modes of God on the same level as other modes of his nature. And since no mode is independent or self-determined, no mode as such can be free. It is no more possible to say 'God acts from the liberty of his will,' than to say 'God acts from the liberty of motion-and-rest.' Innumerable things follow from God's will and intellect—and innumerable things from the modes of his extended being, from motion-and-rest as a mode of the Attribute of Extension. But 'motion-and-rest,' 'intellect,' and 'will' are nothing but modes of God, and as modes they are dependent and determined. God's freedom consists in the absolute self-determination of his whole nature and in that alone [3].

NOTE.—For Spinoza's attitude to the prevalent Christianity, cf. especially Epp. 43, 73, 75, and of course, above all, the Tr. Th. Also, on *Evil* and *Error*, see below, Bk. II. ch. 2, § 2 (1 C); Bk. III. ch. 1; and the correspondence between Spinoza and de Blyenbergh, Epp. 18-24, and 27 (Spinoza's Letters are 19, 21, 23 and 27); also cf. Ep. 78.

Ep. 73 was written in answer to Ep. 71, in which Oldenburg had asked Spinoza for a clear statement of his opinions on certain subjects, so that the Tr. Th., if republished with such a statement, might give no offence. The letter is so important that I append a translation. 'With regard to the three heads, on which you beg me for an open expression of my opinion, I reply: (1) My views as to God and Nature are very different from those which the modern Christians are wont to maintain. For I hold God to be the immanent

---

[1] Cf. perhaps C. M. ii. 8, § 1.
[2] E. i. 17 S.
[3] Cf. e.g. E. i. 32 and C. 1 and 2.

BOOK I.  cause of all things, and not (as they say) the transient cause [a]. I affirm with Paul that all things are in God and move in God. Perhaps in this I agree with all the ancient philosophers, though they expressed it differently: and (so far as one can conjecture from certain traditions, much adulterated as they are) with all the old Hebrew masters. It is a complete mistake to suppose, as some do, that the *Tractatus Theologico-Politicus* tends to identify God and Nature, understanding by "Nature" (as these critics do) an ⟨inert⟩ mass or corporeal matter.

(2) 'I am persuaded that the authority of the divine revelation can be supported solely by the wisdom of its doctrine, and not by miracles, i.e. by ignorance, as I have explained at sufficient length in Tr. Th., ch. 6. I content myself here with adding that the main difference which I recognize between Religion and Superstition is, that Religion is based on wisdom, Superstition on ignorance. And it is because people defend their creed by miracles, and so turn even a true faith into superstition, that the Christian is distinguished solely by the opinion he holds, instead of by Faith, Charity, and the other fruits of the Holy Spirit . . .

(3) 'Lastly, it is not, as I believe, absolutely necessary to salvation to "know Christ according to the flesh": but it is necessary to know the eternal Son of God, i.e. God's eternal wisdom, which has manifested itself in all things, especially in the human mind, and most of all in Jesus Christ. For this wisdom alone teaches what is true and false, good and bad: without it, therefore, no one can attain to the "state of blessedness." . . . But that God took upon himself the nature of man, as some churches have added to this doctrine: this, as I explicitly stated in the Tr. Th., I cannot understand. To confess the truth, such an assertion seems to me as self-contradictory as it would be to say "the circle has put on the nature of the square."'

[a] 'Transient' is to be understood literally as a cause which passes over into an effect outside itself. Contrast Zulawski, l. c., who interprets it as a cause whose action is momentary and fleeting.

# CHAPTER III

## GOD AND HIS ATTRIBUTES (NATURA NATURANS)

### § 1. THE ATTRIBUTES AS 'LINES OF FORCE,' OR FORMS IN WHICH GOD'S OMNIPOTENCE MANIFESTS ITS FREE CAUSALITY TO AN INTELLIGENCE.

God in his free causality, as 'natura naturans[1],' is absolute power which is always in action in all

---

[1] On *Natura Naturans* and *Naturata*, cf. K. V. S. i. 8 and 9 (below, p. 88, note 3). Spinoza makes a somewhat different use of this old Scholastic Antithesis in the Ethics. There (E. i. 29 S.) he explains the distinction as follows:—

'In God, as the free cause of himself and therefore of all things, we must distinguish two aspects. God, as the free *cause*, as "id quod in se est et per se concipitur," is Natura Naturans. God, as the inevitable consequence of his own essential being, as self-*caused*, is Natura Naturata. God therefore (or his Attributes), as the ground of God (or his modes in their eternal and necessary coherence), is Natura Naturans: the eternal system of God's modes, which is the consequent of the free causality of Natura Naturans, is Natura Naturata.'

Cf. E. l.c., 'Per *Naturatam* autem intelligo id omne, quod ex necessitate Dei naturae, sive unius cuiusque Dei attributorum sequitur, hoc est omnes Dei attributorum modos, quatenus considerantur ut res, quae in Deo sunt, et quae sine Deo nec esse nec concipi possunt.' Erdmann (V. A. p. 134) strangely stops the quotation at 'res,' and so misinterprets Spinoza. Natura Naturata is not the world of sense-perception: but the universe in all its articulation as a perfect understanding would grasp it, if that understanding apprehended it as the *effect* of God's causality.

Logically, God as cause or ground is prior to God as effect or consequent. 'Deus omnibus rebus prior est causalitate' (E. i. 17 S.; cf. also K. V. S. ii. Praef. § 5). Natura Naturans is logically prior to Natura Naturata, or could be conceived without

ways[1]. It is his 'actuosa essentia' which all things express—or rather, are—in various determinate forms. The force to be and to persist in being which each thing has—the living energy which constitutes each thing's individuality [2]—is but a fragment, as it were, of the omnipotence of God. And the actual present existence or non-existence of any thing—its coming to be or ceasing to be in the 'communis ordo naturae,' as an event in the spatial and temporal series—this too is the effect of God's omnipotence. For God is the efficient cause of the 'essentia' and of the 'existentia' of all things [3]: and he is the 'causa essendi,' the cause which sustains them in being [4]. God is thus the 'inner vital force of the world [5];' but he is more, for he is also that which the force animates. There is no matter on which God works, or which he informs. All that is, is God: and God is all that is.

The Attributes or forms of God's omnipotence are not it, though not vice versa: just as the nature of a triangle, as given in its definition, is logically prior to the properties which flow from it, or to that which it is understood by the developed geometrical intelligence to be. But the full being (and therefore the full understanding) of the ground is impossible without the full being (and understanding) of the consequent. The triangle's nature would cease to be itself if its properties were to change or vanish; nor could it be understood if we were ignorant of them. So Natura Naturans has its fulfilment in Natura Naturata; and it is only the full understanding of the eternal system of God's modes which would render possible a complete knowledge of God and his Attributes. This, at any rate, seems to be Spinoza's meaning, though his words at times suggest that Natura Naturans is prior *really*—and not merely *logically*—to Natura Naturata, so that the full being and the full understanding of God as ground would not require the being or the understanding of God as consequent.

[1] Zulawski brings out the identity of God's 'essentia' with his power extremely well; cf. e.g. Zulawski, §§ 1, 6, &c.

[2] E. iii. 6, 7, and 8; and see below, Bk. II. ch. 3, § 2.

[3] E. i. 25.

[4] E. i. 24 C.

[5] Camerer, p. 2.

consequences of God's nature—they *are* that nature: and each Attribute expresses the whole nature of God under some one of its ultimate characters (above, pp. 22, ff.). No Attribute therefore is derived from any other, nor is any *deduced* from the nature of God. Each is coextensive with God, each is exclusive of every other, and each must be conceived ' per se.' 'It is essential to Substance that each of its Attributes should be conceived "per se." For all the Attributes which it has, have always been together in it ("simul in ipsa semper fuerunt"), nor could one have been produced from another: but each one expresses the reality or being of Substance.' (E. i. 10 S.)

But within the world as we know it, God's nature is manifested in two distinct systems; or God's free causality, his omnipotence, is actual in two separate lines of force. As a 'res extensa,' God is the free cause of the system which we know as the corporeal universe; its inner constitution, its movements, changes and properties are simply the effects of God's omnipotence working in a single line of force. And God is known to us as a Being infinite in his power of thinking[1]: as a 'res cogitans,' God is the free cause of the whole system which necessarily flows from the Attribute of Cogitatio.

§ 2. THE ATTRIBUTE OF EXTENSION. SPINOZA AND DESCARTES.

Spinoza, although he attacks the Cartesian conception of 'Extension,' yet develops his own view from the starting-point of that of Descartes.

God, according to Descartes, is not himself corporeal

---

[1] Cf. E. ii. 1 S., 'ens virtute cogitandi infinitum'; E. ii. 21 S., 'cogitandi potentia'; E. ii. 7 C., 'Dei cogitandi potentia aequalis est ipsius actuali agendi potentiae'; K. V. S. i. Dial. 1, § 11, and ii. 19, § 6.

or extended: for the corporeal is divisible, and divisibility involves imperfection [1].

But God created matter, and at the same time implanted in it a definite quantity of motion and rest—a quantity which he maintains always the same [2]. The fundamental characters of the material universe are its extension in three dimensions, its divisibility (which follows from its extension), the mobility of its parts (which is due to the motion and rest which God implanted in it), and the variation of its figuration which is the consequence of this mobility [3]. All the other qualities of matter—the 'secondary' qualities—Descartes rejects: they are simply appearances to us, produced by (indicative only of) extension together with the motion and figuration of the parts of the extended [4].

Spinoza follows Descartes in rejecting the secondary qualities—nothing real in the corporeal universe, except figures and motions, corresponds to them [5]—and therefore in calling the corporeal or material universe 'res extensa.' But the 'res extensa' is no creation [6] of God: it is God, an Attribute of God's nature, a form of his being. As such it is not divisible [7]. Nor is it a lifeless

---

[1] Desc. *Princ.* i. 23.
[2] Ib. ii. 36. On motion and rest, and quantity of motion, as Descartes held these conceptions (and as Spinoza in the main followed him), see Pollock, pp. 103 ff. And see below, ch. 4, § 3.
[3] Ib. ii. 23; cf. above, p. 31, note 1.
[4] Cf. e.g. Ib. i. 69; ii. 4; iv. 197 ff.
[5] Cf. e.g. E. i. App.
[6] Cf. K. V. S. i. 2, § 5, note 3. 'To "create" is to posit a thing both as regards its *essentia* and as regards its *existentia*: to "generate" is to cause a thing to come to be only as regards its *existentia*. (Hence there is now in nature no creation, but only generation.) If then God creates, he creates the nature of the thing together with the thing.... But we cannot strictly say that creation has ever taken place.'
[7] It is only imperfect apprehension—the attempt to 'picture' to which we are so prone—which leads us to regard corporeal Substance as divisible. In its real nature, as properly apprehended by Intelligence and not by

# NATURA NATURANS

mass, in which God implanted 'motion and rest.' As an Attribute, it is a form of God's actuality—a line of force in which his omnipotence manifests itself[1]. And 'motion and rest,' on which the figuration and indeed all the properties of the material universe depend, are not put into it *ab extra*, but together are the primary or most fundamental mode of its being[2].

### § 3. THE INFINITY OF ATTRIBUTES. THE ATTRIBUTE OF THOUGHT. GOD IS SELF-CONSCIOUS.

The same God who is to our intelligence an extended thing—a corporeal universe—is also to our intelligence a thinking thing, a spiritual or ideal universe. His omnipotence manifests itself to us in a second line of force, which is articulated in the system of souls or consciousnesses. Every mode of God, every thing, which we see and feel as a body, is also a soul[3]: though it does not follow that we as a fact experience both the extended and the soul-side of all the modes which come within our range.

Since God's omnipotence is absolutely unlimited, his nature absolutely complete, a complete intelligence would recognize in him *all* Attributes, in his active causality *all* lines of force[4]. No number can exhaust this 'allness';

Imagination, it is Substance under one of its Attributes; and, as Substance, necessarily indivisible. All the arguments against the corporeal nature of God show only that if you misapprehend 'Substantia extensa'—if you try to divide it—you get into inextricable confusion; they do not show that Extension in its real nature is not an Attribute of God. Cf. above, pp. 30 ff; E. i. 13 and C; E. i. 15 S.

[1] See Epp. 81 and 83 (in answer to Tschirnhaus).
[2] See below, ch. 4, § 3.
[3] Cf. E. ii. 13 S. 'Omnia, quamvis diversis gradibus, animata ... sunt.' In the context this applies to the 'individuals' or *complex* bodies (see below, pp. 82 ff.); but it is true, according to Spinoza's position, of all bodies whatever, and indeed of all modes of any and every Attribute.
[4] Cf. above, pp. 38 ff.

Book I. we must say simply that God's nature or omnipotence is complete, or 'consists of' an infinity of Attributes or lines of force. And, since this is so, every mode of God—as it really is, for a complete experience [1]—would be 'expressed' in an infinity of ways. But whilst Extension and Thought can be understood by a human intelligence, the other Attributes cannot. The spiritual and corporeal sides of things are at least *possible* objects of our experience: but we cannot experience the other 'ways of expression' of God's modes. We do not find in our experience, e.g., creatures which show themselves as modes of three or more Attributes in the same way as man shows himself as a mode both of Extension and of Thought. The conclusion that God 'constat infinitis attributis' is not reached empirically, but *à priori* from the conception of an absolutely infinite Being [2].

The primary characteristic of Cogitatio is thought proper. The Intellectus (intelligence or understanding as an activity) is the fundamental mode, of which all the other modes of Thought (e. g. volition, desire, passion) are dependents. An act of will or a desire presuppose in the subject an 'idea'—a conception—of the object willed or desired [3]. Now it is the distinctive feature of an 'idea,' or act of thinking, that it exhibits two sides of

---

[1] Cf. E. ii. 7 S. '... Quare rerum, ut in se sunt, Deus revera est causa, quatenus infinitis constat attributis....'

[2] See Ep. 64 in answer to Schuller, who had propounded problems suggested by Tschirnhaus. Although, when Spinoza wrote the K. V. (above, p. 39, note 5), he seems to have thought that we might in time learn some other Attribute of God, no trace of this belief survives in the Ethics, and Ep. 64 directly repudiates it. The doctrine of the 'Infinity of Attributes,' though Spinoza could not logically discard it, remains incompletely assimilated in his philosophy, and serves only to project shadows of confusion within it. Tschirnhaus, with singular acuteness, pointed out these difficulties from the first, and Spinoza never adequately answers them. See below, Bk. II. ch. 1, § 4.

[3] E. ii. Ax. 3.

its being. Its formal or real being is its being as an act of thought: and for this it depends entirely upon other acts of thought: the system of 'ideae' (like that of 'corpora') is a closed system, complete within its own Attribute, Cogitatio. But every 'idea' is also, by its very nature, an idea of an 'ideatum': it reflects or represents or expresses something other than the act of thinking which it is—its formal essence *is* the objective essence of its 'ideatum,' just as it itself may have an objective essence as the 'ideatum' of another idea [1].

Thus the 'idea'—the act of God's thinking—which is the 'soul' of an extended thing, at the same time reflects that thing. God, in being the 'soul' of a thing, thinks the thing, whose soul his act of thought is. The idea which in its formal being is a mode of God's thinking, a fragment of the spiritual or soul universe, has a content which expresses a corresponding extended side of the same mode—or is the 'objective' being of a mode of Extension. It is the same thing, one and the same mode of God, which is both body and soul (and an infinity of other 'expressions'), both 'ideatum' and idea. The intelligence of God is thus one and the same as its objects: it is the soul-side of them, and is thereby, for God, the reflection or apprehension of them [2]. And since for a complete experience every mode of God would exhibit all forms of being, God's intelligence, which is complete,

---

[1] Cf. above, p. 7, and E. ii. 8 C. On *Esse formale* and *Esse obiectivum*, see especially Desc. *Medit.*, Resp. ad primas obiect., and Resp. ad secundas obiect., p. 75 (specimen of synthetic geometrical method), def. 3, '*Per realitatem obiectivam ideae* intelligo entitatem rei repraesentatae per ideam, quatenus est in idea....' Hence, the phrase 'esse obiectivum ideae' is slightly ambiguous. It may mean (1) the being of a thing as it is in its idea, i.e. the content of an idea; or (2) the objective being of an idea, i.e. the idea as it is when it forms the content of another idea.

[2] Cf. E. ii. 7 S.

Book I. is the reflection or apprehension of all God's Attributes and all the modes in which they are articulated.

Thus the Attribute of Thought on its formal side is coextensive with Substance in the same sense as every other Attribute [1]. But since, as thought, it necessarily has a content—or is the 'esse obiectivum' of its 'ideata'—it is, in a sense, 'wider' than any other Attribute: in fact, coextensive with *all* the Attributes of God [2].

God, in his being as a 'res cogitans,' is thus aware of himself and all that follows from himself: and since all consciousness involves self-consciousness, since in thinking or knowing we necessarily know that we know [3], God is aware of his own thinking: or is self-conscious in the sense that he is conscious of his consciousness of himself [4].

---

[1] Cf. E. ii. 1 S.

[2] Cf. Ep. 70, Tschirnhaus's criticism, stated by Schuller. For a consideration of this criticism, see below, Bk. II. ch. 1, § 4. Cf. also the very important statement in K. V. S. App. 2, § 9. Not only the modifications of Extension, Spinoza there says definitely, but all the modifications of all the infinite number of Attributes, have their soul, which is an idea, i.e. a modification of the Attribute of Thought.

[3] Cf. above, p. 7, and E. ii. 21 S; ii. 43 and S.

[4] See Loewe, pp. 287 ff., and below, Bk. II. ch. 1, § 3.

# CHAPTER IV

## GOD AND HIS MODES (NATURA NATURATA)

### § 1. DEGREES OF PERFECTION OR REALITY.

GOD, as the necessary consequent of his own free causality, is Natura Naturata—an ordered system of modes, following with coherent necessity from Natura Naturans. But, though all things follow with the same inevitable necessity from God's nature, they differ from one another in degree of perfection or reality; and indeed the difference is one not only of degree but also of kind. 'For although a mouse and an angel, sadness and joy, depend equally on God, yet a mouse cannot be a species of angel, nor sadness a species of joy[1].' 'The criminal expresses God's will in his own way, just as the good man does in his; but the criminal is not on that account comparable with the good man. The more perfection a thing has, the more it participates in the divine nature[2] and the more it expresses God's perfection. The good have incalculably more perfection than the vicious; and therefore their "virtue" is not to be compared with the "virtue" of the vicious ...'

It is in 'natura naturata,' the eternal system of modes, that these degrees of perfection or reality are exhibited. For there is an order in the sequence of the modes from God's nature, and on that order their degree of perfection

---

[1] Ep. 23.
[2] Ep. 19 '... eo etiam magis de Deitate participat....' Cf. E. iv. App. cap. xxxi.

BOOK I. depends. The order is not a temporal, but a logical one. There is no before and after, no temporal succession, in the relation of the modes to God; all modes are the eternal consequents of God's causality. But there is a logical priority and posteriority; and on this their degrees of reality depend. 'That effect is the most perfect which is produced by God immediately; and the more mediating causes which any effect requires, the less perfect it is[1].'

§ 2. FORMAL STATEMENT OF THE ORDER OF THE MODAL SEQUENCE.

(i) *Immediate Infinite and Eternal Modes.*

Any thing which is the direct consequent of an Attribute of God, will share the Attribute's eternity and infinity:—i.e. since it follows immediately from the Attribute, and since the Attribute involves no negation of being in itself, the mode's reality within the Attribute's field of being will not be limited. Its being will express itself fully: its existence will not be circumscribed in time or space, or by any limiting condition[2]. Thus,

[1] E. i. App.
[2] E. i. 21. Omnia quae ex *absoluta* natura alicuius attributi Dei sequuntur, *semper* et infinita existere debuerunt, sive *per idem attributum* aeterna et infinita sunt.' (The italics are my own.)

*Absoluta*, as opposed to 'quidquid ex aliquo Dei attributo, quatenus modificatum est aliqua modificatione, sequitur': — the modes, therefore, of which Spinoza is talking, are the direct or immediate consequents of the Attribute. Their existence and their nature, since they follow immediately from the Attribute, are coextensive with it. Their existence is not duration for a limited time, but never begins or ceases (*semper*). [On Eternity and Duration, see below, Bk. III. ch. 4, § 2. See also A. E. Taylor in *Mind*, N. S. no. 18.] They have the infinity of which modes are capable (see above, p. 29)—i. e. they are infinite 'vi causae cui inhaerent,' or infinite *per idem attributum*. And they are 'eternal,' so far as their existence follows from the *Attribute's* essence in which their essence is involved.

# PARTICULAR THINGS

e.g., if 'motion[1]' follows directly from Extension, or is the immediate mode in the Attribute of Extension, there will be nothing extended which is not—whatever else it may be besides—at any rate in motion; and motion can never cease to be within the sphere of Extension.

### (ii) *Mediate Infinite and Eternal Modes.*

Any thing which follows from an Attribute of God as modified by an eternal and infinite modification, must itself be infinite and necessary in its existence[2].

Thus, if e.g. in the extended universe there is a direct consequent of the totality of motion and rest, that consequent will itself be infinite and eternal; i.e. its being and its existence will be coextensive with motion and rest, and, so far, with the Attribute.

### (iii) *Particular Things.*

'Particular things are nothing but states or modes of God's Attributes in which these are expressed in a certain and determinate manner[3].' What is their place in the modal system of 'natura naturata'? Are they infinite or finite modes? Eternal or contingent in their existence? We are here face to face with the central difficulties of Spinoza's system. Much in his theory will receive its fuller development in the course of subsequent chapters: much is undoubtedly open to criticism; and much must

---

[1] I say 'motion' (and not 'motion and rest') merely for simplicity: see below.

[2] E. i. 22. 'Quidquid ex aliquo Dei attributo, quatenus modificatum est tali modificatione, quae et necessario et infinita per idem existit, sequitur, debet quoque et necessario et infinitum existere.' (Necessitas existentiae = aeternitas: E. i. 23 dem.)

E. i. 23 is the converse of i. 21 and 22. 'Omnis modus, qui et necessario et infinitus existit, necessario sequi debuit, vel ex absoluta natura alicuius attributi Dei, vel ex aliquo attributo modificato modificatione, quae et necessario et infinita existit.'

[3] E. i. 25 C.

remain obscure from difficulties of interpretation. Meantime I will try to state as clearly as possible the double conception of particular things and of their dependence on God which Spinoza develops[1].

### (A) *Particular things as infinite and eternal.*

So long as the causality of God works through the mediation of infinite and eternal modes, its consequents must themselves be infinite and eternal[2]. Now *in a sense* particular things are infinite and eternal—i. e. 'vi causae cui inhaerent.' As modes their reality is dependent upon the Substance of which they are the 'affectiones,' or which sustains them. Their reality in that dependence is timelessly actual: their 'essence' *in and through the modal system or the Attribute* involves their existence: and *in and through the modal system* their essence is complete or infinite.

The particular bodies and ideas, that is, so far as they are comprehended in their respective Attributes—viewed by reason in their modal systems—have an actuality which flows timelessly and necessarily from their essential nature: i.e. an existence which is eternal. This actuality or existence is not indeed the inevitable consequent of the 'essentia' of each single thing by itself—for then each would be a Substance[3]: but it follows inevitably from the Substance in which the 'essentiae' of all particular things are sustained. The actuality of each particular thing thus seems to be the necessary consequent of the whole modal system, or 'natura naturata,' through the one Substance which this implies. The 'essentia' of each particular thing is 'eternal,' or inevitably is actual, only in so far as it is involved in the whole

---

[1] I am indebted to Camerer in this section perhaps more than usual, though I have not entirely followed his views.

[2] E. i. 22.

[3] E. i. 24 (cf. especially the dem.) is directed against this misinterpretation.

## PARTICULAR THINGS

system of 'essentiae' which together express, and necessarily express, some Attribute of God [1].

And in this necessary coherence of their modal system, the 'essentiae' of particular things are complete or infinite. Their 'infinity' is the infinity of the system which sustains them, of the context apart from which they are not capable of full reality: and their 'eternity' is the necessity of their actuality as the consequence of the system in which their 'essentiae' are complete [2].

If, then, we regard the particular things as forming 'natura naturata'—i.e. as they in their reality are, as expressing God's nature in a coherent and inseparable modal system—we must conceive them as sharing the infinity and eternity of the Attributes and immediate modes. Their existence or actuality, from this point of view, is not occurrence in the time and space series, but the timeless being or self-assertion which they possess as expressions of God's power [3].

---

[1] Spinoza says (Ep. 10) that he does not *call* the 'essentiae' of particular things 'aeternae veritates,' because he does not wish to imply that they have no existence outside the mind. They are eternal truths, i.e. eternal realities. Cf. e.g. E. i. 17 S., where the 'essentia' of a man is called an 'aeterna veritas': and i. 20 C. 1, where Spinoza says that 'the existence of God, like his essence, is an eternal truth.'

It clearly will not do to use the conception of the eternity of the body of scientific knowledge —the reciprocal maintenance of true principles in a systematic explanation of the world— as more than a very inadequate illustration of the kind of reality and actuality of which Spinoza is thinking. 'Natura naturata' is not a system of thoughts, but a system of things which amongst other characteristics have an ideal (or thought-) side. Perhaps Spinoza's meaning is best illustrated—I can hardly say elucidated—by a reference to TdIe, VVlL. i. pp. 33 ff.

[2] Cf. E. v. 40 S. 'Ex quibus, et simul ex prop. 21, part. 1, et aliis, apparet, quod mens nostra, quatenus intelligit, aeternus cogitandi modus sit, qui alio aeterno cogitandi modo determinatur, et hic iterum ab alio, et sic in infinitum; ita ut omnes simul Dei aeternum et infinitum intellectum constituant.'

[3] E. v. 29 S.; ii. 45 S.

But the particularity of the particular things, when they are so regarded, seems to vanish in the system. Completely real and eternal they may be, but individually distinct they are not. In the timeless actuality of the modal system, in the completeness of 'natura naturata,' there is no individual 'essentia' or 'existentia' except that of the whole system.

The 'essentia' of every thing, as a mode comprehended in one of the Attributes of God, is, it is true, on its actual or existing side, a force which makes for assertion of the thing's individual self: a 'conatus, quo unaquaeque res in suo esse perseverare conatur[1].' But this 'individualistic' force is what it is, only as a partial expression of God's 'actuosa essentia' or 'potentia': just as the individual 'essentia' of the thing is only a mode or partial expression of God's 'essentia.' Individuality of essence and existence belongs in any real sense to God, and to God alone[2].

(B) *Particular things as finite and transitory.*

On the other hand, if you take the particular things out of the system, and regard them as particular, their completeness vanishes and their eternity disappears. For although their essence is in its actuality a force which makes for self-assertion, and though that force is not in its self limited for its activity to a finite period of time[3]; yet no single thing can, taken by itself, maintain its individuality through all time, nor resist indefinitely the action of the other single things against which it has to assert itself. And, though every thing in its context—in its dependence on its modal system—is complete, yet every thing by itself is but a part which is incomplete in

---

[1] E. iii. 7.   [2] For developments and modification, see below.
[3] E. iii. 8.

essence and power, or finite in nature and transitory in existence[1].

The same abstraction, therefore, which holds the modes apart from their system, and which gives them individuality, seems necessarily to destroy the fullness and permanence of their being. If we treat the parts of 'natura naturata' as independent of the whole, as having a distinctive character of their own, we are necessarily negating some of their real being: and that means that they have become to us finite or incomplete realities[2].

It is in this incompleteness and transitoriness that particular things appear to us in our ordinary experience. The 'communis ordo naturae[3]' presents itself to us as a complex of particular things acting and reacting on one another, coming into being and passing away, the products of infinite series of finite causes, and the starting-points of similar infinite series of finite effects. The 'ways of picturing things,' the categories of measure, time, and number, form the framework of the experience in which we arrange these events. The 'real' world, as we thus apprehend it, is a world of separate things, of a definite size and shape, occurring at definite places and at definite times. In place of the unbroken unity of Substance—a unity which was maintained in the modal system of 'natura naturata,' and so seemed to render the individuality of the modes of that system impossible—we have the multiplicity of the phenomenal world, in which the distinct character of each part and its occurrence at a particular time and place seem unintelligible and fortuitous, although the interaction of the parts is ascribed to necessary and universal laws.

This world of isolated and perishable things, with its

[1] Cf. e.g. E. iv. 4 dem.
[2] Cf. e.g. E. i. 8 S. i. 'Quum finitum esse revera sit ex parte negatio, et infinitum absoluta affirmatio existentiae alicuius naturae....'
[3] For the phrase, cf. E. ii. 29 S. and C., ii. 30 dem.

BOOK I. apparently arbitrary sequences—arbitrary as regards the natures of the connected events—this world of the unscientific experience is largely illusory. We shall find that Spinoza places it as the object of the lowest grade of apprehension[1]. But it is not through and through illusion: or, if it is, there must at least be a real basis of the illusion. It must in fact be explained as the— inadequate and partial—appearance of 'natura naturata.' It will become intelligible only in so far as it is traced to the intelligible system of modes[2].

### (C) *The twofold causality of God.*

The 'essentiae' of particular things which have a timeless actuality in the Attributes of God, have also an actuality or existence which shows itself as their appearance in the temporal and local series[3]: and their distinctive nature as it appears, and their actions in this phenomenal world, are the inevitable consequents of the causality of God, just as is their permanent 'essentia.' The causality of God determines not only the 'essentia' and 'existentia' of every mode in the system of 'natura naturata,' but also the determinate state of each thing from which its actual existence here and now, and its actual operation, inevitably flow[4].

---

[1] I have been obliged to anticipate Spinoza's theory of knowledge, and must refer the reader to the chapter on that subject for fuller explanation of what I have said here.

[2] Cf. TdIe, VVlL. i. pp. 33 ff. The 'series rerum fixarum aeternarumque,' on which the 'series rerum singularium mutabilium' depends, seems partly to correspond to the conception in the Ethics of 'natura naturata' as the basis of the 'communis ordo naturae.' But in the TdIe, Spinoza is still very strongly under the influence of Bacon, from which he has almost completely freed himself in the Ethics. See however Pollock, pp. 140 ff. On the whole question see below, pp. 119 ff.

[3] Cf. E. ii. 8 and C; v. 29 S. On the whole subject, cf. K. V. S. ii, Appendix 2, § 11, with Sigwart's notes.

[4] E. i. 26 and 27; i. 28; i. 29 dem.

As members of 'natura naturata,' the particular things exhibit a complete and timeless 'essentia,' which is mediated by mediate and immediate eternal and infinite modes. How they can yet maintain their individuality in that system is a question which forces itself upon us already, and which will recur with increased difficulties when we come to consider Spinoza's ethical doctrine.

At any rate, this their eternal nature, with its timeless actuality or force of self-assertion, expresses itself—imperfectly—in a temporal and local existence : and its occurrence with all the characteristics attaching to it (its special present nature, the time and place of its manifestation, its actions and passions, &c.) is determined by a system of necessary law, or by a causality of God, which cannot be reduced to the causality exhibited in 'natura naturata.' The particular things as they appear in the phenomenal world cannot be regarded as mediated by infinite and eternal modes; for they themselves are finite and transitory in their appearances. If you endeavour to trace the cause of the occurrence here and now of this particular thing or this particular event, you are led backwards from finite to finite thing or event; and your explanation resolves itself into an infinite chain of causes and effects, each one of which is itself finite. Or, as Spinoza expresses it[1], every single thing which is finite and has a determinate existence, must have followed from God or one of his Attributes so far as it was affected by a modification itself finite and determinate in existence. And this again must have been determined by a similar finite and determinate mode or cause, and so on *in infinitum.*

NOTE.—The difficult Scholium to E. i. 28 is intended to emphasize the absolute causality of God in all his works, even the most mediated of them. God, as Spinoza puts it elsewhere, is the immanent and

---

[1] E. i. 28 dem.

Book I. not the transient cause; or he is the cause of all things in the same sense in which he is the cause of himself. In this Scholium, Spinoza divides the 'effects' of God into two classes: (i) those things which follow of necessity directly from his nature (i.e. the immediate modes); (ii) those things which cannot be or be conceived without God, but which are mediated in their necessary sequence by the immediate modes (i.e. the mediate infinite and eternal modes; and also the particular things, so far as they are distinguished from these).

With regard to (i), God is their absolutely proximate cause, though not—as is sometimes said [1]—a cause the same in kind as its effects (cf. E. i. 17 S.) For whereas God can be and be conceived apart from his effects, they cannot be or be conceived apart from God. With regard to (ii), God may be called the 'remote' cause of the single things *only in the sense* that they follow mediately and not immediately from his nature. God cannot be called their 'remote' cause, if by that term we understand a cause which is in no way conjoined with its effects.

### § 3. THE MODAL SYSTEM OF THE ATTRIBUTE OF EXTENSION. WHOLE AND PARTS.

#### (1) *Modal System of Extension* [2].

As modes of the Attribute of Extension, all bodies have a certain magnitude, i.e. they are all extended in three dimensions. This—their extension—constitutes their substantial nature, and they do not differ in substance from one another. The division of corporeal Substance is not a division *of* it, but in it: the 'parts' of it, the separate bodies, differ from one another not 'really' or substantially, but only 'modally.' The distinctness of separate parts of the corporeal Substance rests upon the diverse states of those distinguished parts, and not upon divisions of that substratum which sustains the states [3].

[1] Is Spinoza thinking of the orthodox doctrine of Angels? cf. K. V. S. 1, ch. 9, where the immediate modes are called by a Hebraism 'Sons of God.'
[2] Cf. E. ii, after prop. 13 (VVlL. i. pp. 88 ff.).
[3] Cf. E. i. 15 S. sub fin.

## MODAL SYSTEM OF EXTENSION

The quantity or amount of extension which the various 'bodies' include may differ, but its kind or quality does not [1].

---

[1] E. ii. (after prop. 13) Lemma 1. 'Corpora ratione motus et quietis, celeritatis et tarditatis, et non ratione substantiae ab invicem distinguuntur.' Lemma 2 dem. 'In his enim omnia corpora conveniunt, quod unius eiusdemque attributi conceptum involvunt . . .' i.e. they are all modes of Extension, and have therefore a certain — varying — magnitude.

On the whole subject of Spinoza's Physics, see Thomas, pp. 153 ff., Camerer, pp. 61 ff., and Pollock, pp. 103 ff. Pollock is particularly clear and convincing on 'motion-and-rest,' for which cf. also K. V. S. i. 2, § 19, note 6, and ii. 19, § 8.

Though there is some difficulty with regard to Spinoza's conception of the *simplicissima corpora* —the elementary corpuscles—I cannot admit that Spinoza's words are so obscure or inconsistent as Camerer maintains.

Spinoza says definitely in two places that these *corpora simplicissima* differ from one another 'solo motu et quiete, celeritate et tarditate,' i.e. in the degrees of their motion-and-rest. And, in view of this distinct declaration, the definition of Composite Bodies, which immediately follows (VVlL. i. 90), must be interpreted to cover *all kinds* of Composite Bodies; i.e. those in which the components are themselves composite, as well as those in which the components are the elementary corpuscles. Those words of the definition, which at first sight seem to imply that the elementary corpuscles differ in magnitude ('Quum corpora aliquot eiusdem *aut diversae* magnitudinis . . .'), must be taken to refer to those composites whose components are composite. The words of the Scholium (VVlL. i. 91), 'Atque *hucusque* Individuum concepimus, quod non nisi ex corporibus, quae solo motu et quiete, celeritate et tarditate inter se distinguuntur, hoc est, quod ex corporibus simplicissimis componitur,' must not be unduly pressed. The fact that Spinoza reiterates his declaration that the elementary corpuscles differ only in motion-and-rest ought to suffice to prevent a too pedantic interpretation of *hucusque*. 'Up to this point' Spinoza *has* treated of primary compounds—with the single exception of the two words ('aut diversae') introduced to render the definition of Composites wide enough to cover all classes of Composites. And though the *hucusque* is a little incautious, yet the reiteration of his view of elementary corpuscles *in the very same sentence* leaves no doubt of Spinoza's meaning.

I cannot think that Camerer is right in the difficulties which he finds in Ax. i. (VVlL. i. p. 89).

BOOK I.  Further, as modes of Extension, all bodies are actually in motion or actually at rest, and are capable of various degrees of motion [1].

The conception of motion and rest was borrowed—as Pollock shows—from Descartes, and in Descartes it appears to be the direct descendant of the Aristotelian κίνησις and ἠρεμία [2]. From certain expressions of Spinoza —cf. e.g. Ax. 2 with Ax. 1 and Lemma 2, dem. (VV1L. i. p. 88)—we might suppose that 'motion and rest' is only an inexact expression for various degrees of speed. But, strange and obscure as the conception may be, he seems to have followed Descartes in regarding 'rest' as the contrary (not the contradictory) of motion [3], and any given degree of motion in any body (i.e. its velocity) as the resultant of the combination of that body's motion and rest [4]. If a body moves more slowly than another, that means that in the proportion of its motion to its rest, the rest-factor is relatively predominant.

Within the Attribute of Extension, motion and rest together form an immediate infinite and eternal mode [5], i.e. every body, besides its extendedness, must (however rudimentary its nature) exhibit a certain velocity, and that is the resultant of the co-operation of its 'motion and rest,' which belong to it because it is a mode of

It is no doubt true that Spinoza does not 'explain' how motion is involved in Extension, or how the 'nature' of an elementary corpuscle is its degree of motion-and-rest. But that is because Extension is for him an Attribute of God, and therefore a form of God's omnipotence; or (in other words) because motion-and-rest is for him the *immediate* mode of Extension, and not (as with Descartes) something implanted in matter or connected with it through the mediation of a Creator. (Cf. above, p. 69.)

[1] E. l. c. Ax. 1 and 2 (VV1L. i. p. 88), Lemma 2, dem.
[2] Cf. Desc. *Princ.* iv. 200.
[3] Desc. *Princ.* ii. 37. Cf. K. V. S. ii. 19, § 8, note 3.
[4] Desc. *Princ.* ii. 44.
[5] Ep. 64.—In K. V. S. (ii. 19. 8, and App. 2, §§ 14, 15) Spinoza speaks of motion and rest as two modes.

## MODAL SYSTEM OF EXTENSION

Extension [1]. The differences of all the bodies in the extended universe ultimately depend upon the differences of their degrees of motion, i. e. upon the quantities of motion and rest and the proportion between them, which they, or their ultimate component corpuscles, contain [2].

It is in this sense, that all bodies are '*mediated*' by the mode of 'motion-and-rest'; for their distinctive characters, their union, their 'thingness' and their sensible properties, are ultimately all derived from the variations of their motion-and-rest.

Thus, when two or more corpuscles, *which are at rest*, whether of the same or of diverse magnitude, are pressed together by the surrounding corpuscles, so as to lean on one another—or, when two or more corpuscles, *which are in motion*, whether their degrees of velocity be the same or different, so combine their motions that they form a system of motions balanced in a definite proportion—in either case we have what we call *one* composite body, or an individual formed by the union of these corpuscles [3].

'Hardness,' 'Softness,' 'Fluidity,' of bodies depend upon the stability of this coherence. Thus, if the component particles lean upon one another in respect to large surfaces, the combination is stable, and we call the body 'hard'; if in respect to small surfaces, it is unstable, and we call it 'soft.' For the component particles can then shift their position; i. e. though they still rest upon one another and therefore still form a single

---

[1] Spinoza—as we have already seen (above, p. 69)—rejects the view of Descartes that God at the Creation implanted motion and rest in extended matter. Motion and rest are a mode, which is the direct consequent of the nature of Extension.

[2] E. ii. Lemma 1. Cf. K. V. S. § 14 of App. 2 to Part 2; also the interesting and important *Zusatz* to the Preface to Part 2.

[3] Def. of composite bodies, VVll. i. p. 90. See above, p. 83, note 1.

Book I. individual thing, the shape of the whole can easily be changed. If within the system of balanced motions the separate motions of the component particles have free play, the 'individual' is called 'fluid [1].'

The 'hardness' or 'softness,' therefore, of bodies depends upon the magnitude of the conjoined surfaces of corpuscles in a state of rest. If the surfaces are not contiguous—if the corpuscles are not 'leaning upon one another,' but in motion—then, so long as the particles are kept united in a system by the balance of their motions, we have an 'individual' which is 'fluid.'

'One Thing,' therefore, is not 'one' or a 'thing' in virtue of some mysterious substratum or thinghood: its unity, its individuality is constituted solely by the coherence of its parts. So long as this coherence is maintained, even though some of the parts drop out and others take their place, its unity and individuality will persist [2]. So long as the same balance of the proportions of motion to rest in the parts is maintained, those parts may grow larger or decrease in size, without affecting the nature of the composite individual [3]; and, under the same condition, the body will retain its individual nature and form, even though some parts of it change the direction of their motions [4]. Finally, the whole body can change the direction and the amount of its total motion—e. g. it can walk in any direction or be at rest—without losing its individuality, provided that the component motions of its parts can still maintain their relative directions and their relative degrees of velocity [5].

Thus an individual, which is but a compound of the primary corpuscles, can yet maintain its identity under

[1] VVlL. i. p. 90, Ax. 3.
[2] VVlL. i. p. 90, Lem. 4 and dem.
[3] Id. ib., Lem. 5.
[4] Id. p. 91, Lem. 6.
[5] Id. ib., Lem. 7.

considerable variations of its components; it 'can be affected in many ways,' without losing its characteristic unity. It is held together by mechanical laws[1], and yet can fulfil the functions of an organism. Still more is this the case with individuals 'of the second and third and more complex grades,' i.e. those in which the component parts are themselves complex bodies or 'individuals.' These 'can be affected in still more ways,' admit of still greater variations, without losing their identity. If we proceed on this plan, through more and more complex grades of individuals in which the unity comprehends more and more complex and articulate subordinate individuals as its parts, we shall ultimately conceive the whole extended universe as a single individual, whose form and nature is constituted by the balance of the motions of all bodies. Within its identical and persistent individuality it will comprehend the infinite variety of changes and processes which make up 'the face of the corporeal universe[2].' Since every single body has its motion and its individuality in dependence on this total order or system, this—the 'facies totius universi'—must be regarded as a mode which follows from the nature of God in priority to the single bodies. It is in fact a 'mediate infinite

---

[1] This statement will undergo some modification later on. The individuality of a compound body is due to the *balance* of the motions of the parts, and appears as a 'conatus, quo unaquaeque res in suo esse perseverare conatur.' The distinctive character of every individual thus supervenes on the combination of its parts, and is not simply and entirely given in the parts as such.

[2] E. ii. Lem. 7 S. 'Et si sic porro in infinitum pergamus, facile concipiemus, totam Naturam unum esse Individuum, cuius partes, hoc est omnia corpora, infinitis modis variant, absque ulla totius individui mutatione.' Cf. Ep. 32 (below, pp. 92, 93).

In Ep. 64, Spinoza gives as an instance of a mediate infinite and eternal mode 'facies totius universi, quae quamvis infinitis modis variet, manet tamen semper eadem'; and refers his correspondent to the Scholium just quoted.

Book I. and eternal mode' in the Attribute of Extension[1]; *mediate*, because dependent upon the mode of motion-and-rest; *infinite and eternal*, because the direct necessary consequent of this immediate infinite and eternal mode. It is indeed as the direct consequent of the mode of 'motion-and-rest,' which is always constant in amount[2], that the 'facies totius universi' retains its identical character—'manet semper eadem[3].'

Thus, all the properties of bodies depend upon the varieties of their motion-and-rest, and must be referred ultimately to the immediate infinite and eternal mode in the Attribute of Extension, viz. motion-and-rest.

But the motion-and-rest of any single body is not derived directly from the immediate mode, but is mediated for it by an infinite chain of other finite bodies themselves exhibiting motion-and-rest; i.e. every single body gets its properties (not directly from the mode of motion-and-rest, but) *mediately* through the mediate infinite and eternal mode of the Attribute of Extension—the 'facies totius universi,' of which all single bodies are parts. The particular proportion of motion to rest which characterizes each single body is transmitted to it through an infinite chain of finite corporeal causes[4].

---

[1] Ep. 64, loc. cit.

[2] Cf. Pollock, pp. 103 ff. Desc. *Princ.* ii. 36. C. M. ii. 11, § 2. K. V. S. 1, 9, § 2; and Ep. 32.

[3] It is instructive to compare K. V. S. Part 1, chs. 8 and 9. The distinction between mediate and immediate infinite and eternal modes is not expressly drawn there. The (immediate) infinite and eternal modes, which Spinoza calls 'Sons of God'—motion and the infinite intellect—are regarded as the 'universal' part of 'natura naturata,' and as the cause of the 'particular' part, i.e. the *res particulares*. 'Motion' is treated provisionally as an immediate effect, creature, or son of God: but in a late footnote we are told that Spinoza 'hopes to find the cause of motion,' i.e. to mediate it.—The authenticity of this footnote has been questioned: but see Sigwart, Tr., p. 58, note.

[4] Cf. VVII. i. p. 88, Lem. 3, and E. iii. 2 dem.

## (2) *Whole and Parts*[1].

It is only within the modal apprehension of Reality, that the conception of corporeal nature as a single individual, of which all bodies are parts, is legitimate. The category of Whole-and-Parts does not apply to Reality as such: for there are no departments or fragments of Reality whose being is sufficiently independent to make them its 'parts.' Spinoza will not allow that 'whole' is anything more than an 'ens rationis' (='ens imaginationis'), or that it is a less abstract conception than that of 'universal[2].'

But the modal apprehension of Reality, though not an ultimate or completely adequate way of regarding it, is valuable and necessary. The universe *is* a 'whole of parts' from one point of view, though this category does not completely express its nature.

And as the conception of the Attributes as Systems of Modes, or Wholes of Parts, is vital to Spinoza's philosophy, it will be as well to consider in this place Spinoza's most complete statement of his views on the subject. This is to be found in Ep. 32 (Nov. 1665). A month or two before, Spinoza[3], in referring to the miseries of the war between England and Holland, had observed to Oldenburg that he had learnt to study human nature in all these troubles without applying praise or blame, without either laughing or weeping at men's follies. He had reflected that man, like everything else, was but a part of Nature; that we are ignorant as to the way in which each part is congruent with its whole, and all the parts cohere with one another; and that this ignorance—and

---

[1] On the conception of Whole and Parts in Spinoza cf. Busolt, pp. 144 ff.

[2] Cf. above, p. 42; K. V. S. i. ch. 2, Dialogue 2, § 9; and note the cautious language even of Ep. 32, which expressly treats of Nature as a whole of parts.

[3] Ep. 30.

this alone—encourages the mistaken notion that there is 'good order' and 'confusion' in the universe. Because we see the world inadequately and in a mutilated view, some things appear to us useless, disordered and absurd. We first impose our limited notions of order and value, and then condemn what does not fit in with them. In response to an appeal from Oldenburg [1], Spinoza (in Ep. 32) explains why he believes that each part of Nature is congruent with its whole, and coheres with all the other parts of Nature within the Whole.

First, he reiterates his warning: there is no beauty nor ugliness, no good order nor confusion in Nature [2]. It is our Imagination, which finds things 'beautiful' or 'ugly,' 'well-ordered' or 'confused.' But there is all-pervading order in things in a different—non-teleological—sense [3]. All things do as a matter of fact cohere, as modes, to form a single system within their Attributes; and we may distinguish parts and wholes—subordinate systems—within this totality, according to the degree of coherence exhibited; according to the internal congruence, or absence of friction, which forms a sort of natural grouping. 'I regard things as parts of a whole,' Spinoza says, 'so far as their natures reciprocally are congruent, thus producing an inner agreement so far as is possible; on the other hand, so far as things are discrepant with one another, each of them forms a distinct idea of itself in our mind, and each therefore is regarded as a whole, and not as a part.' Thus e.g. the constituent elements of the blood—lymph, chyle, &c.—are regarded by us as its parts, simply

---

[1] Ep. 31.
[2] Spinoza's meaning may be illustrated by a sentence which Bosanquet (*Logic*, ii. p. 106) quotes from Huxley. For Spinoza's philosophy, as for 'purely physical science,' there would be in a catastrophe that extinguished life on the surface of the globe ... 'no more disorder than in the sabbatical peace of a summer sea.' Cf. also E. i. App.
[3] Cf. Oldenburg's remarks in Ep. 33.

because 'the motions of their particles so fit in with one another—in proportion with the respective magnitudes and figures of those particles—that they obviously combine together to form a single fluid. But so far as we regard the particles of lymph as discrepant in their figure and motion with the particles of chyle, we consider lymph and chyle each as a whole and not as a part. Now, suppose a worm living in the blood, endowed with *sight* to discriminate the particles of lymph, chyle, &c.[1]; and with *reason* to observe how each particle rebounds from the impact of another, or communicates a part of its motion to the other, &c. The life of such a worm in the blood would correspond to our life in this part of the universe. Each particle of the blood would be to it a whole, and not a part; and it could not know how all the parts were regulated by the general nature of the blood, and forced to accommodate themselves to a mutual congruence on a definite proportion as that nature demands. For, if we suppose' (in order to make the analogy complete) 'the blood to present the nature of a closed system; clearly its general state would persist for ever, and its particles would undergo no variations, except such as could be explained as the consequents of the nature of the blood alone, i.e. from the proportion of the motions of the lymph, chyle, &c., to one another; and so the blood' (which the worm cannot conceive as a single whole) 'would be in reality a whole always, and never a part.'

But, as a matter of fact, the blood is not a closed or self-dependent system. There are very many other external causes, which modify the laws of its nature (and which are in turn modified by it); hence other motions and variations arise in the blood, i.e. motions, which are not the consequents solely of the proportion

[1] I follow the reading of the Autograph in the possession of the Royal Society.

BOOK I. of the motions of its parts to one another, but of the proportion of the motion of the blood as a whole to the motions of the external causes. And therefore the blood gets the position of a part, and not a whole.

'Now all the bodies of Nature ought to be considered in a similar way. For all of them are surrounded by other bodies, and all are reciprocally determined to exist and work in a certain and determinate manner, viz. so that in the whole universe the same proportion of motion to rest is always maintained [1]. Hence it follows (i) that every body—*taken as a particular thing existing here and now*[2]—is a part of the whole universe, is congruent with the whole, and coherent with all the other parts of the whole; (ii) that—since the nature of the universe is not, like that of the blood, limited, but absolutely infinite —the changes of the parts of the universe, which can follow from this its infinite (nature, or) power, must be infinite.

'But if we regard each body in its relations to its Attribute, as regards its substantial nature [3], then each part has a still more intimate union with its whole. For' (cf. Ep. 4, to which Spinoza refers) 'since Substance is essentially complete, each part of the whole corporeal Substance belongs to the whole Substance, and can neither be nor be conceived apart from the rest of that Substance.

'This is why I hold the human body to be a part of the universe: and as regards the human mind, that too I conceive as a part of the universe. For I maintain that there is given in the Nature of Things an infinite power of Thinking, which, *quâ* infinite, comprehends in

---

[1] Cf. above, pp. 87, 88, on the direct dependence of the 'facies totius universi' on the immediate mode of motion-and-rest.

[2] 'Quatenus certo modo modificatum existit.'

[3] 'Ratione substantiae' contrasted with 'quatenus certo modo modificatum existit.' For this distinction, cf. above, pp. 76 ff.

itself ideally[1] the whole of Nature—its thoughts proceeding in the same manner as Nature itself, its "ideatum." And I hold the human mind to be this same power (not quâ infinite and perceiving the whole of Nature, but) quâ finite, i.e. so far as it perceives only the human body: and it is in this sense that I conceive the human mind to be a part of a certain infinite intelligence.'

### § 4. THE MODAL SYSTEM OF THE ATTRIBUTE OF THOUGHT.

The modal system of Thought is exactly parallel[2] to the modal system of Extension, as Spinoza always insists. But we have not the data which would enable us to trace the correspondence with any certainty in detail: in particular, we are not told what is the mediate infinite and eternal mode in Thought, corresponding to the 'facies totius universi' in Extension. We can, however, sum up what Spinoza says—completing the account to some extent conjecturally—as follows:—

The Attribute of Thought comprehends in itself all forms of conscious or spiritual activity—feeling, willing, desiring, &c.; but just as all modes of Extension ultimately presuppose as their ground the mode of motion-and-rest, so all the modes of Thought presuppose that mode which Spinoza calls 'intellectus.' The primary mode of Thought is the idea: volition, feeling, desire, &c., are all derivatives of apprehension, in the sense that the apprehending of an object must be logically prior to any feeling, willing, or desiring[3]. All the other modes

---

[1] *Obiectivè*.

[2] Or rather, the two systems are one and the same from different points of view. The so-called 'parallelism of the Attributes' is a misleading term; see below, pp. 134 ff.

[3] E. ii. Ax. 3. 'Modi cogitandi, ut amor, cupiditas, vel quicunque nomine affectus animi insigniuntur, non dantur, nisi in eodem individuo detur idea rei amatae, desideratae, &c. At idea dari potest, quamvis nullus alius detur cogitandi modus.'

of Thought are, in fact, as we shall learn, confused forms of the idea. Hence the primary characteristic which constitutes the soul-side of things is their 'apprehending': the 'intellectus infinitus' (in distinction e.g. from voluntas, cupiditas, amor, &c.) is the *immediate* eternal and infinite mode in the Attribute of Thought[1]. As, in the Attribute of Extension, if we conceive the primary constituent modification from which all qualities of extended things ultimately follow, we get the notion of 'motus-et-quies,' or the unvarying quantity of motion-and-rest: so, in the Attribute of Thought, if we conceive the primary form of Cogitatio from which all characteristics of thinking things are ultimately derived, we get the notion of the 'infinitus intellectus'—the completeness of an act of apprehending which would comprehend all reality[2].

The *mediate* infinite and eternal mode of Thought, which corresponds to the 'facies totius universi' in Extension, is—I think—the 'infinita idea Dei.' 'God, as Thought, can think an infinity of things in an infinity of ways; i.e. can form an idea of his own essence and of all things which necessarily follow from it. But what lies in God's power is necessarily actual. There is, therefore, necessarily given in God such an idea' (E. ii. 3 dem.). And this idea is, and must be, unique (E. ii. 4). In other words—God necessarily has a complete and unique apprehension of the universe, both in its eternal coherence and in its temporal order. This unique 'infinita idea' is the thought-side of all bodies and all

---

[1] Ep. 64. It follows (cf. above, pp. 70 ff.) that the soul or idea, which every thing is as a mode of Thought, is at the same time the *apprehension of* the corporeal side of the thing. The human soul, e.g., is by its very nature the apprehension of the human body.

[2] Cf. the significant expressions, E. i. App. sub fin., 'omnia quae ab *aliquo* infinito intellectu concipi *possunt*'; i. 16, 'omnia, quae sub intellectum infinitum cadere *possunt*.' (The italics are my own.)

## MODAL SYSTEM OF THOUGHT

the modes of all Attributes: it is the complete system of all the 'souls,' the ideal counterpart of the 'facies totius universi [1].'

Now our body, both in its eternal and in its temporal being, is a part of the 'facies.' Similarly, we should expect our mind, both in its eternal being (as an intelligence) and in its temporal being (as an emotional and volitional consciousness), to be a part of the 'infinita idea Dei.' But at this point Spinoza's language becomes inconsistent and obscure. Our mind in its eternal being—'quâtenus intellegit'—is a part of 'the eternal and infinite intelligence of God' (E. v. 40 S.; cf. ii. 11 C); or again, 'the human mind is a part of a certain infinite intelligence' (Ep. 32).

To some extent no doubt current theological language

---

[1] Cf. E. ii. 3, 4, 7 C, 8 and C. In this connexion, cf. the remarkable note to the Preface to Part 2 of the K. V. Spinoza there refers to a 'complete idea' which apprehends the nature of all beings in its totality — 'their nature, as it is comprehended in their essence'; and he expressly distinguishes this idea from 'the apprehension of each particular thing which comes to actual existence,' which is the soul of that thing.

Sigwart (in his notes ad loc.) rightly recognizes in this late addition to the K. V. an important anticipatory sketch of the earlier propositions of E. ii (cf. also below, p. 128, note 3). But I cannot agree with him when he identifies the 'idea Dei' of E. ii. 3 and 4 with the 'complete idea' of the K. V., and says that the 'ideas of actually existent things' are considered *for the first time* at E. ii. 9 ff. For this interpretation seems to me to make a sharp severance between 'Idea of Essence' and 'Idea of Existence,' which is neither the doctrine of the Ethics, nor *necessarily* implied in the passage of the K. V. in question. In the Ethics, at any rate, and probably also in the K. V., the 'idea Dei' is the complete apprehension both of the eternal essences and of the existences of things.

It is true that there is in the K. V. a greater *appearance* of such a severance than in the Ethics. But that appearance is precisely a mark of the comparative immaturity of this anticipatory sketch.

On the whole question of 'essence' and 'existence,' see also below, Appendix to Bk. II, pp. 221 ff.

would lead Spinoza to speak of the 'infinitus intellectus Dei,' where his strict terminology would have required 'Dei infinita idea.' But the real source of the inconsistency lies deeper. There is a fatal trend in Spinoza's philosophy towards abstraction, in spite of all his struggles towards the conception of a concrete unity. Thus, things in their temporal being—the actual world of the perceptive consciousness—either turn into illusions, or slip back into the world of eternal timeless necessity, the universe of science. And it is only a symptom of this general tendency that the mediate infinite and eternal modes resolve themselves into the immediate. The 'facies,' indeed, presents a brave appearance of comprehending in its systematic unity all the varieties of the phenomenal corporeal world. But look closer, and it is nothing but a balance of motions. The secondary qualities and the thingness of the distinct bodies have, as we know, long been resolved. The immediate mode, 'motus-et-quies,' alone remains. And the case is the same with the mediate mode of Thought, except that it makes even less show of resistance. Our actual mind with its emotions, volitions, desires, is *quâ passional* unreal. In its reality it is a part of the 'infinita idea Dei'; but in the completeness of that 'idea' all passion vanishes. The complete consciousness, therefore, of which ours is a fragment, is a purely active (i. e. a purely thinking) consciousness—an 'infinitus intellectus [1].'

The fact that Spinoza is all the time struggling to avoid an abstraction of this kind, increases the difficulties of interpretation, though it adds incalculably to the value of his work. *In his intention at least* the consciousness, of which ours is a fragment, fuses in its single intuition all the variety of the lower forms of Thought. The 'infinita idea Dei' is the infinite love, as well as the

[1] See below, pp. 111 ff., 119 ff.

infinite intelligence, of God—not the abstraction of intelligence without emotion or volition, but the fusion (so to say, at a higher power) of all forms of consciousness. But this is a subject the full consideration of which will occupy us in the sequel [1].

[1] See below, Bk. III.

# APPENDIX TO BOOK I

## DIFFICULTIES AND CRITICISMS

Book I.
Object of
this Appendix.

It will be convenient to pause at this point in our exposition of Spinoza. We have attempted to state his general conception of the ultimate nature of Reality—to explain his fundamental metaphysical positions. The attempt has led us a little beyond the limits of the First Part of the Ethics. For the conception of Attributes and Modes, and of degrees of perfection and reality in the modal sequence, would have been unintelligible without an outline-sketch of the inner articulation of Extension and Thought. To this extent, therefore, we have been compelled to treat of Spinoza's physics and psychology in order to give a clear account of his metaphysical principles. When we again take up the thread of the Ethics, we shall find ourselves occupied with Spinoza's physics and psychology so far as he expressly applies them to the nature of man to serve as a basis for his ethical theory. The attempt to present Spinoza's thoughts as far as possible without interruption has led to the suppression of a great deal of criticism which inevitably suggests itself. But though I have not constantly formulated objections to Spinoza's views, I have felt them perhaps as strongly as the reader; and I propose to devote this appendix to expressing some at least of the difficulties in question.

Two considerations render this criticism especially difficult. In the first place, I can but repeat in the main

# DIFFICULTIES AND CRITICISMS

what other and more capable writers have said before me. By making my statement as short as possible, I hope to earn the reader's pardon for this repetition. After all, it is impossible to pass over essential criticisms merely because they have been made before. In the second place, I can but criticize Spinoza as I interpret him; and I am deeply sensible of the inadequacy and probable erroneousness of my interpretation. Still, this is a risk which all history of philosophy must run. If I have blundered in my interpretation, my errors will stand out clearly in this attempt at criticism; and so other writers will, it is to be hoped, avoid similar pitfalls.

*Appendix.*

It is the object of philosophy to interpret experience so as to render it intelligible. A philosophy is successful so far as it enables us to 'think' experience, i. e. to take it in as a coherent system, as a whole which is interconnected by an immanent necessity. This—I have assumed—was the object of Spinoza, and it is from this point of view that I propose to examine the results we have reached. But the demand for intelligent apprehension, which we have made on philosophy, requires further explanation. A philosophy is not necessarily condemned, if it fail to 'think' experience through and through, to render it 'intelligible' in all its details. Such a demand would be preposterous, and would condemn all philosophies in advance. The detail of experience cannot be rendered transparent for human knowledge. Nothing short of infinite or absolute knowledge could completely apprehend the infinite or whole Reality. What we can attempt, and what all philosophies claim to do, is to gain a rational and consistent view of the general nature of Reality—to render experience intelligible in its main outline. And so far as a philosopher fails to do this, he may justly be criticized. But failure does not consist merely in leaving details un-

*Principle of criticism.*

explained and in their special nature unconnected with the general principles. Deficiencies of this kind are inevitable; in a metaphysical theory; and since they detract nothing from its value, it need fear no criticism on thier account. No one, e. g., can be expected to show exactly how and why finite existence, error, evil, change, are and consist with the general nature of Reality. To attempt to 'deduce the finite from the infinite '—if Spinoza had really attempted anything of the kind—would betray a serious misunderstanding of the powers of human thought. Or again it would be a mistaken zeal which, assuming a finite piece of experience, should endeavour to show in detail its exact coherence in the nature of things. So long as it can be shown that the detail of experience does not positively collide with the general conditions of Reality as established in a theory, but is in principle consistent with an intelligible view of things—so long, the existence of outstanding facts, the failure to resolve them, to render them transparent, does not of itself destroy the value of the general theory. If the general nature of Reality has been consistently and intelligibly thought out, and if it has been shown that the features which are not in detail comprehended in the general theory are yet in principle not hostile—then so far the theory maintains itself against criticism. But a philosopher lays himself open to attack if his general theory is inwardly inconsistent, or—and this is another side of the same fault—is incomplete, inadequate to comprehend the whole outline of Reality. And again he may justly be criticized if he offers an explanation of the details which conflicts with his general principles. Or, lastly, his theory is untenable if it forces us to conceive the general nature of Reality in such a way that the details of experience—all or some of them—cannot conceivably for any apprehension be intelligible: if, that is, we can see that

# DIFFICULTIES AND CRITICISMS

even the fullest understanding would but render the discrepancies and the conflict between details and general theory more certain[1].

*Appendix.*

Now, at first sight, Spinoza's doctrine seems to fulfil the task of philosophy in an eminent degree. All the manifold of experience, all the apparently isolated fragments of the world, would seem, for his theory, to fall into place as the necessarily interconnected content of an unbroken unity. So continuous, so absolutely of one piece (it would seem) is the fabric of experience, that no part or parcel of it can 'be' or 'be conceived' without carrying with its being and intelligibility the being and intelligibility of the whole. Indeed, the theory goes further: it gives us (not a system of necessarily co-active members, but) a Substance of which all things are but phases or states, whose distinctness and independence are only apparent. For such a theory, the necessary interconnexion of the manifold is but the unfolding of the immanent being of the One. Reality, so apprehended, offers to thought's passage a reflex of thought's own nature. To 'think' Reality—if such were its being—would be possible through and through; for thought would pass from point to point without ever meeting with an obstacle, without ever crossing a chasm. The limits, which constitute the particularity of the different elements of experience, will—if properly understood—carry the Spinozist over the differences of things, and show him that these so-called 'things' are but modes or states of the self-identical, continuous, and all-inclusive Substance. For they are but 'limits,' and a 'limit' is but a 'negation': it leaves the positive Real untouched in its complete or unlimited being. To 'think' the universe in the spirit of Spinoza, is (it would

*Does Spinoza's theory satisfy the requirements of a metaphysical theory of the universe?*

---

[1] I am indebted to Bradley, *Appearance and Reality*, more than usual for the view developed in this section. Cf. *App. & R.* 2nd edition, pp. 562 ff., pp. 184 ff., &c.

BOOK I. seem) to grasp its multiplicity in so coherent and transparent an apprehension that the multiplicity transmutes itself in the process into absolute unity: unity so absolute, that 'unity' and 'wholeness' are terms inadequate to express it[1].

But to a closer inspection, the apparent coherency of the Spinozistic Reality seems to vanish. Elements show themselves as not intelligibly connected—confront us as mere data, which (not only *are not* mediated, but) refusing to enter into the general harmony of the doctrine, stand out as features which can be shown to be discordant with Spinoza's conception of the general nature of Reality. The texture, which seemed so absolutely of one piece, reveals itself as a patchwork, and the colours of the patches (if the metaphor will be excused) 'swear' with the 'ground' of the pattern. This, at least, is a criticism for which there seems to be justification in Spinoza's doctrine. How far the criticism really applies will be discussed in what follows.

I proceed to examine Spinoza's theory in detail—so far, that is, as my exposition has advanced.

### (1) *Substance and Attributes.*

Spinoza does not render

In his conception of Attributes, Spinoza has attempted to reconcile the absolute unity of Reality with its absolute

---

[1] I hope I may be permitted to quote a paragraph which seems to me to express the essence of Spinoza's doctrine. I do not wish for a moment to imply that the views of the author are those of Spinoza, but the paragraph taken by itself puts one essential side of Spinoza's theory more clearly than anything I have seen. 'For me every kind of process between the Many is a state of the Whole in and through which the Many subsist. The process of the Many, and the total being of the Many themselves, are mere aspects of the one Reality which moves and knows itself within them, and apart from which all things and their changes and every knower and every known is absolutely nothing.' Bradley, *Appearance and Reality*, 2nd Edition, Explanatory Notes, p. 609.

# DIFFICULTIES AND CRITICISMS     103

fullness of content. God, or the Reality, is wholly and transparently One: yet in that Oneness he comprehends all the ultimate characters which complete knowledge could find in the Real. It will not do, therefore, to conceive his nature as exhausted in any one or two or finite number of ultimate characters. The Reality is not merely extended (material), nor merely spiritual (ideal), nor merely both: it is all forms of positive being. But neither will it do to conceive the irreducible variety of these ultimate characters as a variety of God's unity; for that unity is unbroken. How, then, does Spinoza conceive the relation of the Attributes to one another and to God? A later philosophy might have thrown the variety upon the apprehending consciousness; but this resource was not available for Spinoza. It is the ultimate nature of the Reality which is concerned. To appeal to the apprehending consciousness, would reduce the Attributes to Appearance, and God to the Thing-in-itself. Spinoza therefore insists that the Attributes express God's essential nature. The variety is *somehow* God's variety. And, since we are here dealing with the general theory of the nature of Reality, we have a right to demand that the 'somehow' should be made consistent and intelligible. But to the question 'How?' we can find no answer in Spinoza: he merely asserts the fact. 'It is essential to Substance, that each of its Attributes should be conceived *per se*; for all the Attributes, which it has, have always been together in it, nor could one have been produced from another; but each expresses the reality or being of Substance [1].' The unbroken unity of Substance, then, has an infinite variety of sides of its being. It is extended, ideal, and so forth; but there is no principle on which this variety is intelligible as the variety of the one Substance. We have seen that it will not do to lay

APPENDIX. intelligible the 'togetherness' of the Attributes in God.

[1] E. i. 10 S.

BOOK I. stress on the relation of the Attributes to the apprehending consciousness—for that would reduce them to Appearance; or, if not, would at any rate merely throw the problem a step further back. If the variety is unintelligible as the variety of God's unity, how does it become more intelligible when variety alone or variety and unity together are made the objects of an intelligence? We must therefore admit that there is a serious defect in Spinoza's general theory of the nature of Reality. The unity of Substance which seemed so absolute—the unity which was more than the unity of a system—resolves itself into a mere 'togetherness' of an infinite multiplicity. The Reality falls apart into a substratum without character, and characters which have no principle of coherence in a substratum [1].

Nor could he have done so, with his conception of God as excluding negation, and Attribute as complete in its own kind.

The failure of the theory so far is a failure to render the moments of the conception of the general nature of Reality intelligibly connected as the moments of a single principle. Spinoza's starting-point, his fundamental conception, shows an inner disruption, contains elements which, as a matter of fact, he has not made rationally coherent. Could they be dissolved in intelligible union? Or is there an insuperable contradiction within Spinoza's conception of God?

This is a difficult question to decide, but on the whole the answer must be that the moments of the conception, as Spinoza defines them, are irreconcilable—that there is an inner contradiction in his conception of God. God is conceived by him as absolutely positive because absolutely real: as excluding all negation from his being. And this exclusion of negation or determination conflicts with the conception of God as comprehending all the ultimate characters of affirmative being within himself.

---

[1] The difficulties connected with the infinity of Attributes and with the preponderance of the Attribute of Thought will be considered below, pp. 134 ff.

## DIFFICULTIES AND CRITICISMS

This is the general conclusion to which, I think, we must come; but some explanation is required.

The criticism based on Spinoza's exclusion of negation from God may easily be carried too far—to portions of Spinoza's theory where it no longer applies[1]. But it does apply here, because the Attributes are *not only in a sense determinate, but further must retain that determinateness in the unity of God's nature.*

The Attributes, though complete or indeterminate in their own kind, are not absolutely indeterminate or complete, for they are distinct from one another, and therefore involve a certain negation of reality[2]. Now if the Attributes were not ultimate forms of God's being—if, in fact, they were Modes and not Attributes—there would be no necessary contradiction here. For though each Attribute would be distinct, defined, and thus, in a sense, negative in relation to God, God would not be negative in himself. The Attributes would not carry negation into the nature of Substance. For Substance would possess all positive forms of being, and in that totality of affirmative essence all limitation would have been absorbed. But with that absorption, all would have become one; i.e. the unity of God's nature would be a unity without differences. The distinctions which the intellect apprehends in conceiving the Attributes would be distinctions which it *makes*, and does not *find*. The Attributes would have no more reality than the Modes. As Attributes, as distinct ultimate characters of Substance, they would come to be when the intellect apprehends; they would not 'always have been together in Substance,' nor would each 'express the reality or being of Substance.'

God—we may repeat with Spinoza—is completely real, and comprehends in himself all affirmative being. And in God there can be no defect, no limitation, no

[1] See below, pp. 108 ff.    [2] Cf. Ep. 36.

imperfection. Somehow in him all negation is absorbed and overcome. But so far as this is our conception of God, all forms of being—all distinct and therefore limited characters—must be, as such and in themselves, only partly real. They cannot retain their character as features of God; and in their distinctness they are partly unreal. God is neither an 'extended' nor a 'thinking thing': and God does not '*subsist of* an infinite number of Attributes.' And each Attribute is not 'complete' even in its own kind; for, if it were, it would remain a distinct independent feature in the nature of God, and the unity of all the Attributes would of necessity be external. God would be Extension and Thought: and in being Extension he would *not* be Thought, in being Thought he would *not* be Extension. Extension and Thought would lie together in his being, and his nature would hold them conjoined, but not intelligibly as one.

To sum up what has been said :—(1) Substance and Attributes, the two moments in Spinoza's conception of God, involve the fusion of absolute unity and complete variety of character. Spinoza merely states the togetherness of the Attributes in God as a fact; and again he merely states as a fact that God comprehends in unbroken unity infinite variety of ultimate characters. (2) And Spinoza's conception of Attributes, or again of Substance, renders the intelligible coherence of the two moments of his complete conception of God impossible. There is an inner contradiction in his conception of God as at once excluding all determination and comprehending an infinite diversity of ultimate characters. Either the Attributes are not *ultimate* characters—not each complete in its own kind, not forms of the essence of God—or God involves 'negation,' i.e. is not absolutely one, but a togetherness of many. To accept either limb of this antithesis would destroy essential parts of Spinoza's doctrine. It seems, therefore, that Spinoza has failed

# DIFFICULTIES AND CRITICISMS

to give us a consistent theory of the general nature of Reality.

*Appendix.*

### (2) *Substance and Modes.*

In the conception of 'natura naturans,' there is thus a combination of two conflicting moments—a combination which Spinoza simply asserts as a fact, and could not render intelligible and consistent. Is there a similar defect in Spinoza's conception of modes?

Spinoza seems to maintain that 'natura naturans' both 'is' and 'is conceived' apart from 'natura naturata,' whilst the latter can neither 'be' nor 'be conceived' apart from the former; i.e. that whilst God in his substantial nature is absolutely prior to and independent of his modes, they are wholly dependent upon him [1]. But this is logically untenable, as indeed Spinoza himself clearly shows in another connexion [2]. If the modes are the necessary consequents of God, God himself in his substantial nature (as 'natura naturans') must *in some sense* be characterized by the modal being which expresses his causality. The modes are 'states' of Substance: and *somehow* Substance must contain within its unity the ground for its modal multiplicity. I have spoken of 'natura naturata' as a 'system' of modes, and again of the 'modal systems' of Extension and Thought. But the notion of system, though Spinoza seems to avail himself of it, is not logically possible to him, at least as anything more than a provisional, inadequate, and misleading conception of the coherence of modes in Substance. 'Natura naturata' is not a system. For the modes are nothing but states of Substance; and Substance is not differentiated—still less divided—in them. A 'system' seems to postulate some sort of independence in its members, but here all independence vanishes when the modes are conceived 'as they really are' in the Attributes of God, i.e. as 'natura

*The modes are states of Substance. The unity of Substance is not, and could not be, systematic.*

---

[1] See above, p. 65, note 1.  [2] E. i. 33 dem. and S. 2.

BOOK I.    naturata.' 'As they really are' they merge themselves in
the undifferentiated unity of Substance, and we are left
And there with no rational answer to the question 'How—on what
is no intelligible principle—can Substance, in spite of its unity, reveal
explanation of itself in an order of diverse states?' We are told simply
the possibility of that Substance 'is modified,' or that the modes are 'in'
God God.    But it is precisely this 'having states' or 'being
'having modified' that is so inexplicable, this being of a multistates' or
'being plicity 'in' an absolute unity which requires explanamodified.' tion.

But to       Yet it is possible to press this line of argument too far,
demand
explana- and I think myself that this criticism is mistaken. It is
tion in
detail is true that without negation you cannot have articulation,
mistaken, and that without articulation you cannot have systematic
and
Spinoza unity.  And it is true that Spinoza sometimes speaks of
has indi-
cated the 'natura naturata' as if it were a 'system,' and of God or
general God's Attributes in relation to the modes as if they were
principle. wholes of parts. But he has taken care to guard himself,
and expressly disclaims the conception of whole and
parts as an ultimate category[1]. And the real significance
of his conception of modes is just that it implies a unity
which is more than systematic—indeed above the
relational form altogether. Spinoza's Substance is one
(not as a unity of diverse but related elements, but) as
a unity which has overcome and taken into itself the
distinctness of its diverse elements, and this absorption
is so complete that in it there remain no 'elements,'
no distinctness, no articulation. How in detail this is
accomplished we are not told[2], nor is it fair to demand
an explanation of this kind. But Spinoza *has* given
us the general principle, and in the main and up to

---

[1] Above, pp. 89 ff.
[2] Spinoza's treatment of error and evil indicates the way in which the negation and imperfection in a partial reality is absorbed and expanded into the positive completeness and perfection of the Reality. See below, Book II. ch. 2; Book III. ch. 1, § 1.

a certain point I do not think we have a right to complain[1].

The general principle rests on the conception of degrees of Reality or Perfection; and this again is made possible for Spinoza by the distinction which he draws between Negation and Privation[2]. And though Spinoza does not attempt to work out in detail the conception of the modal Reality as the self-evolution of God, yet some such view seems to be indicated by various passages to which I have referred[3]; and in his theory of knowledge and conduct we find him applying a principle of estimation which involves a conception of this kind[4].

Put shortly, what Spinoza maintains is this:—all things are absolutely dependent on God, and in that dependence absolutely real; and yet there are grades of perfection or reality in things, and so far therefore there is variety within the unity of God. God is absolutely complete and positive in his being; and yet that being is not abstractly one, for it is manifested in forms which are limited and finite, and there are infinite degrees in their relative perfection. And Spinoza can consistently

---

[1] Cf. Ep. 21 and Sigwart, Sp., pp. 130 ff.

[2] Ep. 21. 'Adeo ut Privatio nihil aliud sit, quam aliquid de re negare, quod iudicamus ad suam naturam pertinere, et Negatio nil aliud, quam aliquid de re negare, quia ad suam naturam non pertinet.'

[3] Cf. e.g. E. i. 28 S; Epp. 19, 23; E. i. Appendix; above, p. 73.

Yet, at the end of E. i. App., Spinoza seems expressly to disclaim any attempt to show any principle for the infinite variety of God's works. 'Iis autem, qui quaerunt, cur Deus omnes homines non ita creavit, ut solo rationis ductu gubernarentur? nihil aliud respondeo, quam quia ei non defuit materia ad omnia, ex summo nimirum ad infimum perfectionis gradum, creanda; vel magis proprie loquendo, quia ipsius Naturae leges adeo amplae fuerunt, ut sufficerent ad omnia, quae ab aliquo infinito intellectu concipi possunt, producenda. . . .' But this disclaimer applies only to an attempt to render the degrees of reality in the universe intelligible in detail.

[4] See below, Book II. ch. 2, § 1; Book III. ch. 1.

maintain this position, because the conflicting aspects of it depend upon different points of view—a difference which he has explained[1].

If we have a scale of more and more complex natures, we, in comparing the richer with the poorer, regard the latter as deficient, i.e. as *deprived* of what they ought to have. But from the point of view of the whole order of things there is no privation in the lower grades of being, but bare *negation*. A stone, e.g., does not see: vision is denied of it, because vision does not belong to its nature. And we should not think of regarding the stone as 'defective,' i.e. as *deprived* of vision. But from the point of view of the whole order of things the same applies e.g. to a blind man—to cases where we, with our partial knowledge, should suppose *privation* or 'defect.' In reality, it is simply *a fact* that a blind man does not see: his blindness is absence of vision, because vision does not belong to his nature in the eternal order of things. In that order, he is not 'deprived' of vision, but vision is simply negated of him. And the negation does not attach to the Reality, for not *it* has anything negated of it: to *its* nature belongs everything, and nothing therefore

---

[1] The same line of argument will *not* reinstate Spinoza's theory of Attributes, because they are 'moments' in the ultimate conception of Reality. *Substance and Attributes* is an attempt to hold together unity and diversity where each is taken as absolute and ultimate. *Substance and Modes* is an attempt to hold together the unity and diversity of Reality from different points of view, one of which alone is taken as absolute. Whether Spinoza succeeds in finding any place for the modal view of the Reality— where its illusion (for it is partly untrue and partly illusory) falls —is another question, which will be considered presently. The reader will observe that I have been obliged to modify the statement of the antithesis of 'Substance and Mode,' with which I started. Cf. (and contrast) above, p. 15. That statement represents, I think, the conception of the antithesis which Spinoza originally formed and endeavoured to maintain, but—if we are to defend him at all—we must shift our ground as he himself shifts with the development of his system.

# DIFFICULTIES AND CRITICISMS

can be negated of it. There is, then, in the whole Reality, APPENDIX. an infinite variety of grades of being, every one of which is free from *defect*, although as compared with others it may be '*without*' some forms of positive being. Whilst 'in God' himself there is neither negation nor privation, yet in the works of God, looked at in comparison with one another and with his completeness, there is *negation* (determination), though not *privation*.

Hence 'privation' or 'defect' in things, is due simply to our abstract and imperfect apprehension. It is an illusion to suppose that things are in any sense 'deprived' of what they might have possessed. But 'negation' (or degrees of reality) in things is true for the modal apprehension, though not the ultimate truth; for to the ultimate apprehension, there are no things, but one all-complete Reality.

God—we may perhaps express Spinoza's position—is absolutely one and perfect in all the states of himself. Everything that is and works reveals the being and working of God. In God's 'essentia' or 'potentia,' all the multiplicity of his states, and all their degrees of perfection, are comprehended and sustained. And in that comprehensive being their distinctions are *absorbed*, but not *left out*. The 'potentia' of God is actual in all the grades of Reality, but it is not divided in them—still less is it 'outside' or 'alongside' of them.

How in detail this is possible, we cannot explain. But the principle of the union of oneness and variety is that the 'limitations' and distinctions are 'defects' and unresolved 'differences' only for an imperfect apprehension; that 'in God,' of whom the modes are states or degrees, all such limitations are overcome, since for a true apprehension they are bare negations which are not negations *of* God.

But the difficulty still remains: what is the ground of Yet the the modal apprehension? And this is a problem for which remains: difficulty

Book I.
what is
the *ground*
of the
(illusory)
modal
apprehension?

no satisfactory solution is (or can be) given by Spinoza. The modal apprehension is in part illusory, and the illusion is a fact—and yet a fact for which no place can be found in Spinoza's conception of the ultimate nature of things. He describes the fact in terms of his general theory, but his description is no explanation; and *if taken as an explanation* it conflicts with his statement of the general nature of God.

For consider: is 'natura naturata' an appearance only to us? If so, how do we come by it? For we are ourselves modes—indeed, in our actual existence, modes in the 'communis ordo naturae.'

Or is 'natura naturata' an appearance of God to himself? That is true, no doubt, for Spinoza, in the sense in which our apprehension is 'God's apprehension so far as he constitutes our mind[1].' But to describe 'natura naturata' as the product of 'God's apprehension so far as he constitutes the human mind,' is to express the fact in the words of the general theory, but not to explain it. It is to transfer the problem with all its contradictions unsolved to a region where they become fixed and insoluble, and conflict with the general principles of the philosophy.

For in order to constitute our mind so far as that is distinct or has a finite apprehension, God himself must enter into the indefinite complex of finite modes[2]. And so we turn in the well-known circle. 'Natura naturata' as truly apprehended sinks back into 'natura naturans,' but in its distinction from 'natura naturans'—as the timeless order of distinct degrees of Reality—it is the product of a partial apprehension, which itself, as the apprehension of a finite mind, implies the world which it constructs.

And the case is worse with the world of presentation—

[1] See below, pp. 127 ff.
[2] E. i. 28 dem.; cf. above, pp. 80 ff., and below, p. 128 and note.

## DIFFICULTIES AND CRITICISMS

the world of things in time and place [1]. This is not, it seems, ever more than a mere illusion. It is the illusory apprehension of a mind, so far as that itself is a member of the illusory world which it constructs. It is expressed by Spinoza in terms of his general theory, when he says that it depends on God so far as he is affected by an indefinite series of finite modifications. But this expression is only a description; and it is a misleading description in so far as it poses as an explanation. An illusion must fall somewhere; for Spinoza, therefore, it must 'be' in God. And the question is how this is possible. It is no answer to this question to say that it is in God so far as God is himself the product of an illusory apprehension, and yet 'God as affected *in infinitum* by finite modifications' is not consistent with God as the 'absolutely complete positive being' which—Spinoza has shown us—an ultimate apprehension demands.

It seems clear, then, that the world of presentation and 'natura naturata' as an order of distinct modes are in some sense 'facts,' which Spinoza has not brought into harmony with his general principles. And so far as his conception of the infinity of completeness is irreconcilable with the indefinite infinity of the finite—so far as there is a gulf fixed between the two forms of God's causality [2]—these 'facts' appear for Spinoza under a form which comes into positive collision with those general principles.

In support of the criticism which I have just advanced, there are some confirmations which it will be well to adduce. Briefly, the point of the criticism was this:—that the modal apprehension of the Reality is (at least in part [3]) illusory, and that Spinoza either attempts

*APPENDIX.*

*Spinoza is far too ready to dismiss things as mere 'illusions.'*

---

[1] See below, pp. 119 ff.
[2] Cf. above, pp. 80 ff., and Camerer, pp. 20 ff.
[3] A complete apprehension of God would, I presume, apprehend his infinite multiplicity in its

no explanation of the fact of the illusion, or—if you take his description as explanation—involves himself in inconsistency in attempting to explain it. Now, if my interpretation of the immediate and mediate infinite and eternal modes[1] is correct—and I am unable to see my way to a better one—all the distinctive features of the worlds of Extension and Thought seem to vanish as 'illusions' one by one, until you are left with the singleness of the Attributes: *a singleness not concrete, but abstract.* Spinoza is indeed far too ready to dismiss things as 'mere illusions.' The secondary qualities of the extended world vanish in his system with hardly a struggle to mark their extinction. The distinctive figures and motions of the particular bodies disappear in the permanent unity and identity of the 'facies totius universi'; and that again, on inspection, shows itself as a mere balance in the proportions of motion to rest. So the complexity of the individual soul reduces itself to forms of the 'idea' proper. Its passions and desires are but confused ideas; its assertions and negations are but the self-assertions and negations involved in its ideas[2]. And the clear or adequate ideas of the individual soul are but thoughts in the 'idea infinita Dei,' and this in turn—since it excludes passions as confused thoughts—reduces itself to the 'intellectus absolutè infinitus.' Or are we to suppose that God's 'infinita idea' includes in itself all (even the confused) ideas—all finite souls with their characteristic particularities, without

single unity without collision or confusion. It would see God as One and as Many, as 'natura naturans' and as 'natura naturata': and there would be no irrational 'at once' or 'together' in this apprehension, but 'somehow'— in a way beyond our experience— the intuition would be intelligent.

But so far as 'natura naturata' is seen as an order or a system or a whole of parts, we have descended at once into a relational (and so far an illusory) view of God.

[1] Above, pp. 82 ff., 93 ff.
[2] Below, p. 132.

# DIFFICULTIES AND CRITICISMS

transmuting them into adequate ideas; and that, similarly, the 'facies totius universi' sustains in its unity, without merging or transforming them, the infinite variety of distinct particular bodies? Such an interpretation is not supported by Spinoza's words, and it would leave the Reality in a far more conflicting and unintelligible confusion than before. The fact seems to be that Spinoza, while struggling to express the conception of God as concretely One, constantly lapses into language which implies that God's unity is abstract. So far as the latter tendency controls his exposition, differences are dismissed as 'illusions,' and his theory becomes hopelessly unintelligible and inconsistent. So far as the former tendency prevails, his philosophy assumes the permanent value which belongs to it. But to a great extent it seems to be true, that Spinoza was unable to develop this—the genuine tendency of his theory—with anything like the requisite consistency and fullness; whilst, unfortunately, the philosophical terminology which he adopts, and especially the geometrical method, rendered it only too easy for him to develop the abstract conception of God's unity clearly and concisely[1].

*Appendix.*

*Conflict in Spinoza between abstract and concrete conception of God's unity.*

In order to explain my meaning I must remind the reader of a familiar truth. The cogency of all geometrical reasoning depends upon the assumption of the nature of space. The connexions which the geometer finds or demonstrates, are connexions of parts within a whole; and they hold only within the sphere of influence of that whole—only because of its controlling nature. In outward form the method, e. g. of Euclid, is *synthetic*. He appears to define the isolated elements and to build them into the fabric of geometry. But in

*The 'geometrical method' tends to make Spinoza's conception of the unity of Reality abstract.*

---

[1] See an interesting article on 'The Philosophy of Spinoza and Leibniz' by Professor Robert Latta in *Mind* (N. S. No. 31).

Book I. reality of course his method is also *analytical*. He starts with the conception of space and unfolds the threads of relational necessity within it. Hence the conclusions which seem to follow, e. g., from the definitions of triangle and right angle and the axioms, really follow from the whole nature of the triangle, of which the definition expresses only a selected part; or from the whole nature of space, which the axioms partly express, and of which the definitions outline some of the elementary forms. Thus geometrical proof, like all proof which works with the category of ground and consequent, is at once synthetic and analytic. It is abstract and hypothetical, for in all its process it is but tracing threads of necessary interconnexion between abstracted portions of its Reality. And so far as the whole which it is analysing has a unity which is more than systematic or relational, its synthesis can never completely reconstruct the whole which its analysis breaks up. This is a characteristic common to all forms of demonstration, but the defects of the procedure are concealed in geometry. The whole which is there being analysed and constructed can (so far as geometry is concerned) remain a relational unity of its manifold, and the destruction of its life which dissection involves is—at any rate for geometry—of no importance.

But the characteristics of geometrical demonstration survive in Spinoza's geometry of Reality, where their inadequacy becomes at once apparent. He *seems* to be arguing purely synthetically, to start with definitions of the simple elements and to construct the whole out of them. The definition of God *seems* to define one simple element amongst others, and to be used like them as a part which combines with the other parts to construct the whole. Really, he is arguing analytically at the same time, and God is the whole which he is analysing. He is working within the general conception of the

# DIFFICULTIES AND CRITICISMS

concrete Reality and establishing the relations—finding the necessary interconnexions—between its parts. And it is a more than doubtful proceeding to work with the definition of God at all. That definition of course in reality is intended as a preliminary statement of Spinoza's general conception of the whole within which he is to demonstrate connexions, *not* as a definition of one element of the whole amongst others. But it inevitably suggests the latter interpretation, and Spinoza himself has, I think, been misled by this procedure. All things *in a sense* follow from the nature of God, just as all geometrical properties follow from the nature of space, or, inaccurately, all the properties of a triangle follow from the nature of the triangle. But they follow from the concrete complete nature of God, space, triangle, and not from the selected abstract nature which is expressed in the definition—*at least not in the same sense*. A triangle is—in relation to space—an abstracted portion of a whole with which other abstracted portions are connected as consequents with ground; and the definition or 'essential nature' of a triangle is, in relation to the concrete whole triangle, in a similar position. Space itself—so far as it is treated as the ultimate subject-matter of a science—is a whole within which all spatial connexions are, and in whose unity spatial relations disappear. Spatial properties and relations 'follow' from the nature of space in a different sense from that in which one spatial element is the consequent of another. No spatial property can be 'deduced' from space as a whole, in the way in which it can be deduced from other properties or parts within the whole. For all such 'deduction' rests upon the controlling conception of the whole, and is valid only within it. And the whole itself cannot appear as one term in the series of conditions and conditioneds.

Now, for Spinoza, God is the ultimate whole within

which all connexions are, and in whose unity all relations disappear or are absorbed. Hence no details—no characters or connexions of the finite—can be 'deduced' from God, in the way in which they can be deduced from one another under the controlling conception of God. But Spinoza certainly speaks as if he were 'deducing' all things from God, in the sense in which the geometer deduces its properties from the definition or essential nature of a triangle. And so far as he does so, the God he works with is an abstract God, the creature of an arbitrary selection, constituted by a definition: one part of Reality amongst other parts. Hence, if I am not mistaken, the rejected elements in the nature of God reassert themselves alongside of the abstract God of the definition: and we get two Gods, each an abstract, partial aspect of the God whom Spinoza is really analysing. The 'God so far as he is affected by finite modifications *in infinitum*' confronts the 'God who is absolutely complete and subsists of an infinite number of complete Attributes.' And these two abstractions conflict with one another, and refuse to re-create the living God in whose unity all differences are sustained and all relations absorbed. The complete God cannot be a union of two abstractions; his unity once broken cannot be put together out of distinct—still less out of conflicting—elements.

The categories of ground and consequent, cause and effect, are quite inadequate to express the immanence of a whole in all its parts; and the immanence of God in all his modes is (as Spinoza has insisted) too intimate to be conceived even under the category of whole and parts. 'Ground and consequent,' 'cause and effect,' are the very scheme of all relations, and hold only of the interconnexions of elements within a unity. But elements and interconnexions of the Real exist only for an inadequate apprehension: an apprehension which assumes the unity as a background and works from point to point within it. So long therefore as we employ these forms of synthesis, we are confined within the conception, at best, of a relational or systematic unity; and, at worst, are driven to an abstract, hypothetical view of things. We are mechanically constructing a whole out of its separate parts; or we are following the grooves of necessary connexion within a whole, which must lose its living unity as a condition of the process. So long, therefore, as Spinoza works with geometrical forms of expression and of proof, with geometrical principles of connexion, he falls a victim to the inherent defect of all scientific 'explanation.' He cannot adequately represent the coherence of Reality, or satisfy the demand of thought for an intelligible view of things. And his failure is aggravated by the geometrical method, because it tends to conceal its own deficiencies—to make him forget that a unity which is sufficient for geometry is totally inadequate for metaphysics. He is compelled to choose between a conception of God's unity as relational, and a relapse into the notion of God as a unity below relation, i.e. the abstract God who maintains his transparent unity by excluding all diversity.

*Note on 'natura naturata' and the world of presentation.*

In this note I propose to indicate briefly how I interpret Spinoza's conception of the relation between 'natura naturata' and the world of presentation ('imaginationis')[1].

---

[1] Since the 'world of presentation' is the world of things 'so far as we conceive them to exist in relation to a certain time and place' (cf. E. v. 29 S.), or 'so far as the mind perceives them *ex communi naturae ordine*' (cf. E. ii. 29 S. & C., 30 dem.), I shall not hesitate to use 'the common order of nature,' 'the world of

Book I. Spinoza does not attempt and fail to 'deduce existence from essence' or 'the finite from the infinite[1].' But there is undoubtedly considerable obscurity (and perhaps inconsistency) in his language as to what degree of reality he attaches to things in the temporal and spatial order. The inconsistencies, if there are any, will engage us later in their proper place. In the meantime, I will state dogmatically the outline of Spinoza's view as I take it to be.

(1) 'Natura naturata' and 'natura naturans' together exhaust Reality; outside them there is nothing. 'Natura naturata' is to include the whole nature of God in its modal being; i.e. it is God the consequent, God, as a complete *modal* apprehension would conceive him. The modes are conceived as dependent on God for their being and conception, and *neither* as identical with God the ground, *nor* as abstracted from their timeless, necessary, and coherent order and as separate things and events in space and time[2]. Further, 'natura naturata' is not a mere world of thoughts, but a world of realities. The essences of things which it comprehends are not to be confused with 'aeternae veritates,' so far as these are the mere thoughts of a mind. Nor again must the essences of things be confused with the mere 'existence' of things, so far as that means their presence to and action upon a sensitive subject[3]. (2) But if so, then temporal existence—things in the temporal order, the 'communis ordo naturae'—is from one point of view nothing (bare illusion), whilst from another point of view it is comprehended and absorbed in 'natura naturata.' The temporal being of 'things' is an abstract moment of their reality, which, along with their abstract thought—being, is com-

---

presentation,' 'the world of time and place,' &c., as equivalent expressions.
[1] Cf. above, pp. 99 ff.
[2] E. i. 29 S.
[3] Cf. above, p. 65, note 1; p. 77, note 1.

prehended in their total being as members of 'natura APPENDIX. naturata.'

Their temporal being is as such illusory. Time is a mere 'auxilium imaginationis[1]'; and indeed the whole framework of the world of temporal and spatial things vanishes in illusion too[2]. It is, e.g., a part of this illusion when we conceive things as contingent and liable to birth and decay. Change and happening, being born and dying—these are illusory products of the illusory 'auxilia imaginationis' which the whole world of presentation involves[3]. But the illusion or error, like all error, is the partial apprehension of the truth. It is deceptive only if taken for the whole truth, and it can become the whole truth by supplementation. If we fill in our defective apprehension, we shall see the 'contingent' as a link in the necessary order, the 'changing' as a partial manifestation of the permanent, the 'limited temporal duration' as *our* mutilation of eternal actuality[4].

Thus the temporal being of things—their existence in the 'communis ordo naturae'—is the product of a partial apprehension. It is really absorbed in 'natura naturata,' though in that absorption its character is transcended and its illusoriness vanishes in truth. And the same applies in principle to the thought-being of 'things.' As conceived e.g. in a scientific understanding, 'things' are not real with the full reality which they possess as modes of 'natura naturata.' The mere conception of things—their 'being' as expressed in a scientific apprehension of the general laws and conditions of the world—is an abstract, relatively unreal, moment in their full being. 'Actual existence' in the world of presentation is the complementary moment which completes their modal

---

[1] Cf. above, p. 31.
[2] Cf. above, pp. 78 ff.
[3] Cf. E. ii. 31 C.; ii. 44 C. 1 & S.
[4] Cf. e.g. E. ii. 17 S.; ii. 45 S.

reality; the idea of which completes and renders concrete their conception [1].

[1] Cf. E. ii. 8 and C. and S. 'Hinc sequitur, quod, quamdiu res singulares non existunt, nisi quatenus in Dei attributis comprehenduntur, earum esse obiectivum, sive ideae, non existunt, nisi quatenus infinita Dei idea existit; et ubi res singulares dicuntur existere, non tantum quatenus in Dei attributis comprehenduntur, sed quatenus *etiam durare* dicuntur, earum ideae etiam existentiam, per quam durare dicuntur, involvent.' And cf. K. V. S. ii. 20, p. 125, Note 3 (No. 6): 'There is no thing in nature, of which there is not in the Thinking Thing an idea *which proceeds from the essence and the existence of that thing together.*' (The italics are my own.) On the whole question, see also below, Appendix to Bk. II, pp. 221 ff.

# BOOK II

## THE HUMAN MIND

## CHAPTER I

### SOUL AND BODY

#### § 1. INTRODUCTION.

In the preface to Part II of the Ethics, Spinoza indicates the plan of the rest of the work. He will proceed 'to explain those necessary consequents of God's nature which will lead us to the knowledge of the human mind and its supreme happiness.' We have left the general theory of Reality, and passed to Spinoza's application of his metaphysical principles to the nature and life of man. But no philosopher interweaves metaphysics, ethics, psychology, and physics so inextricably as Spinoza. Hence, the later books will modify and supplement the metaphysical theory which I have so far endeavoured to sketch; and, on the other hand, I have been obliged (e.g. in treating of the modal system of Extension) to anticipate some of Spinoza's applications of his general principles. So far as possible, I will endeavour to avoid unnecessary repetition. The reader on his side must postpone his criticism of Spinoza's metaphysical theory until he has followed it in its applications, and studied it in the modified form which they give to it.

Book II.   We have seen that, strictly speaking, nothing short of the Whole is self-contained, self-dependent, and individual. From an ultimate point of view there are no parts, no things, no persons. Yet any theory of knowledge or of conduct, or again of physics, must treat the conception of Deus as involving articulation, as a whole of parts. Human apprehension is essentially discursive and relational, even if at its best and ultimately it is also intuitive. And any such theories are bound to have at least a working conception of 'parts' of the Whole. In anticipating Spinoza's outline of physics, we saw that he postulates certain elementary corpuscles; i. e. that he works with conceptions of distinguishable single things, which are relatively independent and individual. In the course of this book we shall have to follow him still further in his development of the conception of individuality. The force of self-maintenance, in which each thing exhibits God's omnipotence, will expand in significance until it serves to stamp a genuine self-dependence and an individual character on the particular things. It may be that this expansion is irreconcilable with the consistency of his metaphysical doctrine; but it is necessary for his ethical and psychological theories. In the meantime, Spinoza himself gives us a working definition of a 'thing[1].' 'By "single things" I understand things which are finite and have a determinate existence. But if several individuals so concur in a single action that all together are the cause of a single effect, so far I consider all of them as one single thing.' Vague as this statement is, it is clear at least that by 'single things' Spinoza understands things actually existing in the spatial and temporal series: modes, not in their eternal order in 'natura naturata,' but taken in isolation and abstraction, as ordinary experience takes them. Presumably, limita-

[1] E. ii. def. 7.

tions of space and time are to be regarded as marking off 'things' in this sense of the word. A body, e. g., is to be counted as 'a thing,' if it has no internal lapse of its appearance or presentation, and no inner break in its extension; any break or lapse would indicate that we have passed to a new 'thing.' The second half of the definition provides for an extension of this conception, primarily in order to meet the case of the human body. The elementary corpuscles which compose an organ, the organs which compose the body, are to be taken from some points of view as together constituting a single thing. A 'complex individual' can be regarded as a 'single thing,' so far as it works as a single cause to produce a single effect. What precisely a 'single' effect means is not, and could not be, defined. But, for Spinoza's purpose, the definition he has given indicates sufficiently the popular conception of a single thing which he wishes to adopt [1].

### § 2. THE HUMAN MIND AS THE IDEA OF THE BODY.

Everything has a soul-side, or is a mode of the Attribute of Thought [2]. Every body is an idea, and its ideal side is at once its 'soul' and the apprehension of its body [3]. This general principle holds of man as of other

---

[1] In E. iv. 39 S., Spinoza just touches on the question of what constitutes 'personal' identity. He explains that when the parts of the body are so rearranged that their inner ratio of motion-and-rest changes, the body has 'died,' i.e. become another body, even though it is not a corpse. And, in support and explanation of this conception, he appeals to an instance of double personality —a Spanish poet who, after an illness, forgot his whole past life, and could not believe he was the author of his stories and tragedies. 'And, if this appears incredible, what shall we say about infants? A grown-up man regards their nature as so different from his own, that it would be impossible to persuade him he had ever been a baby, unless he inferred it from his experience of other men.'

[2] Cf. above, p. 69.

[3] Cf. above, pp. 70, 71.

BOOK II. things; his 'soul' or 'mind[1]' is an idea or mode of Thought, which at once is the ideal side of his body and *in some sense* apprehends the body, its 'ideatum.' Thus Spinoza's conception of the mind rests upon his conception of the interrelation of the Attributes[2], which indeed he fully develops for the first time in the opening propositions of E. ii. The modal system of each Attribute is complete within that Attribute; the chain of causes does not cross from one Attribute to another. But each Attribute coextensively expresses the same nature—the nature of God. The inner articulation of each Attribute is one and the same; or there is, in reality, one modal system, and one only, expressed in an infinite number of irreducible characters[3]. Hence it follows: (i) that the human mind (as an idea or mode of Thought) is neither cause nor effect of the human body (a mode of Extension); and (ii) that the human mind (as an idea) is the soul-side of the human body, the corresponding mode of Extension. Man, that is, is a finite mode of Substance expressed in two only of its Attributes, Extension and Thought[4]. Man's essential nature is modal, not substantial[5]. 'He consists of mind and body, and the human body exists just as we are aware of it'[6]; i.e. the modes constituting his being are a mode

---

[1] Spinoza seems to use 'anima' as the more general term to cover all the grades of soul or life; cf. E. ii. 13 S. 'Nam ea, quae hucusque ostendimus, admodum communia sunt, nec magis ad homines quam ad reliqua Individua pertinent, quae omnia, quamvis diversis gradibus, animata tamen sunt.' 'Mens' is confined to that degree of 'besouledness' which belongs to beings like man.

[2] Cf. above, pp. 22 ff., 65 ff.

[3] E. ii. 5, 6, 7, and C. (In ii. 7 Spinoza is thinking primarily of Extension and Thought; but of course the doctrine holds of all the Attributes.)

[4] Cf. E. ii. 7 S.; 10 C.; 11, 12, 13 and S. For the difficulties, see below, § 4.

[5] E. ii. 10; cf. Ep. 4.

[6] E. ii. 13 C. 'Hinc sequitur, hominem Mente et Corpore constare, et Corpus humanum, prout ipsum sentimus, existere.'

of Thought, and its corresponding extended 'ideatum,' Chap. I.
a mode of Extension.

Man, therefore, is a 'single thing' in the sense explained. His unity, individuality, and self-dependence are, at any rate so far as we have gone, to be taken merely as postulated for the purposes of scientific investigation, and not in the least as ultimately real. It is an abstraction which cuts off man as the perceiving subject from the rest of the universe as his object. Man and his apprehension are really modes of God. It is God who is and moves in all his modes; and somehow, in some sense, it is God who is perceiver and perceived. Hence Spinoza throughout employs a double language; he speaks, e.g., now of *man* as thinking, now of *God quâ constituting the human mind* as thinking, and the latter form of expression is the accurate one. For every idea and every body, as modes of Thought and Extension, are states of God, and it is only by a necessary abstraction that they can be treated as independent things and made the subject of a judgement. It will therefore be best, before proceeding, to translate what has been said into the more accurate form of expression.

The modes of Thought, which are the 'souls' of things, are the 'ideas' which God has or is. God, in thinking this or that thing, constitutes 'its' soul or mind. The totality of God's nature is expressed ideally or 'objectively' in the Attribute of Thought; and to the mediate infinite and eternal modes in each Attribute there corresponds the mediate infinite and eternal mode of Thought, the 'idea Dei[1].' Now this 'infinita idea Dei'—God's complete apprehension of himself—includes and sustains in its timeless coherence all the modes of Thought, whether they are further 'existing' in the temporal order or not. The 'Mens,' that is, of any being (whether now living or not) is, as part of God's appre-

---

[1] E. ii. 3, and cf. above, pp. 94 ff.

BOOK II. hension, eternally comprehended (timelessly actual)[1] in the 'infinite idea' of God; and in that context it is the idea of its 'ideatum' (the body) as itself involved in the coherent totality of which it is a mode. The idea which forms the mind of a man, as a mode of 'natura naturata,' has for its 'ideatum' a corresponding extended mode of 'natura naturata'[2]; and this being or actuality of mind and body is not determined to any particular time or place. But any body which has an actual presence for us in time and place—which enters into our experience, affects our senses—has acquired 'actual existence' in a further sense. It exists for us not only *quâ* involved in the Attribute of Extension, but also as a link in the chain of causes and effects which forms the corporeal side of the 'communis ordo naturae.' And the same applies to every mind with which we come into contact. Thus, the 'esse' of the mind of this actually existent man is that God thinks a mode of Extension (not merely in the context of his all-comprehending and timeless Thought, but also) in a thought in some sense torn from its unalterable context, and appearing as the idea of an actually existent mode of Extension. God, as Spinoza says, constitutes the actual mind of this or that actually existent thing, not so far as he thinks in his infinite and eternal nature, but 'so far as he is considered as affected by the idea of another single thing actually existent, of which idea again he is the cause so far as he is affected by the idea of a third actually existent single thing, and so on *in infinitum*' (E. ii. 9)[3].

---

[1] Cf. E. v. 29 S.
[2] Cf. v. 23 and S.
[3] I have been following E. ii. 8 and S. See above, pp. 119 ff. On the whole conception of soul as the idea of an actually existent mode of Extension, cf. K. V. S. ii. Pref. note 1, and Append. 2, §§ 10 ff. The first passage is so important that I will add a translation of it. Having proved that our soul is a mode of God's complete Thinking, an idea not of the essential nature of things,

Thus the independence, the personal being, which we attribute to any man, is never strictly real. If it were,

but of an actually existent thing (cf. above, p. 95, note 1), Spinoza continues:—

§ 7. 'Every particular thing which comes to actual existence, becomes what it is through motion and rest. This applies to all the modes in substantial Extension, which we call "bodies."

§ 8. 'Their difference from one another arises solely through the different proportion of motion and rest, whereby the one is *thus* and not *thus*, the other *this* and not *that*.

§ 9. 'The existence of this our body, too, springs from this proportion of motion and rest; and of it—just as of all other things—there must be an idea in the Thinking Thing, which idea is our soul.

§ 10. 'This our body, when it was an unborn child, was in a different proportion of motion and rest; and when we are dead it will be in yet another. But none the less, there was an idea of it in the Thinking Thing before we were born, and there will be when we are dead—just as there is now: though by no means the same idea, for our body is now otherwise proportioned in motion and rest.

§ 11. 'Thus, in order to cause such an idea in the substantial Thinking as this our soul is now, there is required ... a body proportioned in motion and rest precisely as ours is, and no other.

For as is the body, so is also the soul. ...

§ 12. 'If, therefore, such a body has and maintains its proportion (as, e.g., a proportion of one to three), then this body (and its soul) will be as ours is now. It will be subjected, no doubt, to constant change, but to none so great as to exceed the proportion of one to three. But just so much as the body changes, the soul also changes on each occasion.

§ 13. 'This change in us, which arises from the action of other bodies upon ours, cannot take place without our soul—which likewise constantly changes—becoming aware of it. And this change [i.e. the soul's change] is what we call "sensation" [i.e. "sensation" is that change in the soul which is its awareness of a change in the body].

§ 14. 'But if other bodies act so violently upon our body, that the proportion of its motion (one to three) cannot persist:—that is death, and an annihilation of our soul, in so far as it is only an idea ... of this thus-proportioned body.

§ 15. 'Yet, since the soul is a mode in the Thinking Substance, it might have known and loved the latter as well as the Substance of Extension: and through union with Substances which always remain the same, it might have made itself eternal.'

Book II. it would imply that some one of God's thoughts could 'be' out of relation to its context—that God could throw himself completely into a single finite mode of his Attribute of Thought and into a single finite mode of his Attribute of Extension: and man would be Substance. The mind of a man is always 'a part of the infinite intellect[1] of God' (E. ii. 11 C.), as his body is a part of the 'facies totius universi'; he himself (as a whole of body and mind) is and remains a 'pars naturae[2].' Such relative independence as we attribute to his mind and body, can only be described—and inaccurately described—by saying 'God, so far as he is expressed by the nature of the human mind, has this or that idea.' So far as that is so—*and it never is strictly and completely so*—'we' are said to have adequate knowledge, to be 'agents,' to reveal 'ourselves' in action. The contents of our mind are really 'ours,' 'we' have a character and a personality. But so far as God in thinking any finite thought is inevitably thinking the other thoughts on which it depends (so far, in fact, as God's thought can never be finite or incomplete), God's knowledge is distributed as it were over all the finite minds which his thoughts constitute, and any one of those minds has but a mutilated fragment of the adequate knowledge which is God's[3]. In proportion, therefore, as there is absolute continuity in all being—as no 'single thing' can really be separated from its context—the human mind and the human body are devoid of distinct being: their individuality is illusory and untrue[4].

Some of the chief further determinations of the nature of the mind are drawn by Spinoza from his account of the human body. The human body is a complex aggre-

---

[1] 'intellectus' *here* = 'idea Dei,' if my interpretation is correct.
[2] E. iv. 4.
[3] See below, pp. 165 ff.
[4] For developments and modifications, cf. below, Bk. III. ch. 4.

## SOUL AND BODY

gate of many complex aggregates[1]. Its 'unity'—when
it is regarded as 'a single thing'—is the coactivity of its
multiple constituents. Every elementary corpuscle has
its soul-side: and the mind is therefore in reality a complex aggregate of many complex aggregates of ideas[2]. The
mind of man *in God's complete knowledge* would thus be the
soul-side of all the modes of Extension which constitute his
body; and, as their soul-side, it would be the complete
apprehension of them all[3]. But what we call our 'mind'
falls far short of this, though it may approximate to it in
various degrees. A human body is 'single' and continues
in its individual identity, so far as the general scheme
or balance of motions is preserved in the coactivity of its
parts. Many of the parts in their special natures are not
necessary to the continuance of the 'individuality' of the
whole; i.e. they are necessary *generically* but not *individually*. And a 'single' human mind is correspondingly incomplete in its inner necessity of detail. We
need not be conscious of all the elements that constitute
our body: 'we'—'our' soul-life, 'our' conscious selves—
subsist for the most part as a vague feeling of bodily
function. The body exists for us 'prout ipsum sentimus.'
And this means that an infinite number of the constituents of our 'mind' never *for us* enter into, or form part
of, our soul-life at all. They form no part of the 'mind'
of an actually existing man, either for himself or for the
ordinary observer. They are 'necessary elements' in it,
no doubt, just as the elementary corpuscles are necessary
elements in our body. But just as many of the latter
are generically and not individually necessary; just as
what we call the 'form' of the body is preserved through
and in spite of a constant flux of its material, a constant

---

[1] E. ii. post. 1; cf. above, pp. 82 ff.
[2] E. ii. 15.
[3] God, in Pollock's phrase, is the 'accomplished physiologist'; cf. Pollock, pp. 124 ff., and Caird's answer, pp. 197 ff.

BOOK II. 'substitution of similars':—so 'our soul-life' persists through and in spite of a constant flux and substitution of 'simple ideas': 'ideas,' which perhaps 'we' never recognize as elements of our 'selves' at all.

The degree of fullness of our conscious being will correspond precisely to the degree of fullness of our corporeal being: and the latter will—in a sense to be explained presently—form the basis for all growth of our knowledge of ourselves and the external world [1].

### § 3. CONSCIOUSNESS AND SELF-CONSCIOUSNESS.

*Voluntas and Intellectus.*

Every idea is an act of thought, and as such involves assertion or denial: i.e. is a judgement. There are no 'faculties' of any kind. 'Faculties' are but abstract universals standing to the particular acts or exercises of function, as 'Lapideitas' stands to this and that stone, 'Humanity' to Peter and Paul [2]. There is, therefore, no faculty of assertion or denial: no 'voluntas' in the Cartesian sense of the term [3]. And the particular assertions and denials are nothing different from the particular acts of thought. For an 'idea' is not a picture 'in' the mind, which we may then go on to affirm or deny, or again content ourselves merely to gaze on. An idea is an act of thought, and the act of assertion or denial is inseparable from the content asserted or denied. 'Idea' means the assertion or denial of a content, or a content *quâ* asserted or denied [4].

*Idea Ideae.*

But an asserted content is itself a something, an event, a mode with an *esse formale* [5], which has an 'objective'

[1] E. ii. 14, and see below.
[2] E. ii. 48 S.
[3] E. ii. 48 and S.
[4] E. ii. def. 3 and Expl.; E. ii. 43 S.; 49 with the C. and S. Spinoza draws the corollary that the Cartesian theory of the freedom of the will—which was based on the supposed distinction between 'voluntas' (the faculty of asserting and denying) and 'intellectus'—is untenable. See below.
[5] Cf. E. ii. 5 for the phrase.

side of its being—is (or may become) the content of another thought. In God—in the completeness of the Attribute of Thought—there must be an idea of every idea. Everything is, on one side of itself, an object of thought, the content of a thought of God, and to this principle the modes of Thought itself form no exception. Hence there must be an idea of the idea which constitutes the human mind: and so far as the latter idea has an independent existence, the idea of which it is the object has a similar independent existence. If in any sense the mind of any man has an individuality, in the same sense the idea of that mind will exist in separation from the total context of God's thought[1]. And 'this idea of the mind is united to the mind, in the same way as the mind itself is united to the body[2].' As the body is by its very nature—on its ideal side—the mind, so the mind is by its very nature—in its 'objective being'—the idea of the mind: i.e. the mind which is the idea of the body is at the same time by its very nature the idea of itself.

We may reach the same result from a different point of view. The assertion of a content is an act of thought, and thought by its very nature is reduplicated *in infinitum* on itself. We cannot 'have an idea' without knowing that we have it, and knowing that we know that we have it, and so on *in infinitum*. If we imagined an idea as a something, a picture e. g., present in our mind at which we gaze, we might suppose ourselves to 'have an idea' without knowing that we have it. But an idea is the very act of thinking: and the character, which distinguishes Thought from all the Attributes, is its awareness of itself and its awareness of that awareness *in infinitum*[3]. The human mind, therefore, just because it is an idea, is also the idea of that idea.

[1] E. ii. 20.
[2] E. ii. 21 and S.
[3] Cf. Tdle, VVlL. i. p. 12; above, p. 7; E. ii. 21 S.; ii. 43.

BOOK II. This awareness of their thinking—the *form* of self-consciousness—is inseparable from all 'ideas' or minds. But its fullness and importance will vary *pari passu* with the fullness of the first ideal content which is its object. In the higher grades of knowledge, our consciousness of our mind expands with the growth of our consciousness of our body and all that the latter consciousness involves and develops [1].

### § 4. SOME DIFFICULTIES.

It will be as well to consider some difficulties at this point. Their discussion will clear the ground for the further exposition of Spinoza's theories.

Is Thought 'wider' than the other Attributes?

And, first, there is a difficulty to which I have already referred [2]—the difficulty as to the Attribute of Thought.

The Attribute of Thought reflects in its ideas the modes of all the other Attributes of God. Does each idea reflect all the corresponding modes in all the Attributes? Or do 'ideae' and 'ideata' run in pairs, so to say—is there a distinct idea for every mode of every Attribute? There is no doubt as to which conception Spinoza himself adopts; but on either interpretation—as Tschirnhaus acutely points out [3]—there seem to be insoluble difficulties.

(1) If the Attribute of Thought is, so to say, 'formally' coextensive with each Attribute, but intensively or in content as rich as them all: then it is impossible to understand why or that the human mind should appre-

---

[1] For the difficulties of this whole question (the Idea Ideae), see below, pp. 138 ff.; and cf. Erdmann, V. A. pp. 174 ff., though I do not altogether endorse his views.

E. ii. 43 looks like an argument in a circle to support E. ii. 21 S. But this is not so. ii. 43 is an application of the general doctrine of ii. 21 S. to the special case of *true* ideas.

[2] Above, p. 72.
[3] Epp. 65, 70.

## SOME DIFFICULTIES

hend only the body. In the content of the idea which constitutes our mind would necessarily be given the 'objective' being of its corresponding mode in all the Attributes.

(2) Spinoza will not admit this, and his answer[1] shows that he conceived each idea of the Attribute of Thought to correspond to one mode in one Attribute; i. e. for Spinoza's own interpretation 'ideae' and 'ideata' run in pairs. It is true, Spinoza admits, that each thing is expressed in an infinite number of ways *in the infinite intellect of God*. But since every Attribute is complete in itself and must be conceived *per se*[2], the ideas of these infinitely-different expressions of a mode have no interconnexion with one another. Hence the infinity of ideas, which reflects each thing, cannot constitute one and the same mind of a single thing, but constitutes an infinite number of minds. The idea, therefore, which constitutes our mind, reflects and apprehends only our body. Its 'ideatum' is a mode of Extension. It is not intensively correspondent to a mode of Substance in all its Attributes.

But, if so—Tschirnhaus urges[3]—the Attribute of Thought is no longer coextensive with each of the other Attributes, but with all together. It is 'wider' than any of them taken singly; and this seems to collide with the definitions of Attribute and of God.

And we may carry this criticism further, if we will. Let us dismiss the postulate of the infinite number of Attributes: still the problem breaks out anew within the Attribute of Thought itself. For we must remember that Thought reflects itself *in infinitum*. Are we to conceive this reduplication of the idea as merely intensive —are we to suppose that every idea, formally one, is, in its content and intensively, turned upon itself *in*

---

[1] Ep. 66.  [2] E. i. 10, to which Spinoza refers in Ep. 66.
[3] Ep. 70.

Book II. *infinitum*? Even then—whatever the value of such a solution—the Attribute of Thought would 'extend more widely' than the Attribute of Extension. For every idea would be obliged to split itself internally into subject and object ('idea' and 'ideatum,' 'esse formale' and 'esse obiectivum ideae'), and this fissure would have to repeat itself *in infinitum*. Is this fissure grounded on a difference within the idea? Then at once for every single mode of Extension we have an infinite number of modes of Thought. Or is the fissure grounded on no difference in the idea? Then the fissure has no meaning and is inconceivable. Hence it would seem that—even if we disregard the infinite number of Attributes—Spinoza is involved in difficulties. For by his definition Thought must be formally coextensive with Extension; and yet by the nature of Thought, as Spinoza understands it, this is impossible.

The criticism is inapplicable in the form in which it is expressed,

I have set out this criticism at some length, because most of the commentators on Spinoza seem to believe it to be valid. And yet I cannot help thinking that it betrays a serious misunderstanding of Spinoza. 'Attributum cogitationis *se multo latius* quam attributa caetera extendere ...,' Tschirnhaus complains. 'Spinoza never answered this objection. Thought is *wider* than the other Attributes,' the modern commentators echo. But how can modes of extension ('wider,' 'narrower,' 'coextensive') apply to the relations of one Attribute to another? The whole criticism rests on the abuse of a spatial metaphor. The Attributes are 'in' God, but God is not a spatial whole, even though Extension is one of his Attributes. God is extended; but his Extension is not comprised along with Thought within a wider Extension. All the Attributes together exhaust God's essential nature, but they are not (except metaphorically) spatially conterminous with it. Such expressions, however useful and however indispensable, are mere metaphors and give rise to ludicrous misunderstanding if pressed.

But it remains true that Spinoza does not (and cannot) render intelligible the being of the Attributes 'in' God[1]. Since Thought and Extension as Attributes express ultimate characters of the nature of God—and since the complete nature of the Real *is not* Thought and Extension —Spinoza is obliged to postulate an infinite number of other ultimate characters. But, because they are 'ultimate,' he cannot admit that in the Reality all these distinct characters are as such transcended and absorbed; and so he is left with a plurality 'in' an absolute Unity, and the metaphorical 'in' leaves the conception totally unintelligible. Thus the criticism is valid, though it has been expressed in a misleading form. It is a mistaken wording of this objection to say that Thought is 'wider' than the other Attributes. But it is true that the thought-side of things is the 'objective being' of the modes of Substance under *all* the Attributes. Hence, *either* the thought-side of a body (e. g. man's mind) must apprehend its 'ideatum' in all the Attributes—and this is not the fact, nor will Spinoza admit it as a logical consequence of his doctrine—*or* the 'order and connexion' of thoughts must correspond (not to the order and connexion of the modes of Extension, but) to the order and connexion of the modes in all the Attributes; i. e. there are modes of Thought which are *not* the thought-side of modes of Extension, and the 'completeness' of the Attribute of Thought is more full than the 'completeness' of any other Attribute.

To talk of the 'parallelism' of the Attributes, their 'coextensiveness' with God and with one another, their being 'in' God—all this, we have seen, is a mere metaphor which becomes misleading if pushed home. To some extent we may justify our use of such metaphors

[1] Cf. above, pp. 102 ff.

BOOK II. by Spinoza's own language, by his treatment of Reality as the subject of the geometrical method, and by his failure to reconcile the plurality of the Attributes as ultimate characters of God with his transparent unity. Still we must not abuse this license. For Spinoza (at times in expression, and always in intention) rises above the spatial way of representing the 'relation' of the Attributes to one another and to God.

Idea Ideae.

In connexion with this subject, it will be well to consider some of the difficulties in Spinoza's theory of the 'idea ideae.' At the basis of the conception of 'idea ideae' lies the conviction—not won without a long mental struggle (cf. below, chap. 2, § 1)—that adequate thought and its object are one and the same, and that, therefore, thought is its own criterion.

But this does not mean that thought is identical with any and every object with which we, in our imperfect apprehension, choose to identify it. The idea which constitutes the mind of Peter *is* Peter's body; i.e. *so far as Peter's consciousness goes*, it is his self for him and apprehends his body 'prout ipse sentit.' The object of Peter's thought *is* his body *so far as his thought apprehends it*. And the idea, which in God's complete intelligence constitutes the mind of Peter, is identical with Peter's body as it really is: it is Peter's self for God, and apprehends his body both in its eternal actuality in the Attribute of Extension and in its temporal existence in the 'communis ordo naturae.' The object of God's thought of Peter *is* Peter's body as it really is. But the idea of Peter which Paul has is *not* identical with Peter; for the 'ideatum' of that idea is not Peter as he is (either for himself or for God), but as he is *for Paul*: i.e. Paul's idea of Peter is adequate only as the idea of an 'ideatum' which is not Peter, not what the idea professes (to Paul's mind) to represent. In Paul the idea of Peter is inadequate, for Paul refers it wrongly to Peter as he is 'really' and unaffected by his relation to Paul[1].

Now when we talk of thought and its object, we usually are concerned with an idea referring to a part only of its 'ideatum,' or referred for us not to its completely adequate 'ideatum.' And when that is the case, thought is (and ought to be) distinguished from its 'object.' Paul's idea of Peter is not Peter *in rerum natura*, but it refers to Peter and is more or less true of him. And in anything short of completely adequate thought, thought and its object are always in this way distinct from one another. They 'agree' with one another in various degrees, but never coalesce and become one. So far as our mind is the inadequate thought of our body (and it always is so to some extent)[2], our mind or our ideas are, as it were, set over against our body, distinct and distinguished from it. We 'know' our body, not as being it—not from within—but as having knowledge 'about' it; and such knowledge remains always to some extent inadequate and untrue and different from its 'object.' In anything short of perfect apprehension, therefore, thought always implies a distinction between itself and its object, and this distinction is never completely overcome. Thought is 'one' with its object in a very imperfect and ambiguous sense. The 'oneness' is a relation between two distincts; a 'oneness' of two, which never by complete coalescence justify the 'oneness' which we ascribe to them.

And even in the oneness of adequate thought and its object, the oneness is a unity of two, though a unity

---

[1] E. ii. 17 S. By 'Peter' I mean Peter, body and mind. Paul's idea of Peter is *not* the same as Peter's idea of his own body, nor as Peter's idea of his own mind. To avoid unnecessary complication, I have hitherto spoken as if 'Peter' meant 'Peter's *body*,' and as if 'Paul's idea of Peter' meant 'Paul's idea of Peter's *body*.'

[2] Cf. above, p. 130.

Book II. which overcomes and sustains the differences. For though in reality my body and my mind are one and the same mode of Substance, yet they are that mode 'differently expressed,' and the different expressions are separated by the absolute separation which (for Spinoza) divides each Attribute from every other. How the identity of these absolute distincts is possible in the transparent unity of Substance—this (we know) is unintelligible in Spinoza's system. But it is a postulate of his theory, which for our present purpose we must simply accept.

But in his conception of 'idea ideae,' Spinoza renders it impossible to maintain *any* difference between thought and its object. The unity of 'idea ideae' is not a unity of two, but a blank unity. And, as such, it does not answer to any possible form of self-consciousness or even self-feeling. 'Mentis idea,' Spinoza says (E. ii. 21 S.), 'et ipsa Mens una eademque est res, quae sub uno eodemque attributo, nempe Cogitationis, concipitur.' But, if so, the idea which is the 'object' is identical with and indistinguishable from the subject-idea. The identity of subject- and object-idea is so absolute, that all possibility of regarding it as a unity of two has vanished. In fact, so absolutely one are they, that they cannot even be conceived as identical: for identity with no difference is a meaningless term.

Yet if we ask what Spinoza intended to establish by his conception of 'idea ideae,' the answer can hardly be doubtful. He intended to restore that unity and continuity in all our thinking, which his conception of the mind as a complex of 'ideae' seems to have destroyed [1].

---

[1] Cf. Camerer, pp. 53 ff.; and below, ch. 2. Throughout, Spinoza implies that 'we' have an experience: that a single and continuous consciousness combines (or contains combined in itself) all the *ideae* which form the complex of our mental life. Cf. e.g. the significant expression 'simulac enim *quis* aliquid scit, eo ipso

# SOME DIFFICULTIES

Without some unity, without some 'self,' Spinoza's theory of conduct and of knowledge could not advance a step: and it does not seem erroneous[1] to suppose that Spinoza intended to find such a unity in the 'idea ideae'—the consciousness of our thinking which every act of thinking involves. But if this was his intention, it must be confessed that he has failed. The process *in infinitum*, which the 'idea ideae' involves[2], augurs ill for such a project. And since the subject-idea *is* one and the same mode of Thought as its object-idea, the former is no more continuously one than the latter, but resolves itself, like that, into an aggregate of many 'ideae.' And, finally, an idea which is in no sense distinguishable from its 'ideatum' has lost the character of a mode of Thought, and cannot possibly do the work of a feeling of self, or a consciousness of one's thinking.

Man, as the identity of mind and body, is a mode of Substance in two only of its Attributes. He is therefore —even as a mode—imperfectly real. And the unity of mind and body, which constitutes his phenomenal being, is no unity of a self. His 'self' is a complex of such unities; but the complex remains a complex for him and for us, and cannot be anything more even for his thought of himself. For that thought of himself—the 'idea mentis' or 'ideae'—is one and the same as the 'mens' which it apprehends; i.e. in any case, it is a complex of 'ideae idearum' and not a single 'idea ideae.' So far as for our experience we are 'one'—possessed of a continuous consciousness of an individual self—that experience to some degree is illusory[3]. The question really is: 'How

*The question really is, 'What degree of unity has a man for himself?'*

---

scit, *se* id scire,' &c. (E. ii. 21 S., and often).

[1] Yet see note 3.

[2] Cf. e.g. E. ii. 21 S.

[3] How there comes to be a 'we' at all—how 'we' can 'experience,' even be the victims of illusion—such questions cannot be answered. For to answer them would be to apprehend completely the Reality, and from the point of view of that complete knowledge to show the

far can we approximate to that complete experience, in which the individual unity which we are in God is realized for ourselves?' And the answer is not doubtful. The corpuscles which form man's body are linked together in the Attribute of Extension, and for a complete understanding: and the 'ideae' which form man's mind are united in the chain of ideas which are the content of the 'idea infinita Dei.' *In and for God* man is one, has a real being and individuality: but *in and for God* man is no longer what he is for himself and for other men. His real being and individuality is God's being and individuality, and is 'his own' only in the sense in which God is all things and all things are in God.

In the actual living man, the 'ideae,' which form the complex of his mind, are associated in various ways; and the corpuscles, which constitute his body, cohere according to an order external to themselves and imperfectly apprehended by man's mind. By training and reasonable living, man may approximate to the experi-

ground of finiteness and appearance. Spinoza's atomistic explanation of the body and mind —if we take it as anything more than a provisional theory—seems to render all unity of man's consciousness impossible (not merely to leave it unexplained, but to cut away all possibility of its being), and his theory of 'idea ideae' cannot restore such unity. But in that theory he evidently assumes that man is *in some sense* 'one,' has a 'self' (above, p. 140, note 1), and his atomistic doctrines are avowedly provisional only (cf. the way in which they are introduced into the Ethics, and the obviously unfinished and outline form in which they are presented). The difficulty may be put thus: from a complete point of view, there is no individual save God; from the provisional atomistic point of view, there is no 'individual' (except in a loose sense) but the elementary corpuscles and their 'ideae.' Yet the individuality of man is neither one nor the other, and is (and must be) taken by Spinoza as in some sense a fact. The doctrine of 'idea ideae' cannot justify this 'fact,' cannot bring it into consistent coherence either with Spinoza's Atomism or with his metaphysical theory. Yet if this is *not* its object, what place has it in the system?

ence and realization of the more real union which he has in God. The chance association of ideas may give place to a reasoned concatenation on intelligible principles: the imperfect coherence of his bodily components may grow in organic unity. He may become less the plaything of agencies 'external' to himself, less the passive theatre in which ideas come and go and group themselves, and more of an agent and a thinker. In proportion as he does so, he becomes *for himself* what he in reality is: a state of God, a mode with the reality which belongs to modes in their eternal order. In this advance he wins freedom and knowledge. He 'acts' instead of being the meeting-point of external agencies; he 'thinks' instead of receiving impressions. He becomes a person: a being with a 'self' and a 'self-knowledge' which is less illusory as the process advances. But this development means the merging of man in God. It is a development only in this sense, and in its completion the developing self is, as an independent self, absorbed. There is no relation of two: no survival of man over against God, no reconciliation of two independent beings or persons. Man is man, only so far as he is God in a state of himself. He becomes real for himself, only in becoming for himself a mode of God. He wins independence and individuality only in the self-dependence and individuality of God. In that absorption, man's being has transcended itself; and yet, except in that transcendence, man has no being. That paradox is the paradox of the finite. *Quâ* finite, it is in part unreal; *quâ* real, it is not finite. In getting reality, 'it' ceases as such to be. It is the nature of the finite to be 'for ever moving restlessly beyond itself' for completion; in that completion, 'it' as such has vanished: and yet except in 'its' absorption, 'it' is nothing real.

The course of man's progress towards freedom and knowledge—towards that absorption in God which is the

Book II.

God self-conscious.

realization and the transcendence of man's self—is traced by Spinoza in his ethical doctrine and in his theory of the stages of knowledge. The progress exhibits two sides—the growth of man's individuality as an agent and as a thinker—and Spinoza's exposition of each side involves his exposition of the other. The ideal of knowledge and of conduct is one and the same, and the paths of its attainment are indissolubly intertwined [1].

A word of caution is necessary with regard to the self-consciousness of God. The question has been much debated as to whether Spinoza's God is 'personal,' is 'self-conscious,' has 'intellect' and 'will.' In one sense all these predicates belong to God, so far as they express anything real. But God is not a person, nor is he self-conscious, nor has he intellect and will, in the sense which those terms would bear if unqualified. We have seen already (above, pp. 62 ff.) that intellect and will, in the sense in which they are ordinarily attributed to man, do not belong to God. The same is true of 'personality[2]' and of 'self-consciousness.' Any of these terms, if applied to God, lose the distinctive meaning which popular thought gives them in their application to man. God indeed is not 'without' these qualities—in the richness of his nature he is not less, but more than human: so far as any human properties express reality, they must be absorbed in God's completeness. Thus God's understanding and its objects are one and the same, for God's understanding is complete [3]. And God's infinite idea of himself (his 'self-consciousness') is 'unique' and absolutely one [4], and *somehow* it includes in itself all the finite minds which are 'parts' of it. But in its uniqueness and absolute self-identity it is

---

[1] Cf. Brunschvicg, p. 103; below, ch. 2, §§ 1 and 2; above, pp. 3, 4.

[2] Cf. C. M. ii. 8, § 1.

[3] Cf. e.g. E. ii. 7 S.

[4] E. ii. 3 and 4; cf. C. M. ii. 7, § 6; and above, pp. 94 ff.

altogether different from the self-consciousness of finite
minds. And in any case the intellect and self-consciousness of God belong to him in his *modal* nature; i.e. he *is* not intellect, any more than he *is* motion-and-rest. They are but partial expressions of his being, consequents of his substantial nature, and that nature is not exhausted in any or all of them.

# CHAPTER II

## THEORY OF KNOWLEDGE

### § 1. IDEA AND IDEATUM.

BOOK II. Spinoza's conception of 'truth' passes through an interesting development. In his earliest philosophical work [1], the external object implants itself, so to say, in the mind as an idea. Thinking is a passion [2]. The reality acts upon (or impresses itself in) the mind, and truth is pure receptivity. This point of view is overcome in the *Tractatus de Intellectus Emendatione*, though there are indications there of its partial survival. True thought, indeed, is pure spontaneity: but the thought which is false or partial seems (according to some pas-

---

[1] In the K. V.; cf. Avenarius, pp. 40, 45 ff. Traces of this view survive even in the Ethics. Cf. e.g. the axiom (E. i. Ax. 6), 'A true idea must agree with its "ideatum",' and its translation into technical (Cartesian) terminology (E. i. 30 dem.), 'that which is contained objectively in the intellect must necessarily be given in nature.'

[2] Cf. e.g. K. V. S. ii. 16, § 5 '(dass) das Verstehen ein reines Leiden ist, das ist ein Gewahrwerden (perceptio) der Wesenheit und Existenz der Dinge in der Seele; so dass wir selbst niemals etwas von einer Sache bejahen oder verneinen, sondern die Sache selbst ist es, die etwas von sich in uns bejaht oder verneint.' Yet, if we compare K. V. S. i. 2, § 24 (see Joël, pp. 62 ff.), it would seem that Spinoza speaks of knowledge as a passion only in the sense that it is objective, forced upon us, necessary truth—not arbitrarily created by our own imagination. But Spinoza's language in the K. V. and in the TdIe is at least less clear than that of the Ethics, and seems to betray a certain wavering in his own view.

# IDEA AND IDEATUM

sages) to be caused by the action of external bodies[1], and not to spring from the spontaneity of the mind. There is thus, it would seem, one kind of thinking ('perception' or 'idea') which is not the activity of the mind, but forced upon it from without.

But in the Ethics, notwithstanding some ambiguous and perhaps inconsistent statements, Spinoza maintains that all ideas (all thinking of any kind), as modes of Thought, are caused by ideas and not by their 'ideata'—not by any objects or bodies. And he expressly defines 'idea' as 'a conception of the mind, which the mind forms in virtue of its nature as a thinking thing'; and he adds 'I say "conception" rather than "perception," because the latter term seems to indicate that the mind is acted upon by its object. But "conception" seems to express an action of the mind[2].'

'An idea is true if it agrees with its "ideatum",' but this is only an external mark, a relation, which tells us little of the nature of a true idea[3]. If, however, we ask what this 'convenientia' means, the answer is at once simple and difficult. An idea *is* its 'ideatum': thought and its object are in a sense one and the same[4]. Every 'thought' (we have learnt already) is a single 'event' with two sides, or every 'body' is a single thing with two aspects. It does not matter which way you put it. 'Body' is at once body and thought, and 'thought' is at

---

[1] Cf. VVlL. i. pp. 23, 28 ff., and p. 30. These and other passages imply that the objects perceived set up 'corporeal motions' or changes in our body, and hence determine us to perceive or have ideas.

[2] E. ii. def. 3 and Expl. 'Per ideam intelligo Mentis conceptum, quem Mens format, propterea quod res est cogitans.'
'Expl. *Dico potius conceptum,* quam perceptionem, quia perceptionis nomen indicare videtur, Mentem ab obiecto pati; at conceptus actionem Mentis exprimere videtur.'

[3] Cf. E. ii. def. 4, Explic., and Ep. 60. For the meaning of 'denominatio extrinseca' ( = 'relation'), see Busolt, p. 104, note 1; and cf. *Port-Royal Logic*, Part I. ch. 2.

[4] E. ii. 7 S.

once thought and body. And though so intimately one that each involves the other, yet on the other hand neither is the cause or the effect of the other. If you emphasize thought-side only or body-side only, you must keep consistently to that emphasis in your explanation. On its thought-side, the mode is causally connected with thoughts (i. e. with other modes on *their* thought-side); on its body-side, it is causally connected with bodies. Hence an idea is at once identical with its 'ideatum,' and absolutely distinct from it; for the different Attributes, e. g. the Attributes of Thought and of Extension, are absolutely distinct from one another. It would seem, therefore, that it is strictly impossible for Spinoza to talk of an 'agreement' between idea and 'ideatum.' For, from one point of view, they are so completely one, that no relation between them is possible—their unity is in no sense a relational unity. And, from another point of view, they are so absolutely two, that they cannot have any community of being whatever. But a relation, even if you call it 'purely external,' implies some community of being in the related terms.

No idea, then, we must say, 'agrees with' its 'ideatum,' but every idea *is* its 'ideatum.' And every idea is true. But since every idea is a *mode* of Thought, no idea is capable of being *per se*: its being and its truth belong to it only in the complete context of God's infinite idea or intellect[1]. No partial idea can (except in that context) be true, for it comprises no content purely in itself: it is not separable as the idea of a separable 'ideatum,' but has its being and its truth only in 'natura naturata.' The only idea, therefore, which is ultimately true, is the 'infinita idea Dei.' And that is true, because it sustains in itself all 'ideae.' It *is* its 'ideatum': it is identical with the modal Reality on its formal side. And its truth is its reality or completeness, its self-containedness. Its

[1] Cf. E. ii. 7 C.; ii. 32 dem.

# IDEA AND IDEATUM

truth, therefore, depends upon its own inner nature, and not upon its object. It is true because it is inwardly real, complete, coherent, adequate, not because it 'agrees with' something outside it. No doubt, it does 'agree with' its 'ideatum' in the sense that it *is* the ideal side of its 'ideatum'; but it involves all the marks of a true idea, regarded simply in itself.

We have thus reached the conception of truth which Spinoza developed partly in the *Tractatus de Intellectus Emendatione*, and fully in the Ethics.

Since an idea is simply an action of the mind's spontaneity, its character must be dependent upon the mind and not upon its object. We must therefore neglect the 'external denomination' of 'convenientia,' and seek the criterion of truth—where alone it is to be found—within the idea itself[1]. 'Truth is the criterion of itself and of the false, as light reveals itself and darkness[2],' in the sense that our own certainty (which *is* our true thinking) is the guarantee that we are thinking truly. We can know that we have an idea which 'agrees with' its 'ideatum,' only by having such an idea[3]. Certainty is the *essentia obiectiva*, i. e. it is the way in which we feel or experience the *essentia formalis*[4].

Hence, for the conception of a true idea as that which agrees with its 'ideatum,' we can substitute the conception of an 'adequate' idea. An adequate idea 'contains in itself all the marks or properties of a true idea, so far as that is considered in itself without relation to its object[5].' An idea is not made true by being brought into agreement with an object. Its truth is something belonging to it internally; a character, which constitutes its real

---

[1] Cf. TdIe, VVlL. i. p. 23. Spinoza's view is summed up in the expression·'Verum, sive intellectus.'
[2] Cf. e.g. E. ii. 43 S.; and cf.
K. V. S. ii. 15, § 3.
[3] Cf. e.g. E. ii. 43 S.
[4] Cf. above, p. 7; VVlL. i. p. 12.
[5] E. ii. def. 4.

Book II. being and distinguishes it from false ideas, as ideas which (*quâ* false) are not real or are deficient in being [1]. And this internal character of a true idea—its adequacy—shows itself in the coherence, the clearness and distinctness, of its content. So long as we conceive clearly and distinctly—so long as the content of our conception is coherent—we conceive truly. An idea is adequate so long as what it affirms does not extend beyond, or fall short of, what is comprised within its conception. Hence if we conceive an absolutely simple idea—an idea involving an affirmation coextensive with its content—our idea must be adequate and true [2]. And so long as the affirmations involved in a complex idea do not extend beyond, or fall short of, its conceived content—so long, that is, as we conceive clearly and distinctly each and all of the simple ideas which the complex idea involves—our complex idea must be true [3]. But not to conceive a simple idea—or again to conceive a complex idea inadequately

---

[1] VVlL. i. pp. 23 ff.; cf. E. ii. 43 S.

[2] VVlL. i. pp. 24 ff., 'Unde sequitur, simplices cogitationes non posse non esse veras, ut simplex semicirculi, motus, quantitatis, &c., idea. Quicquid hae affirmationis continent, earum adaequat conceptum, nec ultra se extendit'....

[3] VVlL.i.p.23. We can see how this view of Spinoza connects with the conception of an Alphabet of Reality, each letter of which is affirmed (so to say) in a simple idea. Two mistakes must be avoided in the interpretation of Spinoza's doctrine: (1) The 'simple ideas' are *not* the ideal side of corpuscles or extended atoms. Spinoza is not an atomist. The idea of a corpuscle is far from 'simple'; it involves an infinite number of ideas of other atoms. They are ideas, e.g., of Attributes and infinite modes, i. e. the 'simple moments' in complex conceptions. Hence in the Ethics, e.g., the conception of God is constructed out of 'simple' ideas, viz. out of the ideas of Substance, Attribute, &c. (cf.Busolt, p. 146, note 56). (2) The 'simple ideas' are not abstract universals. Their objects or 'ideata' are singular individual realities, which 'by their omnipresence and eternity play the part of universals,' but which are not reached by abstraction from particulars; cf. TdIe, VVlL. i. pp. 32 ff.

# IDEA AND IDEATUM

(indistinctly and inarticulately)—this is simply *defect* of knowledge: and in this defect the falsity of false ideas consists. A complete intelligence is incapable of such defect, for the intellect *quâ* intellect forms conceptions, and *quâ* conceiving conceives adequately or truly [1]. The defect is in us, only because we are but a part of a complete intelligence, and the ideas, which it forms whole and in their adequate context, appear in us mutilated and disconnected [2].

As in reality all things and all thoughts constitute a complete unity which has no distinct or separable parts, the only completely adequate idea will (as we saw, p. 148) be the 'infinita idea Dei.' But there will be degrees of adequacy or truth in the subordinate ideas or minds. A finite mind will attain to truth, so far as its thoughts are conceived by it in their coherence in the system of complete thought. And so far as any thought of a finite mind can be in that mind what it is in God's mind—so far as the whole of a thought of God can in any sense be comprised in the thought of a finite mind—to that degree that thought will be adequate or true *even as the thought of a finite mind* [3].

Thus we may say that the more of God there is in man —(the more the thought of God enters into the mind of man, or the more man apprehends God, experiences things from God's complete point of view)—the more man attains to truth, and man's mind to its full being or reality. And we must remember that this will involve an increase in fullness of being or reality of man's corporeal nature [4]. Further, it will mean that man *does* more, acts from within or of himself, is spontaneously

---

[1] Cf. K. V. S. i. 9, § 3; TdIe. VVlL. i. pp. 24, 25, 35; and Ethics, *passim*.

[2] TdIe, ll. cc.; and E. ii. 11 C., 29 C. and S., 43 S., &c.

[3] This is the case with the *Communes Notiones*; see below, § 2.

[4] Cf. E. ii. 13 S.

Book II. the source of more, '*thinks*' more and 'suffers' less, i. e. is less the plaything of external agencies. And this will mean that man realizes more fully his union with God—his oneness with the whole order of things; and finds his peace and happiness in that experience.

Spinoza traces three main degrees or stages of realization of this end. They are degrees at once of man's power of knowing, his 'freedom' or power of action, and his reality or oneness with God[1]. For the present, we have to consider them on their intellectual side, as grades of increasing knowledge.

### § 2. THE THREE STAGES OF HUMAN PROGRESS AS A DEVELOPMENT OF KNOWLEDGE.

#### 1. *Cognitio primi generis, Opinio, or Imaginatio.*

'Imaginatio'—its meaning and origin.

The human body is in causal relation with other (ultimately with all) bodies, and it is subject to the action of these bodies. What we call 'our body' is a complex of corpuscles, all of which are constantly changing—acting upon one another, being acted upon from without. Owing to its complexity, the human body is able to undergo a great variety of changes, to be affected in very many ways: and so long as the balance of the motions of its constituents is maintained, it keeps throughout these changes that unity which, however imperfect, is sufficient to enable us to regard it as a 'single thing.' The subordinate 'individuals' of which the body is composed are of various character, and may be grouped as '*fluid*,' '*soft*,' and '*hard*.' Not only are all the parts of the human body subject to the action of external bodies, but the body itself can act upon—move and arrange and alter—external bodies in very many various ways[2].

[1] Cf. above, pp. 141 ff.
[2] E. ii. Post. 1-4, and 6; above, pp. 82 ff., 123 ff.

And our mind is the ideal side of the actually-existent body. The mind is a complex of ideas, each of which is the ideal side of a component corpuscle of the body. The 'unity' of the mind is the ideal counterpart of the 'unity' of the body. What applies to the body—the variety and change of its parts—applies also to the mind. Its component ideas are as various as their 'ideata': with every change in the body there is at once a change in the mind, with every change in the mind a change in the body[1].

A change of state in body or mind, as presented to the imaginative consciousness, throws us back for its explanation *ad infinitum* along the chains of corporeal and mental causes respectively. In order truly to understand such a presented change, we should have to rise above the imaginative apprehension, and trace the eternal or necessary coherence of the modal systems of Extension or Thought. But, apart from that complete understanding, we have a two-sided event or change, the occurrence of which we cannot fully explain: from one side of which, however, we can (and do) make an inference to the other. Thus, given a change in a bodily state, there must be, as its ideal side, a change in the component ideas of our mind. Or, given a change in our mental state, there must be, as its corporeal side, a change in the component corpuscles of our body. Neither change is the cause or the effect of the other. The two changes are the double effect of a two-sided cause; and the chain of causal connexion is confined to either side of the double series of events. Yet, since for our imperfect apprehension the complete tracing of the threads

---

[1] Above, pp. 125 ff.; and cf. E. v. 1 for the latter half of this statement. Of course, our body is not to our ordinary experience distinctly and fully apprehended in all its detail—nor are all the 'ideae,' which really constitute our mind, our 'thoughts' in the sense that 'we' in our finite being consciously think them; cf. p. 131.

Book II. of causal connexion is impossible; since, moreover, sometimes one, sometimes the other, side of the events is more conspicuous to us, we inevitably fill in the links of explanation as is most convenient. We ought to remember that to intercalate corporeal links in a series of mental changes (or vice versa) is erroneous, and justifiable only so far as each change under one Attribute postulates a corresponding change under the other Attribute. But even Spinoza himself is not always clear and consistent in emphasizing this [1]. As a rule, the bodily changes are most conspicuous, and mental changes are therefore most readily 'explained' as 'effects' of a chain of bodily changes. Really, they are effects of a chain of mental changes which we cannot exhibit, but of which the bodily side is clear to us. We must bear Spinoza's general position in mind, and interpret occasional obscurities and lapses simply *as lapses*: as survivals from his earlier mental history, partly caused, no doubt, by the influence of those popular notions of the relation of body and soul which in his explicit theory he has rejected.

When an external body acts upon the human body and alters its state, that alteration will be on its ideal side an alteration of the mind; i.e. our mind will have formed an 'idea,' which Spinoza would call a 'perception,' except that he wishes to emphasize that it originates in the mind and not in its 'ideatum [2].' If we abstract such an idea from its whole context and causal connexion, its 'ideatum' will be a state of body correspondingly isolated (in a more or less arbitrary manner) from its context. Now every change of state in any body, which is caused by the action of another body, will depend for its

---

[1] Cf. e.g. E. i. App., where Spinoza corrects his own hasty expression: 'Quae omnia satis ostendunt, unumquemque pro dispositione cerebri de rebus iudicasse, vel potius imaginationis affectiones pro rebus accepisse.'

[2] E. ii. def. 3, Expl.; cf. also e.g. E. ii. 48 S., 49 S., &c.

# IMAGINATIO

character upon the nature both of the affected and of the affecting body[1]. Hence, a change of state in our body, which is caused by the action of an external body, will possess a character which is the joint product both of the nature of our own body and of the nature of the external body. The idea of such a change of state will consequently reflect, more or less adequately, the nature of both bodies so far as that is involved in their interaction[2].

Changes in our body, produced by the impact of external bodies, Spinoza calls 'rerum imagines,' although he expressly repudiates the notion that they *are* copies (reproduce the figures) of the external bodies. They are 'rerum imagines' in so far as their ideal sides give us *external bodies as present*[3]. So far as these changes persist in our body after the actual contact with the external body is over, Spinoza calls them 'vestigia quaedam corporis externi impellentis[4].'

The ideas of these 'imagines' or 'vestigia,' Spinoza calls 'imaginationes mentis,' and we are said 'imaginari' so far as we form ideas which are the counterpart or correlates of such bodily affections[5].

---

[1] E. ii. Ax. 1 (after Lemma 3 C.).

[2] E. ii. 16. The proof rests upon E. i. Ax. 4. 'The knowledge of an effect depends upon and involves the knowledge of its cause.'

[3] E. ii. 17 S. Spinoza retains the term partly as a concession to popular language: 'Porro, ut verba usitata retineamus, Corporis humani affectiones, quarum ideae corpora externa velut nobis praesentia repraesentant, rerum imagines vocabimus, tametsi rerum figuras non referunt.'

[4] Cf. E. ii. Post. 5.

[5] 'Imaginationes' *originally* seems to have meant 'ideas' as distinguished from 'impressions,' i.e. 'ideae' of 'vestigia' as distinguished from 'ideae' of the actual present interaction of our body and the external body. But the term includes both in Spinoza's usage; cf. e.g. E. ii. 40 S. 2.

Spinoza is not always quite clear or quite consistent in his terminology. In the following passages, e.g., 'imagines' *seems* to stand for 'mentis imaginationes': E. iii. 18 dem.; iii. 35

Book II.  It is, then, the general character of every 'imaginatio' to be an idea which pictures an external body as actually existent, i.e. as present to us. So far, the world of 'imagination' may be called the 'world of presentation'—a world which we picture as a complex of external things acting upon one another and upon us. One 'imaginatio' persists until another drives it out of the mind; i.e. we go on 'picturing' a thing as present until another 'picture' occurs in our mind which excludes the first. And this persistence of the picture-idea need not cease, even though the external body which initiated our corporeal change is no longer acting upon us; for that change was in part due to our own corporeal nature, and may survive in it (or be reproduced by inner conditions of our body), when its other part-cause is gone [1].

So far as the occurrence of the various 'imaginationes' *happens* in our mind—so far as *we* do not regulate its order—or (to put the matter inaccurately [2]) 'so long as the mind perceives things according to the common order of nature, i.e. so long as it is determined from without (from the fortuitous concurrence of things) to contemplate this or that'—we are said to be *passive* in imagination. The 'imaginationes' are indeed (as we shall see) only fragments of ideas: *our* mind does not form the ideas of which they are mutilated portions. They occur in *our* mind like conclusions apart from their premisses: the chain of ideal causes which forms their context is not present as a whole in *our* mind, but only in some dissociated links [3].

Spinoza's account of the survival of 'imaginationes' and

dem. and S.; ii. 40 S. 1 sub fin.; v. 12. On the other hand, 'imagines' is clearly distinguished from 'imaginationes' in E. ii. 17 S.; ii. 40 S. 1; ii. 48 S., 49 S.;  v. 1, and elsewhere.
[1] E. ii. 17.
[2] E. ii. 29 S.; cf. above, pp. 153, 154.
[3] Cf. below, and E. ii. 28 dem.

# IMAGINATIO

their recall by 'memory' (association) is involved with a Cartesian theory which has long been rejected[1]. But Spinoza is careful to guard himself. Though his theory (he says) gives a possible explanation, he does not insist on it as the only possible one[2].

An external body 'determines' a 'fluid' part of the human body, so that the latter impinges upon a 'soft part'; i.e. the 'Animal Spirits' are set in motion by the action of an external body on our organs of sense, and in their motion they impinge upon the nerves and brain. If this takes place frequently, the surface of the brain is altered, and thus (as it were) certain 'tracks' of an impellent external body are printed in it[3]. The alteration of the surface of the brain causes the 'Animal Spirits' to be reflected from it at a correspondingly different angle[4]. If therefore the 'Animal Spirits' impinge once more upon the brain, whilst its surface is still in this altered state—even though their impact is not caused by an external body, but by their 'own spontaneous motion'—they will be reflected from that altered surface in the same way (at the same angle) as if they had been impelled against it by the external body. Hence we can 'imagine' a body as present, even though it is not acting on us, provided that it has acted on us sufficiently often in the past to cause a more or less permanent alteration of surface in our brain: i.e. we can call up (or have called

---

[1] Cf. K. V. S. ii. 19, § 9; Martineau, pp. 134 ff.

[2] E. ii. 17 S. 'Videmus itaque qui fieri potest ut ea, quae non sunt, veluti praesentia contemplemur, ut saepe fit. Et fieri potest, ut hoc aliis de causis contingat; sed mihi hic sufficit ostendisse unam, per quam rem sic possim explicare, ac si ipsam per veram causam ostendissem; nec tamen credo me a vera longe aberrare...'

Spinoza's criticism of Descartes' conception of the 'seat of the soul' (E. v. Praef.) no doubt rendered him cautious in his use of the Cartesian theory of the 'Animal Spirits.'

[3] And we have a 'dispositio cerebri'; cf. E. i. App. (VVlL. i. p. 74).

[4] E. ii. 17 C. dem.; cf. ii. Ax. 2 (after Lemma 3 C.).

BOOK II.

The contents of imaginative experience.

up in us) a mental picture of an external object without its actual presence. Some kinds of subjective illusion, and some kinds of Redintegration, are thus explicable consistently with Spinoza's general theory of 'imaginative' experience.

To the class of 'imaginationes' there belong all sense-perceptions—every kind of 'direct' consciousness of external bodies and of our own body—and every awareness of our self as actually existent. Of external bodies and of our own body—or again of our own self ('mind') as now thinking and feeling—we can have no 'direct' or 'immediate' knowledge, except that which is (or is based upon) the idea of an affection of our body[1]. No doubt the idea, which gives us an external body as actually existent, involves an inference. It is primarily the idea of a state of our own body, and only secondarily an idea of an external body, viz. only in so far as the idea of the cause is involved in that of the effect. But in the state of imagination this inference is never complete: its premisses are never clearly nor completely present to the 'imaginative' consciousness, and for that very reason all imaginative knowledge is inadequate[2]. I have called this knowledge 'direct' or 'immediate,' because the inference on which it rests is not recognized by the mind in the state of imagination, and is in any case very inadequately performed. In 'imagination' we 'picture' states of our body and interpret them as external bodies acting upon or modifying our own body. But we are not aware that we are making an interpretation, and we stop arbitrarily and erroneously in our regress from effect to cause wherever it pleases us. Thus we suppose ourselves to 'see' an external body A acting upon our own body. This 'sight' is an inference, which (if *per impossibile* it were completed) would lead us through the whole infinite chain of external bodies (B, C, D, .... ∞)

[1] E. ii. 19, 23, and 26.   [2] Cf. E. ii. 28 dem.

# IMAGINATIO

whose changes of motion are implied in that change of motion which constitutes our bodily modification, and is the 'conclusion' from which we are inferring some of the premisses. But we are content to regard A as the source of the change in our body, as the premiss of the presented conclusion, and we suppose ourselves to 'see' A, and not merely to infer it as a condition of our changed state.

The content of the imaginative consciousness grows by accretion and association into an experience which, in its internal order and in its colouring, is peculiar and personal to each mind. Such an experience Spinoza calls *Cognitio primi generis, Opinio*, or *Imaginatio*. The *matter* of its content (as we have seen) is given to it as ideas of the 'affections' of the body; i.e. may be said to depend upon the position of the percipient's body in the 'communis ordo naturae,' upon its power of being 'affected,' its opportunities and its modes of receptivity. Relatively to the mind itself, the matter of such an experience is due to chance. And Spinoza goes further. For, relatively to the nature of the mind—which consists in the power of thinking, i.e. connecting its ideas in an intelligible order the same for all minds [1]—the *form*, in which the matter of imaginative experience is arranged, is due to chance. There is an accretion of the 'imaginationes' of the single 'imagines' into abstract universals (class-ideas), and into the still more abstract 'transcendental terms' (*ens, res, aliquid*), in which, if the mind is not exactly passive—as Spinoza's words suggest—it at any rate does not control the growth by any principles of synthesis which could properly be called its own. Such universals,

---

[1] Cf. E. ii. 18 S. 'Dico *secundo*, hanc concatenationem (i.e. 'memoriam') fieri secundum ordinem et concatenationem affectionum Corporis humani, ut ipsam distinguerem a concatenatione idearum, quae fit secundum ordinem intellectus, quo res per primas suas causas Mens percipit, et qui in omnibus hominibus idem est.'

BOOK II. moreover, vary in each mind with respect to the slight meaning which they possess for it, and the peculiar colouring of this meaning depends on conjunctions which (relatively to the mind) are due to chance.

Imaginative experience is 'natural' to man, in the sense that he is (and must remain), as an actually-existent mode, a 'pars naturae,' subject to the 'communis ordo naturae [1],' and that his mind is the idea of an actually-existent mode of Extension. But in so far as it owes its being (both its matter and its form), to anything rather than the mind of man alone, it is far from expressing man's 'nature,' or being 'natural' to him. It is the product of man's mind under circumstances which annihilate its individuality. It is the resultant of the whole environment in which man necessarily exists, but which decidedly is not his 'self.'

Let us see how the universals of imaginative experience are formed [2].

(1) *Termini transcendentales* (e.g. *ens, res, aliquid*).

The human body—a finite mode with a limited capacity—can form in itself only a limited number of distinct 'imagines' at the same time. If this limit is exceeded, the images (bodily modifications) will run together and become blurred. Now, at any one time there will be present in the body an enormous number of such 'imagines'—both those which are at that moment being produced, and those which have survived as 'vestigia' of the agency of external bodies in the past. The 'imaginationes,' which are the 'ideae' of these 'imagines,' will 'run together'—be confounded and blurred—in the mind, just as their 'ideata,' the 'imagines,' coalesce in the body. The mind, therefore, will 'picture'

---

[1] Cf. E. iv. 4 and C.
[2] Cf. E. ii. 40 S. 1. Spinoza's account is expressed in terms of the *physical* process which is the counterpart of the psychical formation of abstract universal ideas.

# IMAGINATIO

e.g. all bodies confusedly, without distinct perception of any, under a single vague concept—e.g. 'ens,' 'res.' Such concepts are ideas in the highest degree confused, abstract, and empty of meaning. And they may be said to *form themselves* in the mind, inasmuch as the mind does not attempt to synthesize the differences, or to keep the single 'imaginationes' distinct in their unity. There is no mental grasp of the particulars as differences of a universal. The mind is simply overpowered by the multiplicity of impressions and memory-images, lets the distinct features fall, and takes refuge in an abstract notion, which succeeds in covering the whole field only by leaving most of its significant elements out of account.

The same is true in a less degree of *notiones universales* (e.g. *homo, equus, canis*), the abstract class-ideas of formal Logic. If the number of distinct 'imagines' is not sufficient *entirely* to overwhelm the body's capacity for receiving clearly-stamped impressions, but is sufficient to obliterate the smaller characteristic differences, there will be a corresponding loss of distinctness in the mind's formation of 'imaginationes.' Thus, e.g., the innumerable distinct 'imaginationes' of different individual men will coalesce in a single imaginative universal—'man.' The central part, as it were, of this universal picture—the portion in which the single picture-ideas agree—will be clearly stamped, and so far the notion of 'man' will have distinct significance. But the periphery will be blurred; for the points of difference in the single ideas will cancel one another. Hence 'man' will be an abstract notion, and in it much of the characteristic significance of single perceptions of individual men will have vanished.

Thus the universals, under which the matter of imaginative experience is grouped, are the products of a blending which is due to the limited capacity of our mind and body. They are confused, abstract, and less

*Chap. II.*

(2) *Notiones universales.*

significant than the particular ideas which coalesce to form them. And the mode of the blending must be regarded (not as a mode of the mind's activity, but) as due to the feebleness of our mental grasp. The mind does not stamp its own form—its intelligible connexions or principles of synthesis—upon the materials of its experience: it simply admits them as parts of its single consciousness in the manner which calls for least exertion of its own. The formation of such universals can hardly be called a logical process at all. Spinoza treats it as a mechanical coalescence in the mind, not as a synthesis by the mind.

The significant nucleus of each universal varies with each subject, and Spinoza explains to what this personal colouring is due. The peculiar colouring which ideal conjunctions assume in any given person's mind, depends upon the mode in which, in his past experience, ideal elements have been associated in his mental states. In E. ii. 18, Spinoza shows that (according to his general theory) 'If our body has ever been affected by two or more external bodies simultaneously, we cannot in future "imagine" one without the other'; i.e. any element of a single perceptive state, if reproduced, will reinstate the remaining elements [1]. In the Scholium attached to this proposition Spinoza explains that 'memoria' (association) is a redintegration of this kind. 'Memoria' is, he says, 'simply a certain concatenation of ideas, which *involve* the nature of things external to the human body— a concatenation which takes place *in accordance with the order and concatenation of the affections of the human body.*' 'Involve,' i.e. they do not adequately express the ideas of the external things, but contain them confusedly within the ideas of our own corporeal affections [2].

[1] Cf. Bradley, *Principles of Logic*, p. 278.
[2] E. ii. 18 S. '... involvunt; non autem ... explicant,' &c. The italics in the above quotation are my own.

And the 'concatenation' is not the product of a rational function, but due to the conjunction of bodily images and their ideas in the past. Hence this associative reproduction will vary in every man according to his circumstances—his profession, his past environment, &c.; and on this variation the differences in the personal colouring of the abstract universals will depend[1]. The emphasis of the significance of every single idea will lie with each person where such associations place it, and thus the emphasis of the significance of the 'communis imago'—the nucleus of the abstract universal—will vary with every man 'pro dispositione sui corporis,' 'prout rerum imagines consuevit hoc vel alio modo iungere et concatenare[2],' 'pro dispositione cerebri[3],' &c.

The knowledge of every-day life is for the most part nothing but imaginative experience. The rules which we apply to guide our actions, the universal judgements under which we bring every new perception, and which form the tissue of our ordinary thinking, are derived from the two sources of the 'cognitio primi generis,' i. e. from 'signa' or from 'experientia vaga.' We have either taken them on trust, on hearsay, from books or tradition; or we have formed them by an uncritical induction based on incomplete enumeration. If, e. g., I am given three numbers, and wish to find a fourth which shall be to the third as the second is to the first, I shall either apply the rule of three without question— a rule I have learnt and remembered, but do not understand—or perhaps I shall first test the rule in a few instances, and, finding that it works in these, shall then trust it in all others. If my house is on fire, and I pour water on the flames, this is the application of a universal judgement (that water extinguishes fire) which I may have heard from others or made for myself by an

[1] Cf. E. ii. 40 S. 1.   [2] E. ii. 18 S.
[3] E. i. App.

Book II. uncritical induction based on my personal observation. But in neither case—at least in the ordinary course of life—is there any real knowledge, any rational intelligence, guiding my conduct[1].

[1] Cf. K. V. S. ii. 1, § 3; TdIe, VVIl. i. pp. 7, 8; E. ii. 40 S. 2.

From a comparison of these passages (which do not altogether agree) it is clear that '*experientia vaga*' corresponds to Bacon's 'experientia vaga,' and is the knowledge which rests upon the 'inductions' of an uncritical mind. In the TdIe (l.c.), Spinoza defines it as 'experientia, quae non determinatur ab intellectu, sed tantum ita dicitur, quia casu sic occurrit, et nullum aliud habemus experimentum, quod hoc oppugnat, et ideo tanquam inconcussum apud nos manet.' And his instances make his meaning clear; e.g. 'I know that I shall die' by 'experientia vaga,' i.e. 'because I have seen other people like myself die, although they have none of them lived for the same length of time, nor died of the same disease.' Such universal judgements rest upon an observation which makes no attempt to discover the cause of the connexions asserted, or to purify the connexion from irrelevant detail.

'Ex auditu aut ex aliquo signo' is illustrated thus: 'I know "ex auditu" my birthday, who my parents were, and the like.' But under this head, Spinoza includes all knowledge derived from written and spoken words, so long as it rests upon the *authority* of the speaker or writer; i.e. he includes not merely 'knowledge' of particular facts, but 'knowledge' of rules and of general principles, *so long as these are taken on trust* (cf. K. V. S., l.c.).

In the Ethics (l.c.), Spinoza treats 'cognitio ex signis' as a case of 'memoria' (association). A word, like an 'imago,' is in itself a purely corporeal thing—a modification of extension. Its 'essentia' is constituted solely by corporeal movements, and it must not be confused with the idea which it excites, or with the thing which it signifies (E. ii. 49 S.). As, however, the corporeal change set up by a word was accompanied in our body by another bodily modification caused by an external body, the idea of the word and the idea of the external body formed elements in a single mental state. If therefore one is reproduced, the other will be reinstated with it. Thus, e.g., the word 'pomum' is in itself simply a corporeal mode—its 'essentia' is constituted by certain corporeal motions—and its effects are similarly corporeal, changes of motion in the body of the person who hears it. But a Roman, on hearing the word 'pomum,' at once forms an idea which reinstates the 'imaginatio' of the fruit; although the idea of the word is not like the idea

Thus the fundamental characteristic of the imaginative consciousness is its want of independence. Its colouring and the modes of interconnexion in its content are peculiar and personal to each mind. But this peculiarity is not the mark of a strong individuality. On the contrary, it shows weakness of mind, absence of originative thinking. The 'ordo intellectus' is one and the same in all men; but the arrangement of the contents of imaginative experience varies with the environment of the individual, and this, so far as he is concerned, is a matter of chance.

So far as the ideas of imagination go, they are true. If we take them as what they really are, if we do not attempt to find more in their revelations than they really contain, we are not deceived. To be able to picture absent things as vividly as if they were present, provided we are aware that they are *not* present—provided we do not wrongly objectify our pictures—this is a positive power of the mind, and so far reveals a fuller degree of being or reality in it: or would do so, if this power of 'picturing' could be attributed to the mind itself, and not merely to the agency of the total environment or system of which the mind is a part[1]. Nor is there any illusion in our *perceptions*, provided we do

of the fruit, nor has anything in common with it, except that 'his body has often been affected by these two' together (i.e. by the word and the fruit), 'i.e. that he has often heard the word whilst perceiving the fruit' (E. ii. 18 S.).

Words, then, are 'signs' of things, in the sense that the idea of the bodily modification, produced by the written or spoken word, tends to reinstate the idea of the bodily modification produced by the thing which in the past affected our body simultaneously with the word: the idea of the word, and the idea of the thing, formed parts of a single mental state in our past experience. So far, therefore, as we trust to tradition—to written or spoken words—we are trusting to our past mental states, the interconnexion of the elements of which *may have been* arbitrary, and (so far as our own efforts go) *was* arbitrary.

[1] E. ii. 17 S.

not misinterpret them. We perceive, e.g., the sun as if it were about 200 feet from the earth. There is no error in this picturing as such. Error comes in, when we attribute to the sun itself a position and appearance which belongs to it only in its relation to our organs of vision. The imaginative perception of the sun is the adequate idea of its 'ideatum,' viz. of the bodily affection which the action of the sun's rays produces in us. This 'affection' involves the nature of the sun (not *per se*, but only) so far as that communicates with our body. If we know and remember this—if we understand of what 'ideatum' our imagination is the idea—we are not deceived. And the imaginative idea itself is true and not contrary to any true idea. It does not vanish before the knowledge of the real distance of the sun. Even an astronomer will 'see' the sun as 200 feet distant, but the perception will not mislead him, nor (if he knows its nature and cause) will he regard the perception as an illusion to be rejected. It belongs to its own sphere of truth; and, so long as it is not referred where it has no place, it has its own value and in no way conflicts with other true ideas [1].

In their own context and order, then, all the imaginative ideas are true and valuable. And, though *in us* they appear in an arbitrary and contingent series, 'in God' or in the nature of things they follow eternal and necessary laws of production and sequence. There is no chance, no arbitrariness, no error and no falsehood except from the point of view of finite minds with their partial reality and mutilated knowledge [2].

But since we are finite—since our minds are fragments of God's Thought, our bodies fragments of God's Extension—contingency and error find their inevitable home in our lives and in our knowledge. In the stage of imaginative experience (so far as that is taken to include

---

[1] Cf. E. ii. 35 S.; iv. 1 S.  [2] E. ii. 32, 33, and 36.

the whole mental being of any man), the mind is not conscious of its own limits, nor of the sources and true reference of its ideas. An imaginative idea in us is the presentation of a bodily modification which involves the nature of our own and of an external body, but involves their natures only so far as they interact. The full nature of our own and of the external body is contained in the whole complex of bodies, of which the 'facies totius universi' is the complete modal expression. The momentary interaction of two fragments of this totality (two fragments which have no independent subsistence) is an infinitesimal revelation of the natures from which it springs. Yet—so far as we 'imagine' or 'perceive'—it is from the ideas of such momentary changes in our bodily state that we derive all our knowledge of our bodies, our minds, and external bodies. We construct, without criticism or hesitation, our view of ourselves and of the external world on these miserably inadequate data. The whole imaginative experience is built at haphazard upon ideas of affections of our body—'ideas' and 'affections' which 'occur' according to the order and laws of the universe as a whole, and not according to laws regulating our mind and our body alone. We suppose ourselves to be framing our views, but these are framed in and for us by influences and upon data of which we can have at the best a fractional and confused apprehension. Hence imaginative experience gives us a very partial knowledge of ourselves, our bodies, and external bodies, and this partial knowledge turns to error so far as we are unaware and heedless of its fragmentariness [1].

Further, the inadequacy of this knowledge prevents us from understanding the eternal necessity of the order in things. The temporal existence of our own and of external bodies is the appearance of a timeless actuality,

[1] Cf. E. ii. 29 C.

BOOK II. but the 'how' and 'why' of this appearance would be manifest only to a complete apprehension. For our partial view,. the appearance is taken for the reality. Things come to be and last and pass away without any inevitable necessity, and this we take as the truth of the matter. Why they should come to be here and now; how long they will last, or why they should last so long; or, again, when and why they will pass away—all this for us is purely arbitrary. Hence we look at the things of our experience as in truth and in reality 'contingent' and 'corruptible': we have 'only a quite inadequate knowledge of the duration of our own and of external bodies.' Such 'knowledge' as we possess in the stage of imagination depends upon inferences illogically drawn from conjunctions in our past experience imperfectly understood and erroneously interpreted [1].

The conceptions under which we group our imaginative ideas are themselves mere generalized abstractions from those ideas, and are less presentative of the Real than they. Thus we measure and count and arrange in Time; but Time, Number, and Measure are but 'ways of imagining'—abstract conceptions, empty forms for holding together the single imaginative ideas. In themselves, these 'modi imaginandi' have but a slight significance, and they distort the Reality which they are used to represent [2]. And the case is worse with the *termini transcendentales,* and little better with the *notiones universales* [3].

In the Appendix to E. i, Spinoza treats all aesthetic and moral conceptions, and all perceptions of secondary qualities, as so many 'modi imaginandi'—erroneous, therefore, so far as they are referred to Reality as expres-

---

[1] Cf. E. ii. 30, 31, and C.; ii. 44 C. 1 and S. (on the S., cf. Camerer, pp. 85, 86).
[2] Cf. above, pp. 30 ff., 78 ff.,
and on Time, cf. also E. ii. 44 S. (with Camerer's note, l. c.).
[3] Cf. above, pp. 160 ff.

sing the nature of things. Most of them rest upon the fundamental idea—expressed or implied—that 'all things are made and arranged for the benefit of man'; the moral conceptions involve besides the erroneous notion that man is a free agent.

These two conceptions—the conception of an external teleology and of human freedom [1]—are both 'imaginative,' and both attributed to Reality (as adequately representing the truth of things) because of the deficiencies of our knowledge.

We are aware of our desires—that we act in order to secure what we want—but we have no knowledge of the efficient causes of our desire. We suppose ourselves to be moved to action by final causes, and we acquiesce in a teleological explanation of human action. As we are unaware of the ways in which God acts, we attribute human modes of action to him; and we suppose him to be determined by final causes, since under a teleological form of explanation human actions appear to us intelligible.

External bodies, affecting our body by working on our sensory nerves, give us sensations of heat, cold, sound, light, and taste. But of the mechanism which produces these effects we are ignorant; and in our ignorance we attribute these qualities of sensation directly to the external bodies, which are at most their part-causes. And what conduces to our health, or gives us pleasure, we unhesitatingly affirm to be really and in itself 'beautiful' or 'good,' since (we are persuaded) man is the centre and aim of the universe.

Hence we make for ourselves each his own personal world, built around our own convenience, our likes and dislikes, our arbitrary fancies. And through ignorance of the limitations of our imaginative apprehension, we

[1] On the conception of 'freedom,' cf. below, ch. 3, § 3, and Appendix to Bk. II, pp. 228 ff.

turn this private world into the Reality. But we thus become the victims of illusion[1]. For the Nature of Things is neither good nor bad, neither well-arranged nor disordered. It has no beauty and no ugliness; it does not strive to realize our ends, nor fight against them. Sweet tastes and sounds, virtuous conduct and good intentions, no more belong to Things as they really are, than the iniquities of the criminal or the horrors of putrefaction.

### 2. *Cognitio secundi generis, Ratio.*

*Origin and contents of scientific knowledge.*

The mind is the idea of an actually existent mode of Extension. All our experience must ultimately come in and from that apprehension of the body, which this 'union' of mind and body renders necessary. As a thing in the complex of things, each body is affected in various ways, and in the ideas of these changes of bodily state, in this 'feeling of the present states of our body,' we have the basis or first materials of experience. Out of them we make a whole experience, or form our world; out of them our world grows together. One way of such an accretion or construction we have just considered. Imaginative experience makes its world out of these impressions and ideas of our bodily states; it extends, interprets, and connects them on the threads of personal reminiscence, in an order which reflects the groupings and conjunctions which have happened in the subject's past life; on principles of synthesis (if we can call them 'principles') which are foreign to the nature of the mind itself as an intelligence. If we treat such an experience as knowledge of the Reality, we are interpreting the universe from the centre of our personal prejudices, our likes and dislikes, our partial and arbitrary fancies. We have as yet no notion of a world the same for all—an experience which is objective and universal. Our interests

[1] Cf. Tr. P. ch. 2, § 8.

are not in the nature of things, but in the eccentric one-sided appearances which that nature presents to our partial view. Yet, in a sense, we are in direct contact with Reality. We perceive, and our perception is a fact and is real so far as it goes. But our interpretation or development of the 'given' follows no universal principles of reason, and reaches no true and universal result. If we could fully understand our data, we should know the Reality. But, for imaginative apprehension—for the mind whose only resource is to 'picture'—the data present an infinite series of causes and effects, each of which is unintelligible by itself, the totality of which cannot be grasped by a finite mind. We cannot complete the series, and apart from its completion it is, in every part of itself, unintelligible. And yet, so long as we 'imagine,' we are confined to the series.

Nor do the 'Auxilia Imaginationis' bring us any help. Our hasty generalizations, our abstract groupings and uncritical reliance on our experience of past associations, do but fill in the gaps of our world with error. We make a whole of experience with these aids, but the whole is a jumble and a distortion.

Is there any escape? Can we get any firm basis from which to construct a permanent, universal, and true view of things? And, granted the basis, can we develop a true experience from it—are there any principles of construction which are not arbitrary and personal, but necessary and universal?

Spinoza answers these questions in the affirmative. If we could start with one or more adequate ideas, we should be able to construct a true system of knowledge by deduction from them in the order and on the principles of reason. For the 'order of the intellect' is the same in all men, and corresponds to the order of Reality [1].

[1] Cf. above, p. 8 (VV1L. i. 18 S. '... [concatenatio idearum], p. 16, p. 30); E. ii. 29 S.; ii. quae fit secundum ordinem in-

Book II. The principles of synthesis which scientific reasoning exhibits are not the products of chance association, but are the unfolding of the nature of the mind itself: and that nature is one and the same in all men, and is the truth, the counterpart of the Reality[1]. But it *is* possible amongst the data of perception, amongst the 'ideae' of the bodily affections, to find some which must be adequate, and which can therefore serve as the starting-points for the premisses of scientific inference. For, if we consider the cause of the inadequacy of our 'imaginative' ideas, we shall see that with regard to some of those ideas inadequate conception is impossible.

An idea of a bodily modification was inadequate because partial. The full nature of that modification involved the full nature of our own and of external bodies—ultimately it involved the full nature of the universe of bodies. Its adequate apprehension was comprised in the intelligence of God *so far as he constituted the minds of an infinite number of finite things*. In our mind a mutilated portion of that adequate idea had to do duty for the whole, and we had no logical justification to argue from this shred to the whole. For if our knowledge had been supplemented, if the partial idea in us had been restored to its context, in that supplementation and restoration the nature of the partial idea would—for all we could tell—have been indefinitely altered.

But now suppose that there is some character or property which is present in all bodies, and present equally in the whole and in each, and in every part of each, of them. A perception of a fragment of such a property is equivalent to a perception of the whole. Whether we perceive it in our own body or in external bodies, in one or more, in a fragment or in a whole, it is impossible to

tellectus, quo res per primas suas causas Mens percipit, et qui in omnibus hominibus idem est.'

[1] Cf. above, pp. 149 ff.; TdIe, VVlL. i. pp. 23, 24, &c.; E. ii. 40 and dem.

apprehend it except adequately[1]. If we perceive it at all, we must perceive it in its true and complete nature. For since it is common to all bodies, we cannot err by attributing to the external body what is partly due to the nature of our own: in us and in the external body the property is the same. Nor can we err by extending to the totality of bodies what is given to us only in our interaction with one or a part of one. For our idea may be extended and supplemented, but its character will remain unaltered. The property in question is of one piece and texture throughout the corporeal universe. Apprehend any portion of it, and you have apprehended the essential nature of it all. And your knowledge of it will be universal, without being abstract. For it is knowledge of what is present everywhere in the same character, and yet it is knowledge of a concrete singular affirmative being, not of an 'ens rationis' or 'imaginationis' constituted by arbitrary abstraction[2].

But we know that at least some such properties exist, and must be perceived by us. For all things are modes of Substance and all minds are modes of Thought. And all bodies are modes of Extension, and as such exhibit in all their parts and as wholes certain identical and uniform properties[3].

It is on this identical basis of corporeal nature that the so-called 'axioms' of mathematics and physical science rest. They are 'notiones communes' (κοινὰ ἀξιώματα), which all men share, and as such they can form a common starting-point for an objective and universal knowledge[4].

[1] E. ii. 38.
[2] Cf. TdIe, VVlL. i. pp. 32 ff.
[3] Cf. E. ii. 38 C. with Lemma 2, to which Spinoza refers.
[4] The term 'notiones communes' was primarily applied to the axioms of mathematics and mathematical physics. But Spinoza extends it to cover any judgements expressing fundamental, universal, and self-evident truths —truths e.g. concerning God, Thought, and any Attribute or eternal and infinite mode. Cf. E. ii. 46 dem. *with* ii. 38 and C., and ii. 47 S.

Book II. Further, suppose that a property is confined to our body and a closed system of external bodies, with which our body interacts. If this property is present in all the members of the system (and in our own body), and present equally in the whole and in each body and in every part of each—so far as we perceive it at all, we must perceive it adequately. For if we perceive it at all, we perceive its character completely, since its character is confined to the system of bodies in question, and is equally present in every portion of that system. And when any member of the system affects our body in virtue of this common property, our idea of that bodily affection will be a perception of that property: for the two factors which combine to produce that affection are, *quâ* interacting, one and the same in character, viz. the common property in us and in the external bodies[1]. From this there follows the important corollary that the more properties which our body has in common with other bodies, the more apt is our mind to form a greater number of adequate ideas[2].

The contents of scientific knowledge are therefore the 'communes notiones,' which express the common properties of things so far as these are present in an equal degree in every portion of everything; i. e. the 'axioms' which lay down the fundamental truths as to the nature of God, Thought, Extension, Intelligence, Motion, &c.: further,

[1] E. ii. 39. The object of this proposition is clearly to establish the possibility of the adequate perception of 'propria.' All that Spinoza says is: '*If* our body is affected by external bodies in respect of a property common to it and them, peculiar to it and them, and equally present (or of one texture) in the closed system, then our perception of that property must be adequate.' Of course, *if* into the bodily affection the other (not common) properties of our body entered, then we should not get an adequate idea of the 'proprium.' But, under the hypothesis which Spinoza lays down, the adequate perception of 'propria' is necessary on his principles.

[2] E. ii. 39 C.

# SCIENCE

the ideas which express those properties of any system of bodies which are in like manner equally omnipresent within that system and peculiar to it and to our own body: and lastly the deductions from these axioms and notions of 'propria [1].'

*Character and limits of scientific knowledge.*

The content of science with its ordered system of inferences is *so far as it goes* absolutely true: it is a coherent system of adequate ideas, the same for all men so far as they reason and think clearly. There is no error within the sphere of Ratio [2]. For the 'notiones communes' are given to all men in their sense-perception, and their truth is guaranteed by their own clearness and distinctness of conception [3]. From these adequate ideas, science constructs its universe by deductive inference, the truth of which is guaranteed by the nature of the 'intellectus' itself. For it is the essential nature of the 'intellectus' to deduce truly: a true system of knowledge is the unfolding of the 'intellectus' in its own spontaneous activity according to its own 'order,' and the order of the 'intellectus' is the same in all men and represents the order of Reality [4]. We have as good a guarantee of the truth of what rests on reasoning as of what rests on

---

[1] Cf. E. ii. 40 S. 2, and v. 12 dem. 'Res, quas clare et distincte intelligimus, vel rerum communes proprietates sunt, vel quae ex iis deducuntur (*vide Rationis defin. in* 2 Schol. Prop. 40, p. 2) ...'

The 'communes notiones' are called by Spinoza 'fundamenta rationis,' 'ratiocinii nostri fundamenta' (E. ii. 44 C. 2 dem.; ii. 40 S. 1). The Ethics itself is for the most part the product and the example of 'Ratio'; and the geometrical method is the method of science as Spinoza conceived it, i.e. a deductive body of inference after the pattern of mathematics or mathematical physics. It must be remembered, however, that some elements in the philosophical system of the Ethics are the products of 'scientia intuitiva:' see below, and cf. E. v. 36 S.

[2] E. ii. 41.

[3] Cf. above, pp. 148 ff.; E. ii. 43 and S.

[4] Cf. above, pp. 149 ff., p. 171. For the phrase 'ordo intellectus' or 'ordo ad intellectum,' cf. e.g. E. ii. 18 S.; ii. 40 S. 2; v. 10.

BOOK II. reminiscence, for 'demonstrations are in fact the eyes of the mind, with which it sees and observes things [1].'

Science starts with 'notiones communes'—ultimately with the axioms based on the adequate knowledge of God's complete and necessary nature which is involved in all men's every perception [2]—and its inferences move within this sphere. But the characters which such 'notiones communes' comprehend are equally present in all things which exhibit them, and therefore can be and be conceived apart from any particular one. Hence they 'do not constitute the essence of any single thing [3].' It follows, that science comprehends Reality under the form of necessary interconnexions of content, and not as a complex or a system of particular things. The object of imaginative experience—the world of things, with its changes in time and place, its rich variety of individual colouring, its manifold life—becomes for science a timeless system of necessary laws. 'It is of the nature of Reason to perceive things under a certain form of eternity, viz. as the necessary consequents of God's eternal nature [4].' For scientific experience Reality exhibits that timeless necessary coherence, in which there are no coming-to-be or passing away, no contingency or possibility, no distinct or separable parts, no individual things.

And we have here at once the characteristic advance of science on imaginative experience, and its limits. Scientific truth is universal and necessary; and it is our very own—the product of the mind's intimate nature, its own act of thinking. So far it is immeasurably superior to imaginative experience, for that is personal and arbitrary, and does not reveal our own power of thought. But scientific truth is also 'abstract': not, indeed, in

---

[1] E. v. 23 S. 'Mentis enim oculi, quibus res videt observatque, sunt ipsae demonstrationes.' Cf. Tr. Th., VVlL. i. p. 533.

[2] E. ii. 45–7.
[3] E. ii. 37; cf. ii. 10 C. S.
[4] E. ii. 44 C. 2 and dem.

the sense that it treats of unreal abstractions; but in the sense that differences of temporal and local existence do not exist for it. It has no concern with the individualities of which they are the appearance. It comprehends the eternal order and coherence of the permanent omnipresent properties of the Real: but it cannot give us an understanding of the intimate individuality of any thing, nor of the exact unique mode of coherence of that thing in the Whole [1]—supposing, that is, that such an individuality *is*, and is not a mere illusion.

In a word:—science begins the work of intelligible reconstruction of the world of perception, but it cannot complete it. Its analysis has allowed the breath of life to escape from the world, and its reconstruction is powerless to restore it.

The progress from 'imagination' to 'science' is not the shifting of ideas within an unchanging subject. 'We' do not remain the same, and merely exchange one set of ideas for another. The 'we' of science is very different from the 'we' of imaginative experience. Scientific knowledge is on a higher plane than imaginative apprehension, and the mind that 'knows' has a greater degree of reality or being than the mind that merely 'imagines.' Our mind is still the idea of our body in its actual existence, and all our scientific knowledge is ultimately based on our knowledge of our body. But, whilst in 'imagination' our body 'exists as we feel it,' in the stage of scientific knowledge our body exists as we know it, or is 'actual' with the actuality which belongs to the objects of knowledge. We are moving in the world of eternal truths or essences: the body, so far as its knowledge is the basis of our science, is a mode of Extension conceived in its dependence on its Attribute. It exists for us no longer as this unique portion of matter,

[1] E. ii. 44 C. 2 dem. Cf. and contrast *scientia intuitiva*, E. v. 36 S.

occupying this space, occurring at this time, acting and being acted upon by the complex of bodies in the 'communis ordo naturae.' Our 'idea' of it is not an imperfectly-unified complex or succession of feelings peculiar and personal, but an impersonal and universal knowledge. Its properties are those which it shares with all the modes of Extension or with a connected system of such modes: its existence (or its actuality) is its dependence on the eternal nature of things, its being involved in the necessity of God's nature [1]. And our mind (as the idea of this body) is a corresponding eternal mode of Thought, which apprehends as its 'ideatum' the essence of the body *sub specie eternitatis* [2]. We construct our universe no longer round a 'self' such as imaginative experience constitutes. The centre of our world is not the personality which has grown out of chance impressions and conjunctions, moulded by arbitrary reminiscence out of the products of fortuitous influences. The self, which is the centre of scientific experience, is a self which is constituted by the permanent and necessary properties common to all modes of Extension and of Thought. Body and mind 'we' have become identified—in our intellectual activities—with the general interests of knowledge. Nothing is a constituent part of (or concerns) us, except so far as it exhibits the universal nature of some feature of the universe of science. Our being has become intelligible and necessary: but it has identified itself with the being of all intelligences. In attaining to permanent and genuine individuality, 'we' have become absorbed: 'our' body in the Attribute of Extension, 'our' mind in the Attribute of Thought, 'our' 'self' in the being of God. The 'essence' of our body and mind, as forming *this* single thing, cannot be constituted by the 'common properties' which are the Reality

[1] Cf. E. ii. 45 S.; v. 29 S.; v. 31 dem.
[2] Cf. E. v. 40 S., and see below.

for science. It would seem, therefore, that scientific knowledge inevitably destroys its basis: for in the Reality of science there is no room for an individual body or mind. As we attain to scientific knowledge, 'we' (it would seem) must disappear: science can neither recognize nor justify the distinct being of the man of science. The ' essentia' of the body and of the mind of *this* man does not fall within the ken of scientific knowledge. It knows body and mind so far as they exhibit the features common to all modes of Extension and Thought, and not so far as they have a characteristic individuality. 'Scientia intuitiva'—and it alone—can hope to complete the work of science, and to give us a concrete knowledge of the Reality in its living fullness, by restoring the individuality from which 'ratio' of necessity abstracts.

This conclusion, indeed, requires some modification. The statement[1] that the 'fundamenta rationis nullius rei singularis essentiam explicant' must be taken in its context. It means that for science differences of time do not exist, and that therefore 'single things,' so far as their essential nature involves such differences, cannot be explained or justified by science. But the 'conatus' (which is the expression of the 'essentia' of things) does not involve any determinate time[2]. It would seem, therefore, that for science there may be (and is) the 'individuality' of the ἄτομον εἶδος. Thus, 'Humanity' (although not 'Peter' and 'Paul') would be recognized and justified by the scientific understanding as an individuality with an essential nature distinct from (e. g.) the essential nature or individuality of 'Plant.' *This* is the essential nature which is the actuality of things in the Attributes of God[3]: and *this* is the 'individuality' of the scientific

[1] E. ii. 44 C. 2 dem.
[2] Cf. e.g. E. iii. 8.
[3] Cf. E. ii. 8 C.; above, pp. 76 ff.

For modifications, see below, Appendix to Bk. II, and Bk. III. ch. 4.

Book II. thinker and rational agent. Science, therefore, in its least abstract form, would apprehend the essential nature of man's body and mind—i. e. body and mind so far as they exhibit the properties common to all *human* bodies and minds: though this essential nature of the *human* body and mind would tend for science to merge itself in the conception of the properties common to *all* bodies and minds—i. e. science would tend to conceive Humanity merely as exhibiting the properties common to all modes of Extension and Thought [1].

### 3. *Tertium cognitionis genus, Scientia Intuitiva.*

No full account of 'scientia intuitiva' can be given yet.

We have described imaginative and scientific experience as stages in the advance of man as an intelligence—a purely cognitive being. In reality, man is also an emotional and an active being, and no feature of his nature can be safely abstracted from the rest. The stages in his development are not purely and simply stages of increasing intelligence, though they may be regarded from that point of view. The progress is far more complex. We must hope to correct and supplement our account in the sequel.

But the abstraction, which has enabled us to treat 'imagination' and 'science' independently of the practical attitudes which they respectively involve, is no longer possible in the case of 'scientia intuitiva.'

Philosophy was to Spinoza the outcome of a long and painful struggle for satisfaction of his nature. The

---

[1] 'The Life of Reason,' or the 'Life of the Free Man' (which is the practical side of the stage of experience here considered) will occupy us presently. It certainly implies a strong personality in the man who lives it: but, how far such a personality could be reconciled with the characteristics of scientific experience as Spinoza describes them, is another matter. Cf. below, Bk. III. ch. 3, § 1, for further developments.

problem of philosophy was to him the problem of life [1]. And he found the solution of that problem in an ideal which was at once an ideal of knowledge and of conduct. The good for man, he believed, is that complete realization of the nature of things which *is* the conscious oneness with God [2]. Permanent satisfaction for human nature involves that perfect knowledge which is at the same time perfect fullness of being. To know the Reality and to be one with the Reality known—these are the two sides of the one supreme ideal. In the earlier stages of man's progress, these two moments of the ideal, since they are realized in imperfect forms, fall more or less widely apart: but in the consummation of man's nature they come completely together. The full description of 'scientia intuitiva' will not be possible for us—any more than it was possible for Spinoza—until we have followed him in his conception of the emotional and practical nature of man. The ideal development of human nature, in which we have 'scientia intuitiva,' is at the same time that grade of human being in which we are absorbed in the 'amor intellectualis Dei.' The 'perfect peace of mind' which arises from this third kind of knowledge [3] implies the complete satisfaction of our emotional nature. Spinoza's conception of 'scientia intuitiva' is unintelligible apart from his conception of the 'Freedom,' 'Happiness,' or 'Salvation [4]' of man, i.e. man's attainment of the practical ideal. Philosophy in fact, in its highest form, is to Spinoza at the same time and essentially the noblest form of human life: the life of religion.

At present, therefore, we must content ourselves with a meagre outline of the formal nature of 'scientia intuitiva.' Correction and supplementation will come later.

In E. ii. 40 S. 2 Spinoza says 'Besides these two kinds of knowledge, there is given a third—as I shall show in

[1] Cf. above, pp. 1 ff.
[2] Cf. above, p. 4.
[3] E. v. 27.
[4] E. v. 36 S.

Book II. the sequel—which I shall call "scientia intuitiva." And this kind of knowing proceeds from the adequate idea of the formal essence of some of God's Attributes to the adequate knowledge of the essence of things [1].' And in E. v. 36 S. he says 'I thought it worth while to note this here, in order that I might show by this example how great is the power of the knowledge of single things, which I have called "intuitive knowledge," and how much more valuable it is than the universal knowledge, which I attributed to the second grade.' Lastly, in E. ii. 47 S. he says 'Hence we see that God's infinite essence and his eternity are known to all men. But since all things are in God and are conceived through God, it follows that from this knowledge we can deduce very many things so as adequately to know them, and thus form that third kind of knowledge....'

From these passages we can lay down a few general propositions with regard to the third grade of experience. (1) Like the second grade, it involves deduction: but whereas the second grade is content with inferential or deductive knowledge as its end, this uses deduction solely as a means to its final intuition.

(2) Like the second grade, intuitive knowledge rests upon the adequate idea of God or of some of his Attributes. But the second grade is content to develop this initial conception in a system of universal or hypothetical laws. The third grade seeks to attain to an adequate vision of the concrete natures of the single things: i.e. 'essences,' things as modes of 'natura naturata'[2]. No universal knowledge of the fundamental properties of things satisfies it: it demands nothing less than the complete realization ('intuition') of the intimate essential being of all things. It thus aims at restoring

---

[1] E. l. c. 'Atque hoc cognoscendi genus procedit ab adaequata idea essentiae formalis quorundam Dei attributorum ad adaequatam cognitionem essentiae rerum.'

[2] Cf. TdIe, VVlL. i. pp. 32, 33.

the living individuality of imaginative experience at a higher level: a level where contingency is banished, and the certainty and necessity of scientific demonstration unite with the immediacy and concreteness of perception[1].

(3) The third grade presupposes the second, and (in a sense) rests upon it: yet (in a sense) the second grade starts from conceptions which are apprehended by 'scientia intuitiva.'

The latter point seems clear. The adequate ideas, the 'communes notiones,' with which our scientific demonstrations start, are apprehended immediately, by an act of intuition. They form the basis of 'scientia intuitiva' as well as of 'ratio,' and I do not see how we can attribute their apprehension to anything but a knowledge of the third grade.

But the former point is no less clear, and is emphasized by Spinoza[2]. It is the completion of inferential knowledge, which Spinoza calls 'intuitive science': not an intuition prior to, or independent of, reasoning. Hence, if the 'communes notiones' *are* apprehended intuitively, their apprehension, it would seem, is not in the full sense '*scientia* intuitiva.'

Yet the examples which Spinoza gives of 'intuitive science' are not so clear[3].

We may find a fourth number—where three are given—which shall be related to the third as the second is to the first, by deduction from a universal rule; e.g. from the common property of all proportionals which is demonstrated by Euclid (Book VII, prop. 19). But in the case of the simplest numbers—e.g. 1, 2, 3—'every one sees at a single glance (*uno intuitu*) the proportion of the first to the second number,' and so requires no deduction to find the fourth number, viz. 6.

[1] Cf. K. V. S. ii. 2, § 2.
[2] E. v. 28 and dem.; and ii. 47 S., quoted above.
[3] Cf. E. ii. 40 S. 2, and the corresponding passages, K. V. S. ii. ch. 1, and TdIe, VVlL. i. p. 9.

184    THE ETHICS OF SPINOZA

Book II. But here too there is an inference, and the intuition rests on it. For it is the fourth proportional, viz. 6, which 'scientia intuitiva' is supposed to give us; and this is 'inferred' from the relation of 1 to 2 which 'we see at a single glance.' The point of the illustration is brought out more clearly in the *Tractatus de Intellectus Emendatione* (l. c.) than in the Ethics. Spinoza wishes to distinguish a case where we 'perceive a thing by its own essential nature' from a case where we infer a thing from something other than it. There is an inference in 'scientia intuitiva': but the inference is immanent and absorbed in the final intuition. In 'ratio,' the inference remains external to the conclusion, and the knowledge of the conclusion therefore remains discursive. Hence, in the illustration given in the *Tractatus*, stress should be laid on the words ' nullam operationem facientes.' The mathematicians do not require to move outside the terms, but their inference or discursive movement remains within the whole given to them. The same applies to the other instances in the *Tractatus*, and (still more clearly) to the instance in E. v. 36 S.

Spinoza remarks[1], 'Ea tamen, quae hucusque tali cognitione potui intelligere, perpauca fuerunt': and the truth is that such knowledge is *strictly* only possible for a mind which apprehends the whole Reality. For there are absolutely no closed systems in Reality, and the popular instances of 'scientia intuitiva' which Spinoza gives (e. g. the instance of the numbers) are misleading. Fully to 'see' the interrelations of the numbers by an immanent inference which is absorbed in the intuition, would be possible only for a mind which apprehended 'uno intuitu' the whole numerical system (and ultimately the whole Reality or God) in all its articulation. The 'immanence' of the inference, the 'completeness' of the intuition within the conception of the numbers

[1] TdIe, l. c.

themselves—this, *strictly speaking*, is apparent only. Similarly, the intuitive knowledge of the human mind in its essence and in its individual dependence on God (which Spinoza claims in E. v. 36 S.), if it is to answer to the ideal of intuitive science, presupposes a complete apprehension of the total nature of the universe, and a complete scientific demonstration of the coherence and inner articulation of all its properties.

# CHAPTER III

### THE EMOTIONAL NATURE OF MAN

BOOK II.
The translation of the term 'affectus.'

IT is not always possible to find satisfactory English equivalents for Spinoza's terms. The difficulty makes itself felt especially with regard to his psychology: for the broad division into Will, Feeling, and Cognition is subsequent to Spinoza [1]. Thus, we have seen already that the terms 'voluntas,' 'volitio' in Spinoza do not correspond to our will, volition [2]. And the term 'affectus' defies translation. 'Feeling' will not do; for under 'affectus' Spinoza includes 'cupiditas,' which comprehends 'desire' as at any rate one of its main meanings. Nor can we render 'affectus' as 'passion'; for Spinoza recognizes some 'affectus' as 'actions [3].' Nor, lastly, will the term 'affection' help us: for—setting aside the ambiguity of the word—we need it to translate Spinoza's 'affectio.' I have selected 'emotion' as on the whole the least misleading term, if it is understood as roughly equivalent to the German 'Stimmung'—the change of consciousness to a different pitch or intensity, or the being of consciousness at a determinate pitch. No doubt it sounds strange to talk of 'active' and 'passive' emotions, or of 'emotions of desire' ('cupiditatis affectus'): still, if we take the word in its widest meaning, we shall

---

[1] It seems to date from Tetens and Mendelssohn: see Stout, *Analytic Psychology*, i. p. 38.

[2] Above, p. 132.

[3] Cf. E. iii. def. 3 Expl., and below.

not go very far wrong. Spinoza himself uses the kindred word 'commotio' as equivalent to 'affectus[1].'

§ 1. In approaching the subject of human conduct it is necessary once more to consider what shall be our method of treatment[2]. Already we have been forced into conflict with certain popular prejudices. Standards of value resting on an arbitrary teleology, anthropomorphic conceptions of God and of Nature—these we have rejected as fatal to an adequate theory of the nature of things. Against all such prejudices Spinoza has set his face. Reality in its general nature is absolutely self-determining and self-determined. Human standards of value, human conceptions of action and motives of action, are not ideas which are valid of Reality. The nature of things is through and through *intelligible*—there is neither caprice nor blind fate in the universe. But it is through and through *necessary*—God is not influenced by human notions of good and bad, right and wrong: he does not act 'sub ratione boni'; his action is the inevitable expression of his own eternal nature. That eternal nature is a living activity, which in its freedom or self-dependence reveals an immanent order or system of laws; an order which is 'geometrical' or 'logical'—not 'teleological'—in its coherence[3].

But human emotions and conduct have claimed exceptional treatment. In them morality has its life: to them moral judgements apply: they are the sphere of moral valuation. Hence writers have treated the emotional nature and the conduct of man as a subject for

---

[1] Cf. e.g. E. v. 2 'animi commotionem seu affectum ...' iii. Aff. deff., 27 Expl. 'tristitiae ... laetitiae commotiones.'

[2] Cf. above, pp. 12, 13; E. iii. Praef.; iv. 57 S.; Tr. P. ch. 1, § 1 and § 4; Ep. 30, &c.

[3] Cf. above, pp. 58 ff., and below, Appendix to Bk. II.

praise and blame, for pity or satire, for exhortation and command: but not as the subject-matter of a science, not as facts to be explained. They have given us no objective theory of the passions, no scientific treatment of this side of human nature. They have written as though man formed a unique and isolated kingdom within the kingdom of the universe: as though his conduct were ruled by laws of its own, and were independent of the general laws of things.

Their praise and blame, their moral judgements, have been based on ideals of conduct which they have neither examined nor justified. The 'goodness' or 'badness' of a passion from their point of view tells us nothing of the nature of the passion itself. Yet the 'passion' is an event in nature. As a modification of a mode of Substance, it is in some sense a part of the Reality and must have its necessary coherence in the order of things. Its being—what it in reality is—can be understood only in so far as we can trace its necessary dependence as a consequent of the eternal causality of God. If we subsequently set up a standard of moral estimation, and consider the value of the passion as an element in our ideal human life—that is legitimate enough, provided we remember what we are doing. But we can expect no profit from such a valuation, until we understand *what* we are going to value.

Accordingly, Spinoza proposes to treat the emotions (passions, desires, motives of action, &c.) as a subject-matter of scientific investigation: to explain them by the same method which has served in his hands to explain the general nature of Reality and the human mind. The sphere of human conduct is a part of the general nature of things: it is governed by the same laws, intelligible under the same categories. The facts of man's emotional nature and the facts of human conduct must be investigated in the light of the general laws which have already been demonstrated. We must trace the emotions and actions of man as inevitable consequents of the nature of man conceived as itself the inevitable consequent of the nature of God.

Against any 'moralistic' treatment of the emotions Spinoza's criticisms are obviously valid. It is no part of a scientific or philosophic treatment to thrust an uncritical standard of value upon the facts of conduct, and, in place of a theory of human life and nature, to write a satire or preach a sermon. But it seems as if Spinoza wishes to exclude not merely this or that ideal, but all ideals whatever, as subjective and arbitrary. To understand the emotions, he urges, we must consider them as they really are: and 'really' they are effects which follow from the nature of God with a necessity which is 'geometrical' and in no sense 'teleological.' Emotions and the facts of conduct must (like everything else) be conceived under the category of ground and consequent: all conceptions of purpose or final causes are alike arbitrary, subjective, fictitious. If we frame ideals and apply them to regulate our lives, that is for our own convenience only. The ideals are in no sense constitutive of the material to which they are applied. It must be investigated without their help.

If this were Spinoza's meaning, there could hardly be two opinions as to its erroneousness. The value of an emotion is not something which is merely added to it from the outside. Its value is an essential constituent of its being. A 'geometrical' explanation of the emotions would explain (not them, but) a mutilated and abstract portion of them. Their 'esse' is their place in human life, their contribution to human development, their 'value' as constituents of the moral ideal. To conceive *things* under the category of geometrical necessity alone, is to conceive them abstractly, partially and therefore

Book II. untruly: to conceive *man in his conduct* in this way is to make the abstraction glaring.

But here, as elsewhere, Spinoza in part himself breaks through the abstract rigidity of his logical forms and methods, and in part has been misunderstood.

He does not wish to protest against all ideals or standards of value, but against all specifically *human* standards and ideals; i. e. against a method of explanation which would separate man from the rest of the universe. The ideal, which he himself applies in his moral theory, is rooted in his conception of the general nature of things. It is justified for his theory as the legitimate consequence of his metaphysics. His treatment of conduct rests upon his conception of the ideal human nature: an ideal, which is the logical outcome of his view of the place of man in the nature of things. The 'goodness' of an emotion or a line of action is its contribution to the ideal for man: but that means for Spinoza its reality or perfection, the degree of being which it expresses. He has, indeed, protested against the extension of human conceptions of convenience or goodness to the explanation of Reality. The universe is not made for man, nor is it intelligible in the light of human purposes. But the sphere of human life and conduct shares in the reality or perfection of the universe. Hence Spinoza does not hesitate (is, indeed, logically bound) to apply his conception of degrees of reality to it as to all other spheres. And since for him the reality of man is the reality of his mind and body—i. e. his power to think, and know, and do—he is able to give a concrete significance to his ideal standard for human conduct, without introducing into his moral theory a set of conceptions foreign to his metaphysics [1].

---

[1] See below, Bk. III. ch. 1, § 1.

## § 2. THE CONATUS.

God *is* in virtue of the necessity of his own nature : and the 'omnipotence' wherewith God acts or works is only another name for his essence in its actuality [1].

Now, 'single things' are modes of God which express his Attributes in a certain and determinate manner [2]. As states of God, they are absolutely dependent on him. They are what they are, as effects of God's omnipotent causality. Their essence is a modification of God's essence, their existence or actuality a modification of his actuality, their power of action a portion of God's omnipotence. God, that is, is the efficient cause of the essence, the existence, and the persistence in being (duration) of all things. No particular thing exists in virtue of the necessity of its own essence : its essence and its actuality are derivative. It exists or is actual with a necessity which is not its own [3].

But, if now we look at the matter from a somewhat different point of view, we shall reach further results. The essential nature of any thing short of the complete Reality is *in the end* derivative and not self-sustaining. But, apart from this ultimate reduction, things have a relative independence, a *modal* distinctness of being which expresses itself in their existence and actions in time and space. From this point of view, the 'essential nature' of a thing is that, the being and conception of which reciprocally imply the being and conception of the thing [4]. Though, that is, the essence of no particular thing involves its existence absolutely, yet, *given the essence*, you must

---

[1] Above, pp. 55 ff.
[2] E. i. 25 C.
[3] Cf. above, p. 56; E. i. 24 C.; i. 25; i. 26; ii. Ax. 1.
[4] E. ii. def. 2. 'Ad essentiam alicuius rei id pertinere dico, quo dato res necessario ponitur, et quo sublato res necessario tollitur; vel id, sine quo res, et vice versa quod sine re, nec esse nec concipi potest.' Cf. above, pp. 123 ff.

Book II. have the thing, *unless* the 'position' of the thing, which its essence involves, is counteracted by some external cause. So far as the essence of the thing is concerned—within the four corners of its essence, so to say—there is nothing which can destroy the thing: there is pure affirmation of the thing's being[1]. For otherwise the thing's essence would be inwardly self-contradictory, and the thing could never be at all. We may express this by saying that 'everything, so far as lies in itself, tends to persist in its own being[2].' This 'tendency' or 'effort,' therefore—the 'conatus'—is simply another name for the 'given' or 'actual' essence of the thing[3]. It is *in the end* a portion of that complete affirmation of God's essence, which is his omnipotence.

Things in their relative independence manifest themselves in the temporal and spatial order: they come into being, endure for a time, and pass away. Their essences (we have seen) cannot involve their own negation; nor can the mere lapse of time destroy them. What 'destroys' them is the more powerful self-affirmation of other particular things. For they have to maintain themselves over against an infinity of things, each of which is struggling to assert itself in the same way. The modes of God—we may say—in their temporal appearance conflict with one another: or God—to the imaginative consciousness—passes through ever-varying states of himself. Hence the affirmation, which the essence of a particular thing involves, is only a *conatus*: a force, whereby it *strives* to persist in its being. Hence, too, it is in its nature temporal, though it does not involve a determinate period of time[4]. The actuality of things

---

[1] E. iii. 4.
[2] E. iii. 6. 'Unaquaeque res, quantum in se est, in suo esse perseverare conatur.'
[3] E. iii. 7, and dem.

[4] E. iii. 8. 'Conatus, quo unaquaeque res in suo esse perseverare conatur, nullum tempus finitum, sed indefinitum involvit.'

regarded in their relative independence is temporal actuality, and not eternity. Man is a particular thing, whose essence is constituted by modes of Extension and Thought. So far therefore as lies in him, man will tend to persist in his corporeal and mental being. And this 'conatus' is man's 'appetitus,' or 'will-to-be.' Thus man's 'appetitus' is simply his essence 'from which there necessarily follow all those actions which tend to his self-maintenance.' As man's essence is mental as well as corporeal, and as thought is by its very nature turned upon itself, this 'effort' in man is often an object of his consciousness:—i.e. man not only tends to maintain his corporeal and mental being, but is (or may be) also conscious of this tendency. In order to mark this characteristic of man's 'conatus,' Spinoza uses the term 'cupiditas' (desire) in preference to 'appetitus.' For the presence of self-consciousness, he thinks, makes no difference. 'Desire'—like any blind effort—is merely the tendency to self-affirmation which the essence of the desiring thing involves. Hence the term 'cupiditas' covers the whole range of human self-affirmation. It includes all so-called 'efforts, instincts, impulses, desires, and volitions[1].'

§ 3. WILL AND DESIRE.

Man's 'cupiditas' is his essential nature, so far as that is conceived as determined—by a given modification of itself—to do a definite thing [2]. 'Cupiditas' therefore—the tendency to self-affirmation and self-maintenance which is involved in human nature—takes the place in

[1] E. iii. 9 S.; iii. Aff. deff., 1 Expl. . . . 'Cupiditatis nomine intelligo hominis quoscumque conatus, impetus, appetitus et volitiones...' The term 'voluntas' (or 'volitio'), when used strictly, is the purely mental (intellectual) side of 'cupiditas': 'volitio' is the act of affirmation or negation which every idea as such involves; cf. above, p. 132; E. iii. 9 S.
[2] E. iii. Aff. deff., 1.

Book II. Spinoza's system of 'will' in the broadest sense of the term. So far as any action is referred to a man's 'cupiditas' as its cause, it is an act of his will, the inevitable consequent of his essence: if it is intelligible as the effect of man's 'cupiditas' *alone*—if it is the inevitable consequent of his essential nature *only*, so that man's essence is its *adequate* cause—it is a 'free act,' an act of 'free-will' on man's part [1].

In view of Spinoza's polemic against the freedom of the will, this latter statement requires explanation. In order to understand in what sense Spinoza can admit a 'free' action, it is necessary to recapitulate the views of Descartes; for it is mainly against Descartes' conception of free-will that Spinoza's polemic is directed.

Descartes. The 'freedom of the will' was one of the three Articles of Faith which Descartes accepted—one of the three 'facts' which philosophy must believe though it cannot understand [2]. Accordingly, Descartes does not attempt to deduce his conception of freedom. Its justification for him is that, without it, his system could not stand. For he bases his reconciliation of human error and sin with the omnipotence and goodness of God on this 'miracle' of the indeterminate will. He reasons thus [3]: I derive my existence and my being from God. God has created me and endowed me with certain faculties, and it is his power that sustains me in existence. But God is omnipotent, all-wise and all-good: he cannot deceive and cannot be the cause of error or sin in his creatures. Yet I do fall into error and sin; and the explanation must lie in my nature. Of the faculties, wherewith God has endowed me, my intellect is indeed finite (for a *created* intellect must be finite, and its limitation conflicts neither

---

[1] Cf. below, § 4.
[2] Cf. the saying (quoted by Joël, p. 1): 'Tria mirabilia fecit Dominus: res ex nihilo, liberum arbitrium, et hominem Deum.'
[3] Cf. Descartes, *Med. Quarta*; Spinoza, Ep. 21 (VVlL. ii. pp. 94, 95).

with the omnipotence nor with the goodness of the Creator): but it is not misleading. So far as it goes, my intellect contains nothing but true ideas; whatever I conceive clearly and distinctly, is true. But God endowed me further with a faculty of choice, or free-will: a faculty of assent and dissent, assertion and denial. And this of necessity is unlimited, formally infinite, indeterminate. For to limit it in its form would be to destroy its nature, since its whole nature consists solely in this—that, in virtue of it, I can either do or not do a certain thing, can affirm or deny, pursue or avoid a given thing: or rather that 'I feel myself compelled by no external force to affirm or deny, to pursue or avoid, what the understanding puts before me.' This indeterminate faculty of choice is, no doubt, infinitely more perfect in God than it is in me: for in him it is combined with infinite knowledge, infinite power, &c. But *in its form* it is identical in me and in God: as the abstract disjunction of 'Yes or No,' it cannot be increased or lessened (as e. g. my intellect is infinitely increased in God) without ceasing to be itself. Our freedom is grounded on this abstract or indeterminate power of choice, though it is not necessary that our actual choice should be indifferent (indeterminate) in order to be free. On the contrary, an indifferent choice is 'the lowest grade of liberty.' The less indifferently I exercise my choice, the freer I am. The more I identify myself in choosing with *reasonable* motives, the more liberty I exercise.

Since I possess a finite faculty of knowing (which in itself involves neither affirmation nor denial of the contents known), and an unlimited faculty of choosing (which, in itself 'indifferent,' has no natural bias to assert or deny any one content rather than any other), 'error' becomes possible for me. I may commit error, when I affirm or deny beyond the limits of my knowledge. For, in that case, I extend my power of choice to alternatives to which I am indifferent (i. e. I affirm or deny, where I have no clear knowledge to guide my will); and since there is nothing to direct my choice, it may light on the wrong alternative as easily as on the right one.

But error *in respect to God* is mere negation: for 'it cannot be attributed to a defect in his nature, that he has granted me the liberty of affirming or denying those things, of which he has not put a clear idea in my intellect.' *In respect to me*, error is privation: for it is a defect in me that I do not make a good use of my power of choice; that I rashly affirm or deny, where I have no clear idea. For I have the power of suspending my judgement altogether. I may prohibit my 'voluntas' from playing outside the limits of my 'intellectus.'

Spinoza's criticism.

Now Spinoza's account of 'voluntas' completely cuts the ground from under this Cartesian explanation of error, and at the same time shows the absurdity of an indeterminate 'faculty of choice' or judgement[1]. For, in the Scholium to E. ii. 49, Spinoza maintains (i) that our power of understanding is not confined to the intellect, if by 'intellect' we mean the complex of adequate ideas. But if by 'intellect' we mean our whole power of apprehension, then our faculty of assent or dissent is coextensive with it: (ii) that our faculty of assent or dissent is no more 'free' or 'unlimited' than our faculty of sensation or perception. We can perceive an infinite number of bodies, just as we can affirm or deny an infinite number of things—i. e. *one after another*. And in no other sense have we an 'infinite' or 'unlimited' faculty: (iii) that there are no 'faculties' at all. A 'faculty' is nothing real: it is simply an abstract universal conception. It is the single acts of perceiving

[1] Cf. above, p. 132; E. ii. 48 and S.; 49 and C. and S.; and cf. also Meyer's Praef. to Ph.D.

and judging which are real: (iv) that the single acts of thinking, or perceiving, essentially are (or involve) single acts of assertion or denial. For indeed 'to have an idea' is to assert or deny something. There is therefore no 'free power of suspending our judgement.' An act of suspending our judgement is itself an act of perception or thought, and consequently an act of judgement.

We can now see exactly what Spinoza has denied in his polemic against the 'freedom of the will.' There is— he maintains—no faculty of assent and dissent: no power in the mind which issues decrees out of the blank of its mysterious indeterminateness. There are single affirmations and negations, 'mental decrees'[1]: but these are involved in the ideas, which are determined by the infinite chain of ideal causes. Each so-called 'act of choice' is in reality a necessarily determined assertion or denial. There is no 'choice' in the matter. The affirmation or negation is an essential feature in the content affirmed or negated, and the content (idea) is determined as to its nature and occurrence by the necessary series of ideal causes and effects which constitute the modal system of Thought. The 'volitio,' or 'mentis decretum,' is thus—like any ideal or extended event—absolutely determined and necessary. And if we regard it from the point of view of the mind of a 'single thing,' such as man, it is none the less necessary. It is then the necessary consequent of the essence of the man's mind; it is the expression of the man's essence in its tendency to self-assertion, so far as that tendency is considered on its ideal side alone, and not also on its extended side. For that tendency to self-assertion, which is the actuality of man's essence, is expressed also in his extended nature. So far as any manifestation of it is regarded solely as expressed in his extended being, it reveals itself as a determination of his

[1] Cf. E. iii. 2 S. sub fin.

BOOK II. body; and it is the necessary consequent of the laws of motion-and-rest, or follows from the nature of his body as a mode of Extension[1]. And, lastly, so far as we regard any determination of man's total nature as what it is—viz. as a modification of his corporeal and his ideal essence at once—we then refer the 'conatus' to both body and mind, and speak of its manifestation as an 'appetitus,' or—for the reason already given[2]—as a 'cupiditas'[3].

And it is to be observed that—on Spinoza's principles—it is absurd to regard either factor in 'cupiditas' as the cause of the other. The 'volitio' does not cause the bodily 'determination,' nor does the latter cause the former. They are one and the same modification, one and the same mode, expressed under two Attributes. Hence we have (E. iii. 2) 'nec Corpus Mentem ad cogitandum, nec Mens Corpus ad motum, neque ad quietem, nec ad aliquid (si quid est) aliud determinare potest.' Thus the last vestiges of the popular conception of free-will disappear. The mind does not possess a spontaneous power of decision. And the 'decisions' of the mind do not move the body. Nor does the body

---

[1] E. iii. 2 S. sub fin. 'Quae omnia profecto clare ostendunt, Mentis tam decretum, quam appetitum et Corporis determinationem, simul esse natura, vel potius unam eandemque rem, quam, quando sub Cogitationis attributo consideratur et per ipsum explicatur, Decretum appellamus, et quando sub Extensionis attributo consideratur, et ex legibus motus et quietis deducitur, Determinationem vocamus...'

[2] Above, p. 193.

[3] The scheme is—

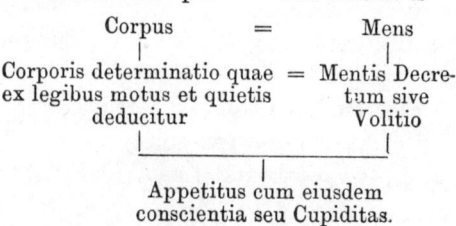

'act upon' the mind and cause it to think. The truth and the reality is simply a necessarily determined succession of modes of man's tendency to self-affirmation. So far as man is aware of these, so far as he feels them as desires, but is not aware of their causes, he traces his actions to his desires and his desires to his own essential nature. He cannot see the dependence of his 'essentia' (and therefore of his 'conatus') on the universe of bodies and minds, its coherence with the Nature of Things: and he therefore supposes that his will-to-be, his desires and actions, originate spontaneously in himself. The notion of our freedom, when traced from its crudest to its ultimate form, is thus the result of that partial or inadequate knowledge which characterizes imaginative experience[1].

## § 4. ACTION AND PASSION.

Within the absolute dependence of all modes, within the necessary determination of all events, there is yet for Spinoza a distinction between action and passion, freedom and slavery. Man is a mode—i.e. through and through dependent on Substance of which he is a state. Everything that occurs in man's mind or body is therefore dependent for its being and occurrence on the nature of God. It is the necessary consequent of God so far as he constitutes man. 'All our "conatus" or desires follow from the necessity of our nature:' but they follow in such a way that 'either they can be understood through that nature alone as their proximate cause, or through us only in so far as we are a part of Nature—a part which cannot be adequately conceived by itself without other individuals[2].'

---

[1] Cf. E. i. App.; above, pp. 169, 170.

[2] E. iv. App. cap. 1. Put in the more accurate Spinozistic terminology (cf. above, pp. 127 ff.), the distinction would be between (1) 'cupiditates,' of which God is the cause so far as he is

A cause is said to be 'adequate' to an effect which can be clearly and distinctly conceived through it alone: 'inadequate' or 'partial' in relation to an effect which cannot be understood through it only[1]. So far, therefore, as any occurrence in our mind or body can be understood clearly and distinctly as the effect of our own essential nature alone, we are its 'adequate' cause. We are then said to 'act'—the occurrence is the necessary consequent of our agency, we (and we alone[2]) are its authors: we are 'free' in respect to it. So far, on the other hand, as any occurrence requires for its clear understanding the conception of more than our own essential nature, 'we' are its 'partial' or 'inadequate' cause: and inasmuch as agencies other than ours contribute to it, we are partly negated in it, or are partly 'passive' in respect to it[3]. God is its author so far as he constitutes other beings besides ourselves.

Man, therefore, is an 'agent' or 'free' in respect to those occurrences which can be clearly conceived as the effect of his own nature (as their proximate cause) alone. He is 'passive,' externally determined, or a 'slave,' in respect to those occurrences which require for their clear apprehension the conception of other causes besides his own nature. Amongst the ideas, which together constitute the complex idea which is the mind, some—we know—are 'adequate.' So far as any desires can be referred to such adequate ideas in us as their adequate causes, they are the necessary consequents of our own nature only; i. e. we are 'agents' or 'free' in respect to them[4].

---

conceived as constituting our mind (and body) alone, and (2) 'cupiditates,' of which God is the cause so far as he is conceived as constituting other minds (and bodies) besides our own.

[1] E. iii. def. 1.

[2] i. e. God, *so far as he constitutes us*, is its author.

[3] E. iii. def. 2; iii. 3 S.; iv. 2.

[4] Tr. P. ch. 2, §§ 7 ff.; E. iv. App. cap. 2. For developments, see below, Bk. III. ch. 1.

## § 5. AFFECTUS AND IDEA. THE THREE PRIMARY PASSIVE EMOTIONS.

By 'emotion' Spinoza understands primarily 'those modifications of the body, whereby the efficiency of the body itself is increased or lessened, helped or hindered, together with the ideas of those modifications [1].' An 'emotion' is an 'action,' if we are the adequate cause of such modifications: otherwise, it is a 'passion [2].'

Every 'idea' in our mind is at the same time a modification of our body, and vice versa. The word 'idea' denotes only the psychical modification, the word 'affectio' only (or primarily) the corporeal event. 'Affectus' strictly denotes both—the whole two-sided occurrence [3].

As, however, for psychology and ethics the event is important chiefly on its psychical side, 'affectus' is used by Spinoza mainly to denote the psychical modification. His chief concern is with the nature of the mind, and he treats the concomitant bodily modifications for the most part as secondary [4].

Taking 'affectus,' therefore, to denote the psychical modification only, it (like other modes of Thought) will be an 'idea' with an 'ideatum.' How, then, does Spinoza distinguish the emotions from the modes of Thought which enter into knowledge and have hitherto been treated by us as the only 'ideae [5]'?

---

[1] E. iii. def. 3.
[2] Ib. Expl.
[3] Cf. above, p. 186.
[4] Thus, e.g., in the Aff. gen. def. (at the end of E. iii) Spinoza defines solely the psychical side of the double event—and moreover the psychical side of the *passive emotions* only.
'... affectus, quatenus ad solam Mentem referuntur, hic definire poterimus.' ... 'Affectus, qui animi Pathema dicitur. ...'
[5] Cf. E. ii. Ax. 3. 'Modi cogitandi, ut amor, cupiditas, vel quicunque nomine affectus animi insigniuntur, non dantur, nisi in eodem Individuo detur idea rei amatae, desideratae, &c. At idea dari potest, quamvis nullus alius detur cogitandi modus.'

Book II.    All 'ideas of bodies'—all modes of Thought which are the apprehension of external things, and give us knowledge of the world—are modifications of our mind, which correspond to bodily modifications derived from the interaction of external bodies with our own body. They reflect both our own body and the external bodies acting upon it. It is to this that their inadequacy (so far as they are to reveal to us the nature of the external bodies) is due : for they 'indicate the actual constitution of our own body rather than that of the external bodies [1].' Such adequate ideas of bodies as we form, are adequate, because in revealing the constitution of our own bodies they *eo ipso* reveal that of the external bodies ; i. e. *what* they reveal is a property common to our own and to the external bodies [2].

Ideas, as entering into knowledge, claim to reveal to us the nature of their objects—claim to be 'true'; and are valued according as they are adequate or inadequate, true or false (less true).

But an emotional idea is simply the reflection of the tone of life in our body or in some part of it. It is the degree of mental being which that tone of life involves, and it claims only to be the consciousness of the lowering, raising, or actual pitch of the vital energy of our body. Its truth or adequacy does not come into consideration at all. The question with regard to it is 'How real or perfect a state of vitality does it indicate ? Is it a feeling of heightened, or of lessened vital energy—a feeling of pleasure or of pain?' Or 'How great a degree of being is summed up in it considered as the feeling from which activities result ? What amount of reality is pressing to assert itself in this desire [3]?' And, lastly, 'Does the emotion result from our own spontaneous self-asser-

---

[1] Cf. E. iii. Aff. gen. def., Expl. and E. ii. 16 C. 2, 24-29.

[2] Cf. above, pp. 172 ff.

[3] Cf. E. iii. Aff. gen. def., Expl.

tion; are we, our essential nature, its adequate cause? Or is it due to the combined activity of other agencies besides our own, so that we are "passive"—only a factor in the totality of conditions which is its adequate cause[1]?'

But, if the 'affectus animi' must thus be distinguished from the 'ideae' which enter into knowledge, the connexion between them is none the less important. The 'ideae' are the primary constituents of the human mind, and all the other modes of Thought—'ideae' in the sense of emotions—are dependent for their nature and occurrence upon them[2]. Our immediate consciousness of the level of vitality in our body and mind (our emotions of pleasure, pain, and desire) is dependent upon a reflective idea of our bodily modification and its cause: and the nature of our emotion—the particular kind of pleasure, pain, or desire which we experience—is determined (in part at least) by the contents of this reflective idea[3]. And it is because the 'ideae' which constitute the mind are some 'adequate' and some 'inadequate,' that the emotions, which depend upon them, fall into two classes—'*actiones*' and '*passiones*[4].'

For the present we will consider Spinoza's conception of the 'passive emotions.' The life of passive emotion is the necessary pendant to the first stage of knowledge[5]; the passive emotions themselves are the 'ideae imaginationis' in so far as these reflect the constitution of our own body[6].

Spinoza recognizes three passive emotions, of which all the others are derivatives: three primary passions, which cannot themselves be further reduced or analysed[7]. So far as man is a mode actually-existent in the 'com-

---

[1] Cf. E. iv. App. cap. 1.
[2] E. ii. 11 dem., and ii. Ax. 3.
[3] See below.
[4] E. iii. 1, 3, and 9; iv. App. capp. 1, 2.
[5] Cf. above, pp. 180 ff., and see below, Bk. III. ch. 1, § 2.
[6] Cf. E. iv. 9 dem.
[7] E. iii. 11 S.; iii. 56; and iii. Aff. deff. sub fin. (VVlL. i. p. 185).

Book II. munis ordo naturae,' his body and his mind are subject to innumerable influences of which they are only the partial or inadequate cause; i. e. he is constantly undergoing modifications in body and in mind, in respect to which he is passive. Such 'ideae'—such mental modifications—are 'confused'; for they are not the effect of man's mind alone [1]. And they are 'passions' just so far as they are confused. They are 'emotional' (and not 'reflective') ideas, inasmuch as they are the immediate consciousness of his own bodily state and do not claim to reflect theoretically the nature of his environment [2]. Now 'his own bodily state' at any moment is the consequent of the infinity of influences acting upon his body, and not solely of the 'conatus' of his own essential nature. In these emotions, therefore, man becomes aware of his own vital energy, his own reality or power-to-be, not as it is in its purity, but as it is under the conditions of the medium of his actual existence—conditions which may hinder, as well as help, his self-realization. So far as he feels an increase of his being—a transition to a higher pitch of his reality—he is said to have the emotion of *laetitia*: pleasure, feeling of heightened power. So far as he feels a depression or diminution of his being—a transition to a lower pitch of his reality—his emotion is *tristitia*: pain, feeling of lessened vitality [3]. And so far as his feeling is simply the consciousness of his actual pitch of being, as the determinate source of this or that definite thought or

---

[1] Descartes (*Princ.* iv. § 190) calls 'Love, Hate, Fear, Anger,' &c., 'confused ideas' or 'animi pathemata' 'in so far as the mind gets them not from itself alone, but because the body, with which it is intimately conjoined, is in some way acted upon.' Spinoza (the reader will observe) has modified this conception of the passions as 'confused ideas,' to meet his own theory of the union of body and mind.

[2] E. iii. Aff. gen. def., Expl.

[3] E. iii. 11 S. and Aff. deff., 2, 3 and Expl.

activity, he is said to 'desire'—to be under the emotion of *cupiditas*[1].

Spinoza is careful to warn us that the emotions of pleasure and pain, though they are 'confused ideas, which affirm a greater or a less vital force of our body (or of some part of our body) than it had before,' do not imply an act of reflective comparison. We do not compare our present with our past bodily state in the emotion of pleasure. It is not a reflective, but an immediate awareness of an altered pitch of our being. The mode of consciousness which is the emotion of pleasure or pain 'affirms something of the body which involves greater or less reality than it had before'; and the mind, in this mode of its consciousness, itself passes to a greater or less degree of its being. But the knowledge of the 'greater' or 'less' shows itself in the form of the emotion, the direct feeling: not in the form of a reflective comparison. We are conscious of increasing or diminishing vitality *simply as feelings of pleasure and pain*. We are not—unless we also theorize and reflect—aware of the reason[2].

Desire ('cupiditas'), though itself a primitive form of emotion, is yet determined as regards its content by preceding pleasure or pain. Man's awareness of his actual pitch of vitality as the determinate ground of action, is always the consequence of a transition which reveals itself to his emotional consciousness as some kind of pleasure or pain. Desire is not a kind of pleasure or pain—it cannot be reduced to them: but it involves pleasure or pain as its condition, it is coloured and modified according to the pleasures or pains which have conditioned it, and its intensity varies with the intensity of the pleasures or pains, loves or hates, which have given it birth[3].

[1] E. iii. 9 S.; Aff. deff., 1 and Expl.; Aff. gen. def., Expl.
[2] E. iii. Aff. gen. def., Expl.
[3] Cf. E. iii. 37.

Book II. But this does *not* mean that man reflects on past pleasures and pains, and forms his desires with a view to secure similar pleasures or avoid similar pains in the future. 'We do not desire anything because we think it good: on the contrary, we think a thing good because we desire it [1].' It means simply that the present state of man's 'self-realization' (his present feeling of himself as a source of activity) is dependent upon his past states. Man's 'conatus' is always fluctuating with the varying influences of his environment. Each fluctuation is on its psychical side an emotion of pleasure or pain—a feeling of heightened or lessened energy—an awareness of the transition of his body and mind to greater or less degrees of being. And the momentary, determinate, static pitch of his vitality—which, as the proximate cause of what he does, is his 'appetitus' or 'cupiditas'— is the resultant of the preceding transitions.

The 'conatus' is the basis of all the emotions. The felt transition to a greater or less degree of reality in body and mind (pleasure or pain) presupposes as its foundation the effort at assertion or maintenance of our bodily and mental being. But it is this same effort (at a determinate state or pitch of itself) which—as the proximate cause of what we do—is our 'cupiditas.'

As all the emotions are ultimately derived from these three, and as these are ultimately forms of man's 'conatus,' it follows that every emotion in every individual—and in every sentient creature—has a peculiar characteristic tone of its own. The animals feel pleasure and pain, and are moved by appetite: but their pleasure, pain,

---

[1] E. iii. 9 S. 'Constat itaque ex his omnibus, nihil nos conari, velle, appetere, neque cupere, quia id bonum esse iudicamus; sed contra, nos propterea aliquid bonum esse iudicare, quia id conamur, volumus, appetimus, atque cupimus.' Spinoza is attacking Descartes: cf. Descartes, *Passiones Animae*, ii. 57, and K. V. S. ii. 3, § 9.

# PRIMARY EMOTIONS

and appetite are as different from those of man, as their essential nature is different from his. And the emotions of each man differ as the nature of each. Each has his own life, his own 'happiness,' with which he lives content: but it is 'happiness' to him, just because it is *his*, is the expression of *his* nature. His life and happiness *are* his 'idea'; i. e. his 'soul.'

And, further, the difference of the objects in which we feel pleasure and pain reflects itself in these emotions themselves, in the desires based on them, and in all the 'passions' which are derived from them. The ultimate ground of 'passion' in us is that we form inadequate ideas; i. e. that we have imaginative experience. Now that experience rests upon an interaction between our body and external bodies, and reflects the nature of the external bodies as well as the nature of our own. Hence the emotions, which that experience brings with it, will get their specific quality not only from the varying nature of the subject, but also from the varying nature of the object. The pleasure which A feels in his experience of anything differs from B's pleasure in the same thing, because A differs from B: and the pleasure of A in one thing differs from his pleasure in another, because they are different things [1]. This double difference—

---

[1] In support of the above, cf. e. g. E. iii. 37. 'Cupiditas, quae prae Tristitia vel Laetitia, praeque Odio vel Amore oritur, eo est maior, quo affectus maior est.'

iii. 51. 'Diversi homines ab uno eodemque obiecto diversimode affici possunt, et unus idemque, homo ab uno eodemque obiecto potest diversis temporibus diversimode affici.'

iii. 56 dem. '... Cupiditas est ipsa uniuscuiusque essentia, seu natura, quatenus ex data qua- cunque eius constitutione determinata concipitur ad aliquid agendum. ... Dantur itaque tot species Cupiditatis, quot sunt species Laetitiae, Tristitiae, Amoris, &c., et consequenter (per iam ostensa) quot sunt obiectorum species, a quibus afficimur.'

iii. 57 dem. 'Laetitia deinde et Tristitia passiones sunt, quibus uniuscuiusque potentia seu conatus in suo esse perseverandi augetur vel minuitur, iuvatur vel coercetur (*per Prop.* 11. *huius et*

BOOK II. based on the varying nature of the sentient subjects and on the varying nature of the objects—runs through the whole emotional life of each man. It causes that infinite complexity in man's emotional nature, which renders a complete description of the emotions impossible. But Spinoza is mainly concerned to understand the emotions, in order to get a basis for his moral theory [1]: and for this purpose 'it is sufficient to understand the common properties of the emotions and the mind,' without attempting to attain to a concrete knowledge of the nature of any individual mind and its emotions [2].

### § 6. DERIVATIVE AND COMPLEX PASSIVE EMOTIONS [3].

(A) Corollaries from Spinoza's conception of the *conatus*.

The mind tends to affirm its being in all its thoughts—whether adequate or inadequate—and is conscious of this its tendency [4]: i. e. the 'conatus' in man takes the form of 'cupiditas' and extends over his whole psychical being.

*eius Schol.*). At per conatum ... Appetitum et Cupiditatem intelligimus . . .; ergo Laetitia et Tristitia est ipsa Cupiditas sive Appetitus, quatenus a causis externis augetur vel minuitur ..., hoc est, ... est ipsa cuiusque natura; ...'

iii. 57 S. 'Hinc sequitur, affectus animalium, quae irrationalia dicuntur (bruta enim sentire nequaquam dubitare possumus, postquam Mentis novimus originem), ab affectibus hominum tantum differre, quantum eorum natura a natura humana differt. ... Quamvis itaque unumquodque individuum sua, qua constat, natura contentum vivat eaque gaudeat, vita tamen illa, qua unumquodque est contentum, et gaudium nihil aliud est, quam idea seu anima eiusdem individui, atque adeo gaudium unius a gaudio alterius tantum natura discrepat, quantum essentia unius ab essentia alterius differt.'

iv. 18, 58 S., 60. App. cap. 30, &c.

[1] Not, of course, that he allows his moral theory to prejudice his theory of the emotions. See above, pp. 187 ff.
[2] E. iii. 56 S.
[3] In this section I have made a free use of Pollock's translation. Pollock, pp. 216 ff.
[4] E. iii. 9.

# DERIVATIVE EMOTIONS

Hence (i) The mind endeavours to 'picture' everything CHAP. III. which increases or aids the body's efficiency[1]; for that which aids the body's efficiency, *on its ideal side* aids the mind's efficiency or power of thinking[2].

(ii) When the mind 'pictures' anything which lessens or hinders the body's efficiency, it endeavours to call up 'pictures' which seclude the existence of the hindrance. The mind, therefore, shrinks from 'picturing' anything which lessens or hinders its own and the body's efficiency[3]; or, more generally, (iii) we endeavour to promote the occurrence of everything which we 'imagine' to conduce to our pleasure, and to remove or destroy everything which we 'imagine' to conflict with our pleasure or to lead to pain[4].

These principles serve to explain the characteristics of *Amor: Odium.* Love and Hate, and the desires which they involve and which are based upon them. Thus, Love is simply 'pleasure accompanied by the idea of an external cause'; Hate 'pain accompanied by the idea of an external cause[5].' In Love, the heightening of the body's efficiency is the effect of an external body, and the heightening of the mind's efficiency (i. e. the emotion of pleasure) is the effect of our idea of that external body; i. e. we refer our pleasure to an external object as its source. In Hate, we refer our 'pain' to an external object as its source. Such being the essential nature of Love and Hate, it necessarily follows (from the principles just stated) that the lover desires in every way to preserve and foster the idea of the external object, and therefore the external object itself; whilst the man, who hates, desires to remove that idea and consequently the external object itself. Hence the desires (i) of doing good to the persons we love, (ii) of harming the persons we hate; (iii) of returning benefits *Ira: Gratia.*

---

[1] E. iii. 12.
[2] E. iii. 11.
[3] E. iii. 13 and C.
[4] E. iii. 28.
[5] E. iii. 13 S.; Aff. deff., 6, 7, and Expl.

BOOK II.  where the love is reciprocal; (iv) of returning injuries
*Vindicta.*  where the hate is reciprocal¹.

*Commise-*  Certain emotions can be traced as further consequences
*ratio.* of these principles. Thus, Pity is a pain felt at another's misfortune; i.e. the pain which we feel when we 'picture' the pain of somebody we love, or—on a principle to be stated presently²—when we 'picture' the suffering of
*Benevo-* any creature like ourselves³. Benevolence is the desire
*lentia.* of doing good to a person whom we pity⁴.

Corresponding to Pity—this sympathetic pain at another's pain—there is the sympathetic pleasure which we feel at another's pleasure. Both these sympathetic emotions are ultimately due to the increase or diminution of our own vitality, which the 'picturing' another's pleasure or pain originates⁵. For similar reasons, we
*Favor.* shall be Well-Disposed to any one, if we imagine him to cause pleasure to a person whom we love or whom
*Indignatio.* we regard as like ourselves; and we shall be Indignant with any one whom we imagine to cause pain under the same conditions⁶.

Connected with these emotions, and partly explicable on the same principles, are *invidia* and *misericordia*—
*Invidia.* Envy (or Malice) and Kindliness (or Goodwill). Envy is hatred so far as that disposes us to feel pleasure in

---

¹ Spinoza has no special name for the *first* 'cupiditas,' but he recognizes it as involved in Love; cf. E. iii. 13 S., 25 and 39. The second 'cupiditas' is called *ira* (E. iii. 40 S. 2; Aff. deff., 36). The third is *gratia* or *gratitudo* (E. iii. 41 S. 1; Aff. deff., 34), and the fourth is *vindicta* (E. iii. 40 S. 2; Aff. deff., 37).

These names cover the whole emotional state, i.e. both the feelings of love and hate (pleasure or pain) and the desires to do good or injuries to the persons loved and hated; cf. E. iii. 41 S. 1.

Cruelty or Barbarity (*Crudelitas seu Saevitia*) is the desire of doing harm to a person whom we love or pity (Aff. deff., 38).

² Below, p. 215.
³ E. iii. 21, 22 S.; Aff. deff., 18.
⁴ E. iii. 27 S. 2; Aff. deff., 35.
⁵ E. iii. 21 dem.
⁶ E. iii. 22 S.; Aff. deff., 19, 20.

## DERIVATIVE EMOTIONS

another's pain, pain in another's pleasure. Since, however, we cannot picture the pain of a being like ourselves without ourselves feeling pain, the pleasure of Envy is always tinged with pain [1]. A Kindly Disposition is the general state of mind, of which *commiseratio* is the single manifestation, and is thus the opposite emotion to Envy [2].

CHAP. III.

*Misericordia.*

Further, from the general tendency of our mind to affirm itself, and to remove all ideas which lessen or hinder its being, there follow the emotions of Self-love or Self-complacency, Humility and Repentance, Self-conceit and Self-depreciation, Over-esteem and Disparagement of others.

We are for the most part ignorant of the nature of things, and apt to take our uncertain and fluctuating opinions for the truth. Since, moreover, we tend to regard ourselves as free agents, it is not surprising that our own actions should cause us pain or pleasure; i.e. that we should 'feel emotions of pleasure and pain accompanied by the idea of ourselves as their cause [3].' Self-love or Self-complacency is 'pleasure bred of a man's contemplating himself and his own active power,' and Humility is 'pain bred of a man's contemplating his own impotence or infirmity [4].' Repentance is 'pain accompanied by the idea of some action which we suppose ourselves to have done by a free resolve of the mind,' and is the opposite emotion to that Self-complacency which is due to the consciousness of an action similarly supposed free. It depends upon custom (i.e. chiefly upon a man's education) *what* actions are subjects of complacency or repentance to him [5].

*Philautia (Acquiescentia in se ipso). Humilitas.*

*Poenitentia.*

---

[1] E. iii. 23 and S.; 24 and S.; Aff. deff., 23.
[2] E. iii. Aff. deff., 23 Expl.; 24 and Expl.; 18 Expl.
[3] E. iii. 51 S.
[4] E. iii. Aff. deff., 25 and 26 (Pollock's translation); iii. 51 S.; 53, 54, 55 and S.
[5] E. iii. Aff. deff., 26 Expl.; 27 and Expl.

Book II.
*Superbia.*

Self-conceit is a consequence of Self-complacency. It is an emotion of pleasure which is due to our 'picturing' our own power or efficiency as greater than it really is. It may be defined as 'Self-love, so far as that leads us to think too highly of ourselves.' Strictly speaking, there is no contrary to this emotion. For, if we picture our own efficiency as low, the act of so picturing it really lowers it, and so we cannot think 'too lowly' of ourselves. Yet we may under-estimate the opinion which others have of our powers, or we may hold back where our equals do not hesitate, and in this sense we may be said unduly to depreciate ourselves. Such Dejection or

*Abiectio.*
Self-depreciation is the contrary of Self-conceit, and it arises from true Humility as Self-conceit springs from Self-complacency [1].

*Existimatio.*
Over-esteem of others is a consequence of Love for another, just as Self-conceit is a consequence of Self-love. It is 'Love, so far as that leads us to think too highly

*Despectus.*
of the person we love.' Its contrary emotion is Disparagement (or Undue Contempt) of others. This may be defined as 'Hatred, so far as that leads us to think too lowly of the person we hate [2].'

(B) Consequences of the 'association' of emotions.

The 'association' of emotions follows the same law as the 'association' of ideas [3]. An element of a single perceptive state, if recalled, tends to reinstate the remainder. But the 'perceptions' of imaginative experience, in so far as they reflect the vital tone of our own body, *are* 'emotions [4].' Hence we may express the principle—so far as it applies to emotions—thus: an element of a single emotional state, if recalled, tends to reinstate the remainder [5]. It follows that anything may be the *accidental* cause (i.e. the cause by 'association') of pleasure

---

[1] E. iii. Aff. deff., 28 Expl.; 29 and Expl.; iii. 26 S.
[2] E. iii. Aff. deff., 21, 22, and Expl.; iii. 26 S.
[3] Cf. above, pp. 162 ff.
[4] Above, p. 204.
[5] E. iii. 14 and dem.

## DERIVATIVE EMOTIONS 213

or pain; and, consequently, the *accidental* object of Love CHAP. III.
or Hate, and therefore also the *accidental* object of the
various forms of Desire[1].

This is the meaning of the emotions of Instinctive *Sympathia*
Attraction and Aversion, and explains how emotions can *or Propensio.*
be excited in us by objects *like* those which give us *Antipathia*
pleasure or pain and excite our desires[2]. *or Aversio.*

Further, an object may combine in itself properties
which are the direct cause of pleasure and the *accidental*
cause of pain, or vice versa. Our feeling towards them
will be mixed: we shall both love and hate them. This
emotional Wavering corresponds to the intellectual state *Animi*
known as *doubt* or *hesitation*. Moreover since the human *Fluctuatio.*
body is highly composite, and since what raises the vitality
of one part may diminish the being of another, it is quite
possible for the same object to be the *direct* cause of
conflicting emotions[3]. From such an emotional tension
arises Jealousy. *Zelotypia.*

Jealousy is a state of emotional tension, in which love
towards an object is combined with hatred towards the
loved object, and hatred or envy towards the person who
has supplanted us in that object's affections. The most
conspicuous instances of Jealousy occur in the relations
of a lover to his mistress, and the passion is intensified
when it is reinforced by the emotion of Regret. If we *Desiderium.*
have once enjoyed a thing, in our thoughts of that thing
we desire to re-enjoy it with all the circumstances of our
first pleasure. So far as any such circumstance is absent
or different, we feel the pain of Longing or Regret. But
a lover, whose mistress has proved faithless, is no longer

---

[1] E. iii. 15 and C.
[2] E. iii. 15 S.; Aff. deff., 8 and 9. Since the efficient cause of the emotions need not be the point of similarity (or the associative cause), associational emotions of this kind may be directed to quite unsuitable objects. Cf. E. iii. 16.
[3] E. iii. 17 S. The emotional and the intellectual 'wavering' or state of tension 'differ from one another only in degree.'

## 214 THE ETHICS OF SPINOZA

BOOK II.

(C) Presentation under the form of time, and its influence on the emotions.

welcomed by her with the same countenance as formerly, and his Jealousy is intensified by Regret[1].

The actual 'picture' of anything is in content the same, whether we refer it to past or future time; for to 'picture' a thing is always to contemplate it as present. The perception of a thing as past or future is a complex idea, in which the image of the thing is conjoined with the image of past or future time[2]. The same applies to the emotional tone of an imaginative idea. The imaginative idea affects us with the same emotional state of pleasure or pain, whether we refer it to a past, future, or present occurrence: for as such and *per se*—as an emotion—it is always actually felt. But, in associating the image with that of past or future time, we bring it into a multiplex and conflicting context. Hence *intellectually* imagination of past or future events is apt to be inconstant, uncertain, hesitating; and *emotionally* our state in reference to events which we 'picture' as past or future is one of fluctuation or wavering[3].

*Spes.*
*Metus.*

Hope and Fear[4] are the wavering and uncertain emotions of pleasure and pain, which arise from the image of a future or past event of whose issue we are doubtful.

*Securitas.*
*Desperatio.*
*Conscientiae Morsus.*

When the doubt is gone, Hope becomes Confidence, Fear Desperation. Disappointment is the emotion of pain, which arises from the image of a past event, about whose issue we had hopes which are now frustrated. The opposite emotion of pleasure, which arises from the image of a past event about whose issue we had fears now shown to have been groundless, is called by Spinoza

*Gaudium.*

*gaudium*—'an agreeable surprise[5].'

---

[1] E. iii. 35 and S.; 36 C. and S.; Aff. deff., 32 and Expl.
[2] E. ii. 44 S.; cf. above, p. 168, notes 1 and 2.
[3] E. iii. 18 dem. and S. 1.
[4] *Metus* is a form of mixed pleasure and pain, and must be distinguished from *timor* (see below, p. 217, note 1), which is a form of *cupiditas* or rather of checked desire.
[5] E. iii. 18 S. 2; Aff. deff., 12-17.

## DERIVATIVE EMOTIONS

In imaginative experience, the ideas—which are the psychical expressions of affections of our body—reflect external bodies as present to us; i.e. the ideas of imagination involve both the nature of our own bodies and the actual nature of the external bodies. If the external body has a nature like our own, the idea of that external body will involve an affection of our own body *which is like* the affection of the external body. Consequently, if we 'imagine' some one *like* ourselves to suffer any emotion, that imaginative idea will involve an affection in our own body *like* the affection in his; and, therefore, our emotion (the idea of our bodily affection) will be *like* his. Hence the mere picturing the emotion of a being like ourselves will rouse a like emotion in us [1].

This explains that form of Pity (and kindred and dependent or corresponding emotions) which refers to all beings *like* ourselves [2]; Pity of this kind is simply a pain which arises in us from picturing a pain in a being like ourselves. Emulation is derived from the same principle: it is the desire for a thing which arises in us, because we picture the same desire as influencing others like ourselves [3]. From this principle (of the 'imitation' of the emotions), combined with the preceding principles, certain further forms of emotion can be explained.

Thus, we feel pleasure in what we picture as pleasing our fellow men, we dislike and avoid what we picture others as disliking and avoiding. Ambition is the desire of winning popularity at all costs, Civility or Deference the desire of conforming to public opinion [4];

CHAP. III.
(D) Consequences of the 'imitation' of the emotions.

*Aemulatio.*

*Ambitio.*
*Humanitas seu Modestia.*

---

[1] E. iii. 27 and dem.
[2] Cf. above, p. 210.
[3] E. iii. 27 S. 1; Aff. deff., 33 and Expl.
[4] E. iii. 29 and S.; Aff. deff., 43, 44. *Modestia* is thus a species of ambitio (E. iii. Aff. deff., 48 Expl.). So, too, the desire of making every one agree with you in your likes and dislikes, adopt your opinions and ideals, is really a form of Ambition (E. iii. 31 C.

BOOK II.
*Laus: Vituperium.*

Approbation and Disapproval are the emotions of pleasure and pain which we feel in picturing the actions of others, according as they have endeavoured to please us, or not [1].

*Gloria: Pudor.*

Hence, too, the reflective emotions of Self-satisfaction and Shame; i. e. the pleasure or the pain with which we contemplate ourselves as the source of an action which we picture others as approving or disapproving [2].

It is this 'imitation' of the emotions which intensifies our Love, Desire and Aversion, when we picture others as influenced by the same feelings towards the object of these emotions. This is the characteristic of human nature which is the common root of Good-nature and of Envy and Ambition: it is owing to it that mankind for the most part pity those who are in trouble, and envy the fortunate. A study of the psychology of children, Spinoza adds, would afford convincing evidence of its prevalence and power [3].

(E) *Luxuria, Ebrietas, Libido, Avaritia, Ambitio. Temperantia, Sobriet Castitas.*

Luxury, Drunkenness, Lust, Avarice and Ambition are simply names to express immoderate degrees of Love or Desire for certain objects and actions. Temperance, Sobriety and Chastity are not passive emotions at all. They express the power of the mind so far as it moderates the above-mentioned forms of Love or Desire. They are forms of Self-control [4].

and S.). Contrast *modestia* as a form of *generositas*; below, p. 219.

[1] E. iii. 29 S.

[2] E. iii. 30 S. (where Spinoza distinguishes *pudor* and *gloria* from *aquiescentia in se ipso* and *poenitentia*. The former emotions arise from sympathetic appreciation of the moral judgements—*laus, vituperium*—of others), Aff. deff., 30 and 31. In Aff. deff., 31 Expl., Spinoza explains that Modesty

(*verecundia*) is the fear of feeling shame which restrains a man from acting wrongly; whilst *pudor* is the shame itself, which we feel when we have done wrong. Shamelessness (*impudentia*), which is usually regarded as the contrary of *verecundia*, is not, properly speaking, an emotion at all.

[3] E. iii. 31, 32 and S.

[4] E. iii. 56 S.; Aff. deff., 44–48, and Expl. The term *libido*, Spinoza explains, is applied to

## DERIVATIVE EMOTIONS

We are said to experience Wonder or Fascination, when our attention is held by the imaginative idea of something new or unique: whilst the idea of something common is called Contempt. A thing which we have never seen before, or which contains unique features, is apt to attract and hold our attention, whilst a thing which is neither unique nor new calls up in our mind the images of the other things which it resembles, and sets our attention wandering to them. Hence the presence of a common or familiar object sets us thinking of what it is not, rather than of what it is. Since the imagination of something new or familiar is not, *quâ* imagination, different from any other imaginative idea, Fascination and Contempt are not emotions, but simply imaginative ideas directed to objects which are to us of a certain kind. But when those objects are the objects of our Love, Hate, or Desire, these latter emotions are coloured by this peculiar nature of our imagination. Thus, e. g., Fascination by an object which we fear is called Consternation, which is a species of Cowardice [1], its distinctive character being

*Chap. III. Admiratio. Contemptus. Consternatio.*

[1] Cf. E. iii. Aff. deff., 42 and Expl.; 39-41 and Expl.; iii. 39 S. and 51 S. Timidity [a] is a special case of Fear (*metus*, see above, p. 214). It is 'Fear, in so far as that disposes a man to avoid by a lesser evil a greater one which he judges to be imminent.' By 'evil' Spinoza means any form of pain or anything which frustrates a man's Longing (*desiderium*). Hence, the 'timid' man is in the contradictory state of not willing what he wishes for, and willing what he does not wish for. Boldness [b] is that form of Desire which incites a man to act in spite of perils which his fellows fear to face. And Cowardice [c] is predicated of the man whose Desire is checked by the fear of a danger which his fellows are not afraid to face. (Though Cowardice, as an emotional state, is opposed to Boldness, it is really a form of Fear, i.e. of pleasure—pain, whilst Boldness and Timidity are forms or states of Desire.) A man is said to be in a state of Consternation, so far as his desire to avoid an evil is checked by the fascination of another evil which he fears to undergo. Consternation [d], there-

[a] *Timor.*    [b] *Audacia.*    [c] *Pusillanimitas.*    [d] *Consternatio.*

BOOK II. that the evil in question fascinates our attention and prevents us from thinking of remedies. Wonder at a man's surpassing prudence or industry is called Worship; Fascination by his anger, envy, &c., is called Horror. Wonder at the industry, prudence, &c., of a man we love is Devotion. Contempt of a thing we hate or fear gives rise to Mockery or Derision, Contempt of folly to Scorn [1].

*Veneratio.*
*Horror.*
*Devotio.*
*Irrisio.*
*Dedignatio.*

## § 7. THE ACTIVE EMOTIONS.

Pleasure is the awareness of a heightened vitality, and desire is the consciousness of our being as the determinate source of activity. Both these ground-forms of emotion may depend in us on our adequate ideas, i. e. may follow from the nature of our own mind only, and may therefore be 'actiones' and not 'passiones' in us. For the mind, so far as it thinks truly or adequately, is necessarily conscious of its own true thinking, or power; and in such consciousness it is aware of a heightened being which springs from itself alone, i. e. it experiences an emotion of pleasure which is 'referred to it, so far as it is active.' And the mind necessarily tends to persist in its being not only so far as it thinks confusedly, but also so far as it thinks adequately; i. e. the mind experiences desire as an intelligence, or so far as it manifests its being in true thinking or in activity [2]. All the 'active emotions' are the effect of, and reveal, our power—the realization of our own nature. Hence all of them are forms of desire or pleasure: none of

fore, although it is a species of Cowardice, may be most simply defined as 'Fear (*metus*), which keeps a man so stunned or stupefied—or so undecided between two equally torturing evils—that he is unable to remove an evil from which he is suffering.'

[1] Cf. E. iii. 52 S.; Aff. deff., 4 and Expl.; 5; 10 and Expl.; 11 and Expl.

[2] '... Cupiditas ad nos refertur, etiam quatenus intelligimus, sive quatenus agimus.' E. iii. 58 dem.; cf. also E. iv. App. cap. 2.

them are forms of pain. For pain implies a decrease of vitality in body and mind, the consciousness of a lessened power of thought. But so far as our power or our being is lessened or hindered, we are 'passive' not 'active[1].'

The actions which follow from the active emotions are all consequences or manifestations of the mind's power to think truly, i. e. of our mind as an intelligence. Spinoza includes them all under the head of *fortitudo*, i. e. he regards them as expressing Strength of Mind. A strong character in its relations to other men is Nobleness (*generositas*)—the steadfast and intelligent endeavour to help others and make friends of them. The same strength of character shows itself also as Strength of Purpose (*animositas*)—the steadfast and intelligent endeavour to promote our own best welfare. Forms of Nobleness of Mind are e. g. *modestia, clementia*, &c.; forms of Strength of Purpose are e. g. Temperance, Sobriety, Presence of Mind in dangers, &c.[2]

---

[1] E. iii. 59 and dem.
[2] E. iii. 59 S. *Modestia*—as Spinoza defines it elsewhere—is a passive emotion, a form of Ambition (p. 215, note 4): it means 'deference or civility to others in order to attain popularity.' Here he evidently intends it to mean 'deference to others so far as that results from an intelligent endeavour to help them and make friends of them'; cf. E. v. 4 S.; iv. 37 S. 1; iv. App. cap. 25, and below.

# APPENDIX TO BOOK II

## ESSENCE AND EXISTENCE—THE CONATUS—CUPIDITAS—FREEDOM—TELEOLOGY—EMOTIONAL AND COGNITIVE IDEAS

Book II.
Object
of this
appendix.

1. In this appendix I propose to consider certain difficulties—both of interpretation and of doctrine—which are involved in Spinoza's account of the nature of man. It was convenient to postpone their discussion in order not to interrupt an exposition already sufficiently complicated, but it will not be unprofitable to examine them here. For such an examination, even if it should force us to admit that Spinoza's views are exposed to unanswerable criticisms, will at least show us where we stand. It will throw our interpretation into relief, and thus clear the ground for the exposition of Spinoza's ethical theories.

The reader will perhaps expect some apology for a discussion which must repeat in its main features the criticisms I have already set out at length[1]. In one sense, it is true, the whole problem of the Ethics is summed up in the question 'How can we conceive the being of a multiplicity in God?' 'What is the good,' it may be said, 'of criticizing the details, when the principle has already been condemned? If the basis of a philosophy is inwardly contradictory, the contradiction must reveal itself also in the superstructure.'

---

[1] See above, App. to Bk. I.

But the real problem for Spinoza is not adequately formulated in a question of this kind. His subject-matter is the concrete unity of Reality in the various degrees and forms of its manifestation. To have criticized his conception of the general principle of that unity cannot absolve us from an examination of his theory in its details. For the full significance of the general principle is revealed only in the complete theory; and it would be rash to assume, without confirmation, that our earlier criticism was sound. It may be that the flaws of the basis will repeat themselves in the superstructure; or perhaps a study of the latter will modify our views of the former. These are questions which critical inquiry alone can determine. And even if after all we encounter the old problem in fresh forms, these forms have an interest of their own, and the examination of them is certainly not a useless labour.

2. I will begin with a difficulty on which we have touched more than once. We have maintained that Spinoza does not sever 'existence' and 'essence.' 'Natura naturata'—the Reality as consequent—is not a world of shadowy essences confronting a world of temporally-existent things. The *mere* existence and the *mere* essence of a thing (its temporal-being and its thought-being) are abstract 'moments' of its full modal being. 'Natura naturata' is the concrete modal system in which the 'essences' maintain themselves with a timeless actuality. Its unity sustains within itself the individual distinctness of the modes: their distinctness does not break the wholeness of 'natura naturata,' but constitutes it [1].

And this interpretation was confirmed by Spinoza's theory of knowledge. 'Science' apprehends the universal nature of things: but it remains abstract, in so far as 'the adequate knowledge of the essence of things'— their intimate individuality—escapes it. It grasps at

[1] Cf. above, p. 95, note 1; pp. 119 ff.

most the specific, not the individual, nature of the modes. 'Natura naturata' is incompletely comprehended by 'science' as a system of universal law, a universe of common properties. For complete truth we must look to 'intuitive science' or philosophy. It alone can grasp the intimate individuality of each thing as the inevitable consequent of the nature of God. In that complete apprehension 'natura naturata' is fully understood. The temporal actuality of things receives its recognition as the partial manifestation of their timeless self-maintenance. Things retain their unique individuality without losing their necessary coherence in God. The 'essences' of things reveal the actuality which is adequate to them. The *mere* 'essences' and the *mere* 'existences' are viewed as what they really are, abstractions from the concrete being of things [1].

This is, I believe, in outline Spinoza's view; a view, which—as I hope to show—is elaborated in the fifth part of the Ethics [2]. But Spinoza is far from consistent; and if this is the theory he intended to express, sometimes, it must be admitted, the intention is very imperfectly realized. For there are passages which cannot be reconciled with this general tendency of his thought. If they stood uncontradicted, they would force us to a widely different interpretation of the Ethics. As it is, we have to face inconsistencies which it is impossible to override, however liberal the use we make of the distinction between 'intention' and 'actual expression.' In other words, an honest interpretation of the Ethics is compelled to recognize here, as elsewhere [3], two conflicting lines of thought. In my exposition as a whole I have followed what I take to be the main stream of Spinoza's philosophy. But it is now my duty to point

---

[1] Cf. above, pp. 175 ff.     [2] Cf. below, Bk. III. ch. 4.
[3] Cf. above, pp. 115 ff.

# ESSENCE AND EXISTENCE

out some of the evidences for the 'undercurrent,' if I may so call it.

In E. ii. 8 we read: 'The ideas of the single things or modes which are not existing must be comprehended in the infinite idea of God, just as the formal essences of the single things or modes are contained in God's Attributes.' The corollary adds: 'Hence it follows that so long as single things do not exist, except so far as they are comprehended in God's Attributes, their " esse obiectivum" or ideas do not exist, except so far as the infinite idea of God exists; and when single things are said to exist not only so far as they are comprehended in God's Attributes, but so far also as they are said to endure' (i.e. exist in time), 'their ideas too will involve an existence in virtue of which they are said to endure.' Now, apart from the use of the expression 'infinita idea Dei,' these passages create no special difficulty. For they could be interpreted simply as distinguishing the conceptual being and the temporal actuality of things as two aspects or factors of their full modal being. And it was in this sense that I understood them, when I quoted this very corollary to support my interpretation of Spinoza's conceptions of 'natura naturata' and the world of presentation[1]. Moreover, the Scholium confirms this. For the illustration, which it offers[2], clearly indicates that 'the

---

[1] Cf. above, p. 122, note 1.
[2] E. ii. 8 S. Having warned us that any illustration is necessarily inadequate, Spinoza proceeds: 'I will try to illustrate the matter as best I can. The nature of a circle is such, that the rectangles formed by the segments of all its chords, which intersect in the same point, are equal. Therefore, a circle contains an infinity of equal rectangles. But none of these can be said to exist, except so far as the circle exists; nor can the idea of any of them be said to exist, except so far as it is comprehended in the idea of the circle. Now suppose that two only of these innumerable rectangles ... exist. The ideas also of these two exist now, not only so far as they are comprehended in the idea of the circle, but also so far as they involve the existence of the rectangles in

Book II. essences of things which are not existing' (of which the proposition and corollary speak) are the abstract conceptual essences—things in their potential being, as involved in the common properties or universal laws which the 'scientific' consciousness would apprehend.

But the use of the expression 'infinita idea Dei'—if we are to take it precisely—suggests a very different interpretation. The 'infinita idea Dei' is, as we have seen[1], a mediate infinite and eternal mode of Thought— 'natura naturata' on its ideal side. The ideas, therefore, 'so far as they are comprehended in the infinite idea of God,' are modes of Thought in their eternal being as modes of 'natura naturata;' and the 'formal essences of things so far as they are contained in the Attributes of God' are modes of the other Attributes in their eternal being as modes of 'natura naturata.' Unless, then, we regard the expression 'infinita idea Dei' as a mere mistake on Spinoza's part—which is assuredly not a likely hypothesis—we must recognize in this proposition and corollary an undercurrent which conflicts with the main stream of his thought. We must see in them one more evidence of that tendency to an abstract conception of the unity of things, which, as we have maintained, constantly thwarts Spinoza's effort to conceive God as a concrete unity[2]. For, follow out the interpretation which is thus suggested, and 'natura naturata' at once becomes a world of shadowy essences, in which the distinctness of the modes is absorbed in a vague identity. And, as the inevitable retribution, a second world of bare existences rises over against the world of essences. A world of 'actual things,' that is to say, acquires a being independent of 'natura naturata' which was to have included all modal reality in itself. The members of

question, whereby the ideas of these two are distinguished from the remaining ideas of the remaining rectangles.'

[1] Cf. above, pp. 94 ff.
[2] Cf. above, pp. 115 ff.

'natura naturata'—the shadowy essences or potentialities of things—step into actuality in the world of temporal existence: and (most strange of all) this process confers upon them an additional reality which distinguishes them from their less fortunate fellows—the modes which remain *in posse* as mere essences. Thus the world of temporal existence, if it is not itself 'real,' at any rate confers an additional privilege, a distinctness and individuality, on the essences which *are* the modal Reality.

And yet, if we ask '*what* is it that is existing in the world of temporal existence?' the answer can only be 'the essences of things.' It is the infinity of possible equal rectangles which acquires 'actual existence' when the intersecting chords are drawn; the infinity of formal and ideal essences which 'also' exists in time. There are no two worlds for Spinoza. The inaccurate language of the proposition and corollary in question is evidence, *not* that he intended to assert this inconsistent confusion as his philosophical theory, but that he was struggling against a conflicting tendency in his thought which he had only partially overcome when he wrote the Ethics.

3. A certain ambiguity in the conception of the 'conatus' confirms the conclusion we have just reached. The effort at self-maintenance, which is the individuality of things, manifests itself in their temporal being, and is—as we have seen [1]—itself temporal, though not involving a determinate period. Yet it is also, and essentially, a part of the omnipotence of God, and follows from the eternal necessity of his nature. It is thus the force wherewith each thing persists in its eternal actuality—the timeless existence which it has in God [2]. For though the term 'conatus' and its implication of time make it clear that Spinoza conceives it primarily as the source of the actual

*The conatus.*

[1] Cf. above, p. 192.
[2] Cf. E. ii. 45 S.; also iii. 6 dem., 7, 8, and 9.

existence of things in the temporal world, yet he never loses sight of its ultimate derivation from the omnipotence of God. And the 'conatus' is thus, in the end, the 'effort' which imperfectly expresses under the conditions of temporal actuality the full self-affirmation of things in their timeless coherence. The two senses of 'existence' or 'actuality,' which Spinoza recognizes[1], are not independent of one another, nor on the same level of reality. However obscurely Spinoza may express himself, temporal existence is an incomplete manifestation of eternal actuality; and the 'conatus' is, in its ultimate conception, the complete self-maintenance which the modes of God involve in their full or eternal being:—not merely their effort at self-assertion in the temporal series.

*Spinoza's treatment of the relative reality of time is unsatisfactory.*

4. To regard 'temporal existence' as a partial manifestation of the actuality of the modes in God; to speak of their 'effort at self-assertion' as the incomplete revelation of their timeless self-affirmation, and of the 'world of time and place' as a partly illusory appearance which adequate understanding would supplement and resolve into the reality of 'natura naturata':—all this, no doubt, tells us very little. Such phrases cannot pretend to solve the problem as to how a timeless Reality comes to show itself under the imperfect form of a temporal succession. They cannot pretend to explain how or why the illusion of time, like other illusions, infects our imaginative experience: for—as we have seen—the mutilated experience, which for Spinoza's theory is the ground of illusion, itself is a product of the illusory world which it creates[2]. Nor can Spinoza even claim to have inquired what degree of truth is expressed in the illusion of temporal succession, what rank of reality attaches to the world of time and place. Whether or no such questions can be asked of any philosophy—whether or no any answer can be made to them—Spinoza, it is clear, never

[1] Cf. E. v. 29 S.    [2] Cf. above, pp. 111 ff.

makes any attempt to formulate them. The complete Reality is, for him, a timeless fulfilment of being, within which there is neither succession nor change as such. Temporal succession and determinate duration are appearances of the Real, but appearances which in their distinctive character are misleading: i.e. which possess a low degree of reality. The supplementation, which would render them adequate expressions of the Real, would so modify their character that nothing distinctive of them would survive.

It is not a satisfactory treatment of the subject, we may agree; but I do not think that more can be gathered from the Ethics[1].

5. The 'conatus' of man, as the determinate state of his being from which activity follows, is called by Spinoza 'cupiditas'—'desire.' This term is intended to cover all forms of human impulse:—the strivings of which man is conscious, as well as those instincts and tendencies which are not present *to* him, but present *in* him as mere vague feelings[2]. We are not to suppose that 'desire' is anything specially distinctive of man. All things in our experience are modes of Extension and Thought—'ideae' of corporeal 'ideata'—and there is no ground for limiting Thought's reflection upon itself to the human soul, the idea of a human body[3]. On the contrary, Spinoza expressly tells us that the substitution of 'cupiditas' for 'appetitus' is a mere convenience of terminology. 'The term " cupiditas " is generally used of men in so far as they are conscious of their " appetitus "'[4]:—but there is no real difference: 'for whether man is conscious of his " appetitus," or whether he is not, the " appetitus " itself remains one and the same[5].'

APPENDIX.

*Appetitus* and *cupiditas*.

---

[1] Cf. also below, Bk. III. ch. 4. below, p. 257, note 4.
[2] See above, p. 193.
[4] E. iii. 9 S.
[3] On the reflection of Thought on itself, cf. above, pp. 132 ff.;
[5] E. iii. Aff. deff., 1 Expl.

228     THE ETHICS OF SPINOZA

Book II.   These statements can only mean this:—all modes exhibit an effort at self-affirmation, which may be called a 'will-to-be' or 'appetitus[1].' The fact that in some modes—e. g. in man—this 'will-to-be' is often not a mere instinctive impulse, but a 'desire' (i. e. an impulse of which they are reflectively conscious) makes no difference to its character. It remains what it was as a blind striving. Reflective consciousness supervenes without modifying it, or is a mere 'epiphenomenon.'

The 'will-to-be,' then, of all modes is one and the same in character: and that character is revealed as fully where no reflective consciousness is present, as where it is. The significance of this doctrine can hardly be doubtful. Its object is to admit the fact of conscious 'desire,' whilst denying the reality of purposive action. We 'desire,' and our 'desire' involves the consciousness of purpose which distinguishes reflective from instinctive effort. But the *effective* factor in our desire is the blind impulse: the reflective consciousness—the conception of a purpose—may seem to the agent to condition his action, but in reality it is the otiose accompaniment of the propelling force[2]. The 'motives,' which condition our action, may include in their content the conception of an end to be realized: but, if so, it is not *as such*—not by their complete content—that they 'move.' The real motive force works in the depths unaffected by the surface-play of our thought.

Spinoza's conception of *cupiditas* completes his polemic against

6. Before we can discuss the question at issue, it is necessary to show how this conception of 'cupiditas' connects with the polemic against the 'freedom of the will,' with which we are already familiar. Spinoza's polemic may be summed up thus:—' we act "purposively" in

[1] The 'conatus' is no doubt called 'appetitus' primarily in reference to what ordinary experience regards as 'living things'—plants, animals, and men.

[2] Cf. e.g. E. iv. def. 7. 'Per finem, cuius causa aliquid facimus, appetitum intelligo.'

the sense that we do that which we consciously desire: but our action is not "free" in the sense supposed, because the conscious desire itself is produced in us by non-purposive causes.' Man *thinks* he acts purposively: and man's conception of an end, or the 'desire' which involves it, is the next link determining his action. Purposive action, in this sense, is a fact. But it is not an ultimate fact: for the 'desire' from which action springs is not itself freely formed, but is determined by an indefinite chain of causes which are not teleological in their *nexus*. Hence man's 'freedom' is illusory: for the basis of the so-called 'free' action, is itself necessarily determined *a tergo* by forces over which man has no control [1]. But what about the *nexus* between the 'desire' and the action? Is that teleological—is the action done 'in order to' realize the 'desire'? If so—and Spinoza's polemic against 'freedom' left the question undecided, or indeed suggested an affirmative answer—there is a break in the causal chain. For the *nexus* up to the 'desire' was throughout mechanical, or at least not teleological: whilst at the 'desire' we suddenly cross over into a different kind of causation. It is here that the conception of 'cupiditas' completes Spinoza's theory and removes the obscurity. The *nexus* between 'desire' and 'action' is the same in character as that between all the other links in the chain. There is no teleological determination—no acting 'in order to' carry out a purpose—no 'freedom' in this sense of the word. 'Desire' moves to action *a tergo* in the same way in which the antecedent ideas called up 'desire.'

Spinoza's own conception of 'action' is thus cleared of ambiguity. Body does not determine mind, nor mind body: but one determinate state of mind and body is the ground of another. A given action, then, is the

APPENDIX. the freedom of the will.

[1] Cf. E. i. App., iii. 2 S.

Book II. resultant of an indefinite chain of conditions (each of which is both corporeal and mental): and the *nexus* between the links of the chain is throughout 'geometrical'—never teleological or purposive. So far as a determinate state of our own body and mind is the adequate ground of an action, we are said to be 'free,' or 'agents': so far as the environment has to be taken in to complete the ground, we are 'passive' or not free. But *ultimately* in any case the only completely adequate ground, and the only 'agent,' is God [1].

'Geometrical' sequence.

7. We are now in a position to examine Spinoza's conception of 'desire' and the motive force which determines action. The first criticism which suggests itself touches a difficulty we have already discussed [2]. Of what nature is this 'geometrical' coherence—the only type of causal *nexus* which Spinoza admits? His own words throw but little light on the subject. It is clear that he intends to contrast it with 'teleological' connexion [3]; and it is clear also that he conceives it as a connexion *by content*, and not by external colligation. By this I mean that the natures of the cohering elements contribute essentially to the coherence [4], and that the connexion is not of the type sometimes called 'mechanical [5].' But it is not clear whether Spinoza was fully

---

[1] Cf. above, pp. 197 ff.
[2] Cf. above, pp. 115 ff.
[3] It is hardly necessary to quote passages in support of this point: but I shall have to inquire presently *what kind* of 'teleological' connexion Spinoza criticizes and rejects.
[4] In this sense I have spoken of the 'geometrical' coherence as a 'logical' *nexus*.
[5] A connexion may be called 'mechanical' in proportion as it approximates to a mere conjunction, in which the natures of the conjoined elements contribute nothing to their coherence.—That the 'geometrical' coherence is not 'mechanical' in this sense of the term, but 'logical,' is (I think) placed beyond a doubt by the whole tenor of the Ethics. Cf. e.g. the identification of *causa* and *ratio*, the constant employment of the example of the triangle as the ground of its properties, and the distinction between *memoria* and *intellectus*.

aware what a 'logical' *nexus* implies. One property of APPENDIX. a spatial figure 'follows from' another, because the positive character of the figure demands for its construction and maintenance precisely these spatial elements with their distinctive characters and mode of interconnexion. The conclusion 'follows from' the premisses, because the positive character of the whole of significance which they express requires for its construction and maintenance precisely these elements with their distinctive significances and mode of coherence. In other words:—every connexion by content (every 'geometrical' or 'logical' *nexus*, therefore) implies a significant whole dominating significant elements. And the coherence of the elements is the expression both of the reciprocal implications of their own natures and of the character of the whole; for it is only within that character that the reciprocal implications *are*. Now, if this is so, every connexion by content implies a domination essentially *teleological* in character. For the 'significant whole' conditions the contents and reciprocal implica-

In *memoria* ideas are 'mechanically' conjoined, in *intellectus* they are 'logically' coherent; and the Reality is re-presented by the *intellectus*—not by the associational reminiscences of *memoria*. The well-known proposition (E. ii. 7)—taken in conjunction with the outline of physics in E. ii. and with the theories of Descartes —seems to have led to the too frequent assumption that Spinoza regards all laws of necessary connexion as conforming to the type of the laws supposed to regulate the transference of motion. But E. ii. 7 gives us only one side of his theory: the converse is given in E. v. 1 and E. ii. 6 C. (to which v. 1 refers). The 'order and connexion' of 'ideas' and of 'things' (i.e. bodies and modes of Attributes other than Thought) are 'the same': the 'order' (and 'connexion') of the modes of Reality, though differently expressed in the different Attributes, remains fundamentally one. But we are not told what the nature of that identical order is, nor how far its different expressions adequately reveal its ultimate character. All we know is that it is 'geometrical,' and we have certainly no right to identify it with the form which it assumes in one Attribute, i.e. as the order of the modes of Extension.

BOOK II. tions of the component elements *as that to which they are the indispensable means*. Its 'being' requires their 'being': and they are what they are, and are reciprocally interrelated as they are, because it is what it is. It is not a mere resultant which they happen to produce, nor an end external to them to which they lead; but an individuality which stamps them with its character. It is the immanent end, which they constitute and maintain, but which determines what they are.

What 'teleology' does Spinoza reject?

The 'final causes,' which Spinoza contemptuously rejects, are external ends: ideals not yet real, but to be realized. The 'purposive' action which he discredits, is action with a view to the attainment of an unpossessed 'better.' God does not act 'purposively,' or from final causes, because that would imply that God is *now* defective[1]. But the necessary and timeless 'sequence' or coherence of the modes in God is the articulation of the divine nature. It is stamped with God's individuality, and draws its being and significance from the totality of significant being which is God. And *in this sense* God acts 'purposively,' or the internal coherence and reciprocal implications of his 'states' are 'teleological' in character. The 'best' is not an ideal towards which God is progressing: still less an archetypal perfection alien to his nature, to which he endeavours to conform. But the complete Reality, which all things conspire timelessly to express, is the 'most perfect being.' The nature of the universe is not the gradual realization of a plan, which God's 'intelligence' has first conceived and which his 'will' puts bit by bit into execution: but it is the timelessly actual manifestation of an ideal Reality, and an ideal Reality which is completely significant as the object of God's intelligence[2]. The modes of God are what they are, and cohere as they cohere, as the necessary expressions of God's individual nature—

[1] Cf. e.g. E. i. App.      [2] Cf. above, pp. 144, 145.

as the indispensable means of its eternal self-fulfilment ; APPENDIX. whilst that individuality is in no sense the 'resultant' of them.

I am aware that this interpretation will seem paradoxical, and I am not prepared to maintain that Spinoza distinctly—still less, consistently—expresses such a view. But I think it is implied in the general tenor of the Ethics, a great deal of which seems to me unintelligible without it [1]. It is wiser, perhaps, in view of Spinoza's own use of the terms and in order to avoid misunderstanding, not to call God's activity 'teleological' or 'purposive.' It does not much matter, so long as we are clear what the 'geometrical' coherence involves. And —unless I am mistaken—it does involve that which, for want of a better name, I have called an 'immanent teleology.'

8. Coming now to the subject before us, much that is implied in Spinoza's polemic against 'freedom' (and especially his conception of the *nexus* between 'desire' and 'action') is irreconcilable with the causality of God as we have been forced to interpret it. It is true that man is never completely 'free,' and that his action is not really 'purposive' in the sense in which he imagines it to be so. But man's 'freedom' is incomplete, because it is a derivative of God's 'freedom': and we have seen that God's 'freedom' or self-determination is in the end 'teleological.' As a derivative portion of God's 'freedom,' the 'freedom' which Spinoza attributes to man should exhibit a corresponding character; i.e. man's 'free action' must 'follow from' his nature, as

'Freedom' and 'purposive action.'

---

[1] Cf. e.g. E. v. 40 S.; and the whole conception of the *amor intellectualis Dei*, on which see below, Bk. III. ch. 4; cf. also Epp. 19, 21, 23. Many commentators find themselves compelled to dismiss most of the fifth part of the Ethics as 'mysticism' (i.e. unintelligible dreams which please the fancy), because they have committed themselves to mistaken interpretations of the 'causality' of God as expounded in the earlier parts of the Ethics.

Book II. God's action 'follows from' the divine nature. Man, that is to say, is 'free' in so far as he possesses an individuality which stamps itself on his 'ideas' and 'movements,' which dominates his 'desires' and activities and their mode of interconnexion. Action 'follows from' desire, not because 'desire' includes an impulse which moves *a tergo,* but because both desire and its issue cohere as 'states' of an individuality, which impresses its significance on them and yet requires their distinctive characters to constitute it. And man's action is not 'purposive' in the way he imagines. For he does not first conceive and then will; nor does his mental volition determine his bodily movement. But it is 'purposive' in a different sense. For the total state (of which the consciousness of an object as desirable is the ideal side) and the total state (of which the bodily movement—the conspicuous feature in an 'action'—is the corporeal side) cohere with a *nexus,* the ultimate ground of which is a dominating individuality. Because man is what he is, he desires (and conceives), he acts (and moves), as he does. His character is not the chance resultant of blind impulses externally associated with activities. It determines the nature and the mode of coherence of the elements which constitute it.

Reflective consciousness in 'desire.'

9. We can deal briefly with the remaining difficulty in Spinoza's conception of 'cupiditas.' Every 'appetitus,' as a modification of our mind as well as our body, is of course felt or experienced by us: it is present 'in' us as a determinate state of feeling. But in 'desire' we are conscious of an impulse *as ours*: the 'appetitus' is present 'to' us, in the sense that we are conscious of ourselves as experiencing a determinate state of feeling. We have seen that Spinoza's account of self-consciousness is unsatisfactory: for he treats it as merely the reduplication *ad infinitum* of 'idea' on 'idea' in such

a way that 'idea' and 'ideatum' always remain indis- APPENDIX. tinguishably one[1]. Self-consciousness, thus conceived, becomes the otiose epiphenomenon of consciousness; the reflective 'idea' is the idle duplicate of the 'idea' reflected. And it is an inevitable corollary of such a view that reflective consciousness can 'make no difference' to the 'appetitus' which it reflects. 'To be aware of ourselves as feeling an impulse' thus becomes identical with ' feeling an impulse.'

But we have seen that, in spite of his theory of 'idea ideae,' Spinoza himself constantly implies a very different conception of self-consciousness[2] and clearly the self-consciousness, which is in some sense a fact, is not the idle shadow which 'idea ideae' would make it. Indeed, Spinoza's own theory should have led to different results. All bodies are ideas: but the ideal side of a body makes a difference. For the idea of a body is its soul or life. The *first idea* is thus not the otiose duplicate of its 'ideatum.' Why then—if 'idea' is related to 'idea' exactly as 'idea' is related to body—should the second and succeeding ideas leave their 'ideata' unaltered? It may seem to add nothing to an idea, that we should have an idea of it, and so on indefinitely. Yet in knowing that we know, we refer our knowledge to a central unity —we constitute a 'self.' Similarly, in reflecting on our impulses and thus ' desiring,' we adopt them as *our own*, as parts of a coherent and centralized plan of life. And this vitally distinguishes them from mere 'appetitus.' Spinoza does in fact make use of this difference due to self-consciousness, although he denies its existence. The different grades of perfection or reality in man and animals or 'stocks and stones' are differences in the grades of their soul-life; and the different degrees of self-dependence or freedom in different men are

---

[1] Cf. above, pp. 138 ff.   [2] Cf. above, p. 140, note 1.

Book II. differences in the coherence of their ideas and, in the end, of their self-consciousness[1].

'Cognitive' and 'emotional' ideas.

10. It remains to point out an obscurity in Spinoza's account of the relation and distinction between reflective (i. e. cognitive)[2] and emotional ideas.

Emotions are secondary thoughts which presuppose the primary or reflective thoughts, though the latter may be present without the former. Active emotions are derivatives of clear thinking. Passive emotions are confused secondary thoughts; i. e. passions are derivatives of imaginative thought[3]. In what sense are the emotions *derivative*? As portions, it would seem, of a total conscious state[4]. Thus, a 'passion' is a part of a total imaginative idea. We are affected in our body by the action of an external body. The result is a modification of our body, which is *eo ipso* a modification of our mind; i. e. an 'imago' which is also an 'imaginatio.' As a cognitive (or reflective) idea, this 'imaginatio' is a confused notion of the external body and a confused notion of our own body. As an emotional idea or passion, this same mental modification (or 'imaginatio') is a feeling of our bodily state.

It is a feeling of 'pleasure' if it is more real, of 'pain' if it is less real, than the modification immediately preceding it; i. e. it is an emotion of 'pleasure' or 'pain' according as we, body and mind, are more or less 'alive'

---

[1] See below, Bk. III. chs. 1 and 4.

[2] I have not hesitated to employ the term 'reflective ideas' to include both cognitive ideas and the ideas which reflect ideas; but I do not think that my use of the term is anywhere ambiguous. Spinoza's theory of 'idea ideae,' which admits no distinction between the two, renders it desirable to use some English term in a correspondingly wide sense.

[3] Cf. E. ii. Ax. 3; E. iv. 9 dem. (above, p. 203). 'Emotions' here, as elsewhere, are loosely taken as *mental* modifications only; cf. above, p. 201.

[4] Cf. also E. v, where the 'passions' resolve themselves by supplementation into clear reflective thoughts.

# EMOTION AND IDEA

in it than we were. And it is a 'desire,' so far as it is the feeling of a determinate pitch of mental and bodily vitality as the source of activities.

But what distinguishes the part-idea, which is a passion, from the part-idea of our own bodily and mental state or transition which remains a cognitive thought? For obviously the imaginative idea may—and often does—stop short at the awareness of the modification as a change *in me*, without going on to refer the change to the presence and action of an external body. This would then be a part-idea; and yet it would be a cognitive or reflective, not an emotional, thought.

The only answer which Spinoza gives is that the emotional idea is *immediate*, does not imply comparison; i.e. *is* a feeling, not a reflective thought[1]. But (i) this merely states a difference without explaining how two things, apparently so different, are yet both entitled to the common name, 'idea[2]': and (ii) it suggests that the emotional ideas are *prior* to the cognitive ideas, which is contrary to Spinoza's explicit doctrine. The total modification (bodily and mental) is no doubt the first condition both of 'emotion' and of 'thought': but 'emotions' would seem to be the simplest and most direct resultants of this, reflective ideas its secondary and derivative consequents.

The whole subject is, however, so vague in Spinoza's statement, that it is wisest to be content with pointing out that considerable obscurity does exist.

---

[1] Cf. E. iii. Aff. gen. def. Expl.

[2] In this respect, Pollock's contention (Pollock, pp. 124 ff.; above, p. 131, note 3) seems to be justified. But I cannot altogether accept his views. Spinoza's use of the term 'idea' is ambiguous, not because it means for him both soul and thought of the body, but because it means both 'reflective thought' and 'feeling'; and because he has not made it clear how he conceives the relation and difference between them.

# BOOK III

## THE IDEAL LIFE FOR MAN

## CHAPTER I

### THE MEANING OF A STANDARD OF MORAL VALUE

BOOK III.   IN the preceding Books we have sketched Spinoza's theory of Reality and of the nature of man. We have now to consider the ethical views which he bases on that theory—to examine his conception of the ideal life for man. But what right has Spinoza to talk of an ideal life, or an ideal human nature, at all? 'Good' and 'bad,' 'perfect' and 'imperfect,' as we know, are terms which have reference to our partial apprehension, and which do not express the nature of things. Neither is there any teleological process in Reality. 'Final causes' and 'purposive action' are mere phantoms of the imaginative consciousness. The Reality is through and through determined with an immanent necessity. There is no progress, no striving to become better: everything which is in any sense real, is eternally what it is as the inevitable consequent of the unalterable and complete nature of God.

Before, therefore, we can attempt to deal with Spinoza's ethical theory, we must review his conceptions of 'perfection' and 'goodness.' We must ask in what sense he allows himself to speak of 'good' and 'bad,' 'perfect' and 'imperfect,' of an 'ideal' human nature

## 'PERFECT' AND 'IMPERFECT'

and life, of 'error' and 'moral evil,' of 'virtue' and 'vice.' He himself is explicit on the subject, and there is no lack of material for answering the question [1].

(i) To begin with, we must reaffirm the conclusions of Spinoza's metaphysics. In truth and in reality there is no perfection and imperfection, no good and bad. The ultimate nature of things is completely real, and its reality is an eternal necessity. There is no possibility or contingency; no ideal, which, as yet unrealized, is capable of realization. Reality is throughout its infinite variety absolutely all that it has in it to be. This, its absolute necessity and fullness of being, constitutes its 'perfection' or 'completeness.' It is not 'perfect' in any sense which would imply the successful realization of a 'best' over against a possible failure [2].

And an examination into the origin of our notions of 'perfection' and 'imperfection' will but confirm this conclusion [3]. In their original significance, the terms *perfect* and *imperfect* seem to have been applied to the products of the arts and crafts. A work was adjudged *perfect* if it completely fulfilled, *imperfect* if it failed to fulfil (or did not yet completely fulfil), its maker's design. Thus, in order to judge a work 'perfect' or 'imperfect' in the strict and primary sense of the terms, it was necessary for the critic to know the mind of the maker. But the terms have acquired a wider and less accurate signification. We have learnt by experience to form 'universal ideas.' We have acquired a general notion e.g. of 'what a house should be' by comparison of actual houses and architects' plans, and by abstraction and generalization from the data compared. Hence,

---

[1] On 'error,' cf. above, pp. 165 ff. On the whole subject, cf. E. iv. Praef., and Spinoza's correspondence with de Blyenbergh, Epp. 18-24 and 27. The Ethics were already written at the time of this correspondence—Spinoza refers to them in Ep. 23.
[2] Cf. above, pp. 59 ff., 232 ff.
[3] For what follows, cf. E. iv. Praef.

Book III. 'a *perfect* house' comes to mean one which answers to our ideal pattern, our universal idea of a house: and a house is *imperfect* for our judgement if it fails to realize our ideal, however completely it may fulfil its builder's design. A further (and an illegitimate) extension of these notions to the works of nature soon follows. We talk of 'failures' or 'faults' of nature, so far as any natural product does not realize the universal idea of its class which we have formed by imaginative abstraction; and we use this universal idea as a pattern or type to which every member of the class in question '*ought*' to conform.

Now in the case of human works the so-called ideal or final cause is—when it is operative at all—the desire or motive of the workman. The builder e. g. 'pictured' to himself the comforts of a house, and this imaginative idea was—in its emotional effect upon him—the basis of the specific desire which issued in the building of the house[1].

If he had had sufficient knowledge, he could have traced the series of conditioning 'ideae' (from which this desire on its ideal side inevitably followed) *in infinitum* backwards. As it is, he is aware only of his ideal—his imaginative idea of home comforts, e.g.—and of his desire as an effort to realize it: and, since he is ignorant of the real determinants of the one and the other, he supposes himself to originate action with a view to an end: and in this supposition of his own freedom he is deceived by partial knowledge[2]. But to the processes of nature we cannot ascribe any purposiveness, not even this illusion of purposive activity which dominates the operations of man. Nature does not 'picture' an ideal and then strive—or suppose itself to

---

[1] Cf. above, pp. 203 ff.

[2] For a criticism of Spinoza's conception of 'cupiditas' and his polemic against 'final causes,' cf. above, pp. 227 ff.

strive—for its attainment. Natural effects all follow inevitably from their efficient cause. And so far as there is any consciousness in nature, it is nature's (i. e. God's) consciousness, which is never partial and inadequate or imaginative; never, therefore, the victim of any illusion as to the character of the causation which controls its processes. Nor is any natural product *for and in itself* 'imperfect' or 'faulty.' *We* class all natural products under the abstract universal idea of 'being': and hence *for us* they are 'perfect' or 'imperfect,' according as they exhibit more or less 'being' or 'reality' in comparison with one another. But in reality—*in and for itself*—every natural product is of necessity all that it has in it to be. *What it has not* in comparison with others, is only *for us* and is no part of its nature. It is not 'deprived of' the greater possession. The 'greater possession' is not its portion, precisely because it is no part of its nature to have it.

The same applies to the terms *good* and *bad*. *Goodness* and *badness* are simply modes of our thought, imaginative ideas, notions which spring from the comparison and generalization of an inadequate apprehension. *In and for themselves*, things are neither 'good' nor 'bad,' but all alike necessarily what they are. *For us*—in relation to our arbitrary types and patterns, as means to our purposes—one and the same thing is good, bad, and indifferent, according to our present circumstances and requirements.

(ii) For the purposes of an ethical theory, the terms 'good,' 'bad,' 'perfect,' 'imperfect' are convenient and legitimate, provided we define the sense in which we use them. They do not express the nature of things as they really are *in and for themselves*: but they express that nature as it is *for us* under the determinate circumstances of the task in which we are engaged. We (in the Ethics) are endeavouring to form an ideal of human

Book III. nature, a pattern for our life and conduct: and 'good' or 'bad,' 'perfect' or 'imperfect,' express things as they are for us *so far as we judge them with reference to this pattern or ideal*. The term 'good' is to be applied to anything which we certainly know to be a means by which we can approximate to the realization of this ideal: anything, which we certainly know to be a hindrance to its attainment, is to be called 'evil.' Similarly men are to be called more or less 'perfect' (or 'imperfect') according as they approximate more or less (less or more) to our ideal. A man, therefore, is 'perfect' in proportion as he is and does what adequately expresses our ideal human nature. This ideal nature itself (which thus determines the use of the terms 'good' and 'bad,' 'perfect' and 'imperfect' within an ethical theory) is to be called 'perfect' in the wide sense of the term. A thing is 'perfect' in this general sense in so far as it is real: its perfection is its essential being, or the totality of its determinate actuality and activity. All that the thing of necessity is and does, so far as depends upon itself, is the manifestation of its affirmative being, its essence or perfection[1]. The ideal human nature, therefore, is 'ideal' or 'perfect' simply because it represents the essential being of man as adequately and fully as possible. We conceive as completely and adequately as possible all that man, so far as follows from within the four corners of his essential nature, of

---

[1] Cf. E. iv. Praef. 'Denique per perfectionem in genere realitatem, uti dixi, intelligam; hoc est, rei cuiuscunque essentiam, quatenus certo modo existit et operatur, nulla ipsius durationis habita ratione. Nam nulla res singularis potest ideo dici perfectior, quia plus temporis in existendo perseveraverit; quippe rerum duratio ex earum essentia determinari nequit; quandoquidem rerum essentia nullum certum et determinatum existendi tempus involvit; sed res quaecunque, sive ea perfectior sit, sive minus, eadem vi, qua existere incipit, semper in existendo perseverare poterit, ita ut omnes hac in re aequales sint.'

necessity is and does. This conception serves as a pattern by which we estimate the goodness or badness—the moral value—of everything which comes under the scope of our ethical investigations.

(iii) But we have not yet freed Spinoza's position from obscurity. For from what has been said it would seem to follow that Spinoza regards the ideal human nature, and the distinctions between ' good' and ' bad ' which rest upon it, as purely arbitrary. *We* conceive a completely real essential nature of man : *we* take this as our pattern of perfection : *we* value all things by its standard. But every man, and every thing, is—in and for itself—completely and affirmatively real, and therefore completely ' perfect.' What right have we to select *our* conception of human nature as most real, to take *our* type as the standard of perfection ? All forms of human nature—and indeed all forms of modal being—seem equally real and equally perfect; and all standards appear equally arbitrary and false.

These objections rest upon a misunderstanding. Spinoza does not hold that all things *in and for themselves* are equally and completely real, or equally and completely perfect. Things are modes, and no mode *in and for itself* can be completely real or perfect. On the other hand, he does hold that all things *in and for themselves* are of necessity as real (and therefore as perfect) as they can be : and further, he maintains that Reality taken in its total being (i. e. *all things conceived in God*) is completely real and perfect.

But so long as we are treating of 'things' ('parts' of nature), we are not conceiving Reality in its completeness and totality, but as a system of modes : and for the modal apprehension (Spinoza always insists) there are degrees of reality or perfection, and indeed specific differences between the ' parts' of nature or the essences of things [1].

[1] Cf. above, p. 73, and pp. 108 ff.

Book III.   In his controversy with de Blyenbergh, Spinoza develops this conception of degrees (and specific differences) of reality as the basis of his ethical doctrine. All things depend absolutely upon God, and in that dependence alone they are real and perfect. But it does not follow—as de Blyenbergh had supposed—that all things are therefore reduced to a colourless uniformity. To make man real only in his dependence upon God does not make man 'like the stocks and stones': it does not deprive man of his essential nature—his power of self-conscious thought. On the contrary, it is in his dependence on God that man's essential being is realized.

The essential being—the distinctive character—of all things is realized in their dependence on God. And the nature of the dependence of all things on God is most clearly manifested in the dependence 'of the most real and perfect and intelligible things' on God. God is a God of the living more than of the dead. His absolute power is manifested most clearly in his control of the relatively self-dependent things. Now, the being of man is primarily the power to think[1]: and this, his essential being, is most fully realized in his dependence on God. Man attains to the fullest personality, or reality, or perfection, of which his nature is capable, in so far as God thinks in him; i. e. in so far as man is clearly conscious of himself and of all things in their union with God. In this 'consciousness of the union which his mind has with the whole of nature[2],' man realizes his essential being; and in *this* realization, therefore, Spinoza finds the ideal pattern of humanity. From this 'knowledge of God'—in which man's dependence

---

[1] i. e., the being of man's *mind*. This perfection of the mind is also of necessity a certain condition of the body. But Spinoza is throughout *primarily* concerned with the nature and ideal state of the mind.

[2] Cf. above, p. 4. TdIe, VVlL i. p. 6.

on God (and therefore man's essential nature) is realized in its completest form—there necessarily flows the 'love of God,' in which man's supreme happiness consists [1]. In proportion, therefore, as knowledge and love of God are absent, man misses his happiness, and his dependence on God sinks to a lower (non-human) level: or his reality is less. Thus, in falling short of the ideal human nature, man is missing (not an arbitrarily-conceived perfection, but) the full realization of himself.

Hence Spinoza—in answer to de Blyenbergh's challenge—places the difference between the 'good man' and the 'criminal' precisely in this difference of level (or rather, of kind) of their dependence on God. In a sense, both are absolutely dependent on God. What they do, they do necessarily, and realize themselves in so doing: more, they both 'serve' God, or fulfil their function in the universe by their works. But there is all the difference in the world between the levels of their dependence; in the value and importance of their 'service,' in the value of the 'virtus' which each exhibits, and in the degree of being or perfection which the nature of each expresses [2]. For the criminal, who 'neither knows nor loves God,' is—in his dependence on God—like an instrument in the hand of the craftsman, which serves his purpose unwittingly and is consumed in the service. He has no insight into his own nature or into the nature of things. But the good man in his dependence on God is—and knows himself to be—at one with the necessity which governs him. He is aware of the real significance of his actions, and is filled with the knowledge and love of the universe, in the order of which he is playing a necessary part. 'The good serve God consciously, and by serving him become more perfect'; for their knowledge and love are increased,

---

[1] Cf. Ep. 21, and below, ch. 3 and 4.
[2] Cf. Epp. 19, 23.

Book III. and their being or perfection *is* knowledge. Hence there is more of God in the good than in the wicked, just as there is more of God in the 'most perfect and intelligible things' than in 'stocks and stones[1].'

(iv) To the question 'why should I obey the laws of morality?' it is sometimes answered, 'to reap the rewards of the righteous, and escape the penalties of guilt: i. e. to please God, enter into the joys of heaven, and avoid the torments of hell.' But God is not a judge—not a *human* lawgiver and ruler magnified in wisdom and power. The question indeed, as formulated, is unanswerable, for it involves misconceptions as to human agency and freedom which we have already discarded, and it implies gross misunderstanding of the nature of happiness. The happiness or bliss of the righteous is not a state of being which may be added to them as the reward of their goodness: it is their goodness itself. The good man does not restrain his evil desires, and live a joyless life in this world, in order that he may attain to a happiness hereafter. The happiness or bliss, which is his in his knowledge and love of God, fills his mind and thus enables him to restrain his lusts[2]. The good man is good, because it is his nature to know and love God, and therefore to live in accordance with that knowledge. And the criminal is evil, because it is his nature to live by the half-light of imagination and to act accordingly. 'The upright man is he who stead-

---

[1] Cf. E. iv. App. cap. 31. In his controversy with de Blyenbergh, Spinoza *to some extent* accommodates his language to the theological position of his opponent. Hence—e. g.—he talks of man 'serving' God, and compares God to the 'artifex,' man to the 'instrumentum.' Some of this inaccurate phraseology necessarily clings to the above sketch of Spinoza's position. But Spinoza himself is fully aware (and warns de Blyenbergh) that all such expressions are from his point of view highly metaphorical. And, in fact, they can be disregarded without essentially affecting Spinoza's arguments.

[2] Cf. E. v. 42.

fastly desires that each should have his own: and in those, whose lives are guided by reason, this desire—as I prove in my "Ethics"—follows of necessity from their knowledge of themselves and of God. And since the thief has no such desire, he is necessarily so far without the knowledge of God and of himself, i.e. without that which principally constitutes our humanity. If you ask further "what can move me to do the works which you call 'virtue' rather than anything else?" I reply that I cannot possibly know which way out of the infinity of ways God may employ to determine you to act thus. It may be that God has impressed on you a clear idea of himself, so that you forget the world for the love of him, and love all other men as yourself: and it is plain that such a state of mind conflicts with all the other states which are called "evil," and therefore cannot coexist with them in one and the same subject[1].'

'The man, who avoids crime solely from the fear of punishment, in no sense works from love, and in no sense embraces virtue. As regards myself, I avoid—or rather strive to avoid—crimes, because they directly conflict with my own particular nature, and would make me to wander from the love and knowledge of God[2].'

Thus the difference between the good and the bad man is a difference of their nature. It is not a difference in the prudence of their calculations, nor a difference which depends upon their *choice* of the course to attain their happiness. The path which each follows is the inevitable result of the nature of each. Its 'goodness' or 'badness' depends upon the 'goodness' or 'badness' of the nature which it expresses: and the 'goodness' or 'badness' of that nature means its relative humanity— the degree of *human* reality which it contains. 'I do not introduce God as a judge; and therefore I value actions by their quality, and not according to the power

---

[1] Ep. 23.   [2] Ep. 21.

BOOK III. of the agent. And the reward, which follows the action, follows it as necessarily as it follows from the nature of a triangle that its three angles must be equal to two right angles[1].'

The line of thought, which has just been sketched, will occupy us in its development during the following chapters. But it is already clear what Spinoza understands by his standard of moral value. Every man acts of necessity according to his nature; and his actions are explicable either as the joint-effects of his own nature together with an infinity of other co-operative causes, or as the effects of his own nature only. The actions of the good and of the bad are alike necessary. They follow inevitably from the nature of the agent in the medium in which he lives and works. But the actions themselves differ inestimably in value according to the richness of being—the humanity of the nature—which they reveal. And though we cannot *blame* the criminal (for he acts necessarily and his nature is not of his own making), yet we can most certainly *pity* him: i.e. we must estimate his nature as infinitely less real, less human, than the ideal pattern of manhood.

(v) But—once more—we must remember that this difference in value, although not arbitrary, is yet dependent upon *our* comparison. In the light of a philosophical view, Reality is one and positive throughout. Every 'part' of nature is all that it can be—is real so far as lies in it to be. There is no defect, no error, no evil. Every part (i) *in its dependence upon the Whole* is absolutely and completely real, and (ii) *taken by itself* is

---

[1] Ep. 21; cf. E. v. 42 S.
Cf. also K. V. S. ii. 25, § 2. 'If we suppose—as some do—that the Devil is a thinking thing, who neither wills nor does anything whatever in any sense good, and therefore opposes God in every way, then the Devil is assuredly very miserable, and—if prayers could help—we ought to pray for his conversion.'

all that it claims to be. It is 'evil' or 'defective' to us, because we neither take it as it is, for what it asserts itself, nor in its necessary union with the Whole. We 'compare' it, and in the comparison throw it together with other things with which it has no real coherence: and then, in so far as it has not what they have, we suppose it to be a mutilated or defective instance of the nature which reveals itself 'more perfectly' in them.

Thus, e.g., the action of Nero in killing his mother, taken simply as something positive—as an external action realizing a determinate intention—was not a 'crime.' Orestes had a similar intention and realized it; yet Orestes is not accounted 'criminal,' or at least not to the same degree as Nero. The 'crime' of Nero consists in the ingratitude, pitilessness, disobedience which we attach to his action when we consider it as the behaviour of a son to his mother; but these defects or negations form no part of the positive nature of the action[1]. Looked at from the point of view of a clear and a complete apprehension, there is no moral quality in Nero's action: it is simply the expression of a certain human nature under the conditions of its medium. But if we look at it from the partial point of view of morality—if we compare it with the actions of other men in the light of the moral standard, and consider how much humanity it reveals—then we are bound to attach negations and defects to it; i.e. we are bound to condemn it.

Thus, it seems, there is nothing arbitrary in the moral standard. If you apply a moral standard at all, you *must* apply the standard Spinoza adopts; i.e. the conception of the most fully real human nature. But if you apply the moral standard, you are not considering the nature of things as such, or as it is for complete knowledge: you are considering their nature from a special point of view.

[1] Cf. Ep. 23.

Book III. The moral categories (we may perhaps express it) are not ultimate, not valid as metaphysical categories. But they are valid and objective within the limits of human conduct and life.

Yet the conceptions of good and bad, perfect and imperfect, true and false, are not for Spinoza on the same plane of validity. Goodness, perfection, truth have a real significance which he denies to evil, defect, and error. For the goodness of the good action (or the truth of the true idea) *is* its positive being. Every idea in its proper place and relations is 'true,' everything in its proper focus and position is 'perfect': for the truth of the idea is its positive content, the perfection of the thing is its being or reality. But every idea (except the idea of the Whole) and every thing (except the Whole) may be confusedly taken; taken for more than it is, or really claims to be; taken in wrong relations. And so far as it is *not* clearly conceived, *not* rightly apprehended, *not* what *our* expectations demand of it, it is 'false,' 'defective,' or 'bad.' Thus 'falsity' or 'badness' is no part of the essence of the false idea or the bad thing.

The form of evil, error, and crime does not consist in anything which expresses essence or being, and therefore God cannot be called its cause[1].' 'Sins and evil are nothing positive[2].'

The badness, therefore, which from a moral point of view we attribute—and attribute rightly—to certain actions, is no part of the actions themselves. The error or falsity, which a fuller knowledge discerns in the confusions of a lower grade of apprehension, is no part of the content of that apprehension itself. A false idea is taken up into a wider or more adequate one:—but the 'falsity' vanishes in that supplementation (if that can be said to 'vanish' which never was), for it was nothing but absence of what the supplementation supplies. Similarly,

[1] Ep. 23.   [2] Ep. 19.

the desires, which in a poorer nature issue in actions that we from our richer humanity condemn as 'bad,' are absorbed in the fuller being and enter into the completer activity of the richer human nature. In that absorption the desires retain what reality they possessed: but they do not appear as 'bad,' for 'badness' was no part of them. It is in this way that the passional content of the imaginative life is transformed into the life of reason in which all 'passion' has become free activity [1].

Thus, whereas complete knowledge is completely 'true,' and whereas everything in so far as it involves any affirmative being *is* 'perfect'; 'falsity' and 'evil' (or imperfection) *do not 'belong' even to partial knowledge and partial or finite being.* They are mere negations and defects which attach to partial knowledge *which poses* as complete (or completer than it is), and to imperfect forms of humanity which yet *claim to be* human: 'claim to be,' that is, *for us* who group all men under the universal idea of humanity, and compare them with our conception of the pattern of manhood [2].

(vi) The finite and the infinite, the false and the true, the evil and the good, *are* not on the same level of being. There can therefore be no 'relation' and no 'conflict' between them, nor again any 'progress' from one to the other, nor any 'deduction' of one from the other [3]. The only Real is the infinite, which as completely real is completely perfect, and as infinite apprehension is completely true. The finite and imperfect, the partial and erroneous apprehension, are not as such real, but limitations of the Real. Man, *quâ* 'imaginative,' *quâ* working towards true knowledge and his ideal perfection —in his finite humanity, in short—is *not* himself. His 'self,' his 'reality,' or his 'truth' is the divinity which he

---

[1] Cf. above, pp. 165 ff., and below, ch. 3; E. iv. 1; iv. 59.
[2] Cf. e.g. E. ii. 35, 43 S.
[3] Cf. above, pp. 141 ff.; Brunschvicg, pp. 178 ff.

expresses: expresses clearly in his complete self-realization, in his imperfection obscurely and imperfectly. As full knowledge contains within itself in a harmonious form the truth of the lesser apprehension, and *is* all that there was of positive thought in that lower stage; so the human mind in its complete activity (in that intuitive understanding which is God's thought thinking in man) absorbs and sustains, whilst it completes and renders fully true, the inferior stages of imaginative experience and the abstract scientific consciousness. Thus, what appears as a progress from 'imaginatio' through 'ratio' to 'cognitio intuitiva,' is the gradual self-revelation of the complete human mind. The lower stages are absorbed in the 'progress': for the progress is the negation of the limitations which constituted them.

The movement from 'imaginatio' to 'cognitio intuitiva' may correctly be called 'dialectical[1],' inasmuch as the advance annihilates its starting-point. It is not a progress from one positive state to another, but the freeing of the only real and positive state by the removal of the barriers which obscured its expression. It is the breaking of complete knowledge through the form of incomplete apprehension: the manifestation of the nothingness of the imaginative stage so far as it was imaginative, i.e. incomplete.

The same principle applies to every side of Spinoza's theory. The world of imaginative experience—the world of 'things,' the 'communis ordo naturae'—is *real* only in so far as it is obscurely and in part 'natura naturata.' When its limitations are removed, it shows itself first as the world of science—a world of objective necessary universal laws. A further removal of unreal (and therefore obscuring) negations shows the world of science as what it really is. Freed from the abstraction of its universality, it reveals itself as the eternal concrete being of God, the

[1] Brunschvicg, l. c.

# EVIL AND ERROR

Reality apprehended by 'cognitio intuitiva.' So, the ideal life for man (his life as an immediate mode or state of God, the life in which God lives in him and he knows himself one with God) is the reality of human nature. It is this, of which the lower stages of apparent human personality are the obscure and imperfect manifestations. From the lowest grade, in which (as e. g. in the criminal) there is hardly a *human* self at all—through the grades of increasing being, in which man wins himself and becomes an agent, instead of being the mere plaything of forces alien and unintelligible to himself—the 'progress' is *unreal*: for the forms, which the developing nature puts off, are constituted by negations which do not really belong to it. It is the real humanity which is breaking through in the apparent development: and that from which it develops is a stage of itself, which (so far as it is anything real or positive) is no starting-point distinct from the final perfection, but is that final perfection itself.

(vii) But though I believe that this interpretation of the Ethics is right, I do not for a moment imagine that the result is an adequate theory of things. On the contrary, if we have cleared away some superficial difficulties and misunderstandings, we have also thrown into relief the main problems which beset Spinoza's position.

I do not wish to dwell on a point which I have already emphasized too often. Illusion, error, and evil are 'facts' in some sense real, and facts which will not come into harmony with Spinoza's conception of the general nature of Reality. Absence of knowledge becomes 'error,' imperfection of human nature becomes 'sin,' only when the one *poses* as complete, the other *claims* to be human. The *pose* and the *claim* constitute the distinctive characters of error and sin; and they are not mere 'negations.' We, in our error and sin and suffering, are not merely *without* fuller knowledge and a larger humanity. The defects involve a positive character in us: and we, in our actual limitations and shortcomings, with our prejudices and obstinate self-will, are *something* for ourselves. And even if this experience of ourselves is illusory, the illusoriness itself is part and parcel of the experience and cannot be conjured away. For, since we are parts of the Reality, our experience—illusoriness and all—is in the end a portion of God's experience. But the God, who is timeless complete and positive Reality, cannot be conceived as the ground of evil, error, or illusion[1]. *As we experience them*, they are in respect to such a God 'mere negations': and yet *as we experience them*, they have a distinctive character and are in some sense real. Nor will it help us to regard evil and error as incomplete stages of life and knowledge which are 'mere moments in a dialectical process.' For even a 'dialectical process' must fall within the Reality. If the process is illusory, some one must experience the illusion. His illusory experience is a fact, and must be grounded in a positive feature of the Reality. In short, 'error' and 'evil' are not 'mere negations'—as Spinoza himself is well aware[2]. They involve a *pose* and a *claim* which distinguish them from the 'less adequate truth' and the 'less complete good.' But this *pose* and *claim*, which constitute the distinctive nature of error and evil, can neither be grounded in the Reality as Spinoza conceives it, nor be dismissed as mere illusions. For the former alternative would bring imperfection and defect into the nature of God, whilst the latter would leave the illusion itself as inexplicable as the 'facts' it was intended to explain.

[1] Cf. above, pp. 111 ff.   [2] Cf. e. g. E. ii. 35 dem.

## CHAPTER II

MAN AS A MEMBER OF THE 'COMMUNIS ORDO NATURAE'—THE BONDAGE OF MAN

§ 1. THE STRENGTH OF THE PASSIVE EMOTIONS, AND THE RELATIVE POWERLESSNESS OF THE ACTIVE EMOTIONS.

WE are said to suffer 'passive emotions' in so far as we are only the partial or inadequate cause of what we feel and do[1]. We are therefore inevitably liable to the passions, so far as we are a 'part of nature, which cannot be conceived by itself in separation from other parts[2].' And it is impossible that man should ever cease to be a part: impossible, therefore, that he should ever attain to a state in which all the changes that he experiences in himself, and all the actions which follow from him, should be explicable as the effects solely of his own nature[3].

In other words, man can never entirely rise above the 'common order of nature,' and become an unaffected spectator of the infinite complex of causes and effects which determines all the events in the world of imagination. He can never cease 'to follow and obey the common order of nature, and to accommodate himself to it so far as it requires of him[4].' Man is, and must always to some extent remain, a plaything of the forces of his environment, at the mercy of the changes and

---

[1] Above, pp. 199 ff.
[2] E. iv. 2.
[3] E. iv. 4.
[4] E. iv. 4 C.

Book III. chances of the order of the world in which—as an imaginative being—he lives[1].

The essential nature of man is a force which makes for self-assertion: so far as man is anything at all, he tends to affirm and maintain his being. But everything which in any sense *is*, tends in the same way to affirm its being. Hence man's 'conatus' is a 'striving-to-be,' which is in conflict with an infinity of other 'strivings-to-be.' Moreover, since 'there can be no single thing in nature than which there is not another single thing more powerful and stronger[2],' the 'force, whereby man perseveres in existence,' is not only limited, but also indefinitely surpassed, by the power of external causes[3]. Now the passive emotions owe their origin and essential being (and therefore also their force, their development, and their persistence) chiefly to the nature of the external causes which excite them in us. Hence the strength and persistence of a passion is determined (*not* by our limited power of self-assertion, but) by the power of the external causes: and this power, in comparison with our own, is indefinitely great. Consequently, a passion may completely overwhelm us. It may entirely dominate our personality and we may become its slaves[4].

Since an emotion is an affection of the body as well as an ideal modification[5], it follows that to check or remove an emotion requires a contrary and stronger emotion; mere knowledge, an idea *quâ* idea, is of no avail. On its psychical side, an emotion is an idea whereby the mind affirms a greater or less vitality of its body: but the psychical side of an emotion is never present apart from the corporeal modification which, together with it, constitutes the whole emotional state.

---

[1] Cf. above, pp. 141 ff.; pp. 166 ff.; pp. 177 ff.
[2] E. iv. Ax.  [3] E. iv. 3.
[4] E. iv. 5, 6.  [5] Above, p. 201.

No reflective idea, therefore, *except in so far as it is also itself a factor in an emotional state*—the ideal modification which expresses a modification of the subject's body—can suppress or eradicate any emotion [1].

Now anything which helps or hinders our being, or which increases or lessens our power of acting, is necessarily an object of our desire or aversion. And what we desire is 'good,' what we avoid 'evil' [2]. But so far as we feel pleasure or pain, and so far as we desire, we can also be aware of these our feelings and desires: for consciousness in man can always be turned upon itself, and become self-consciousness [3]. Hence an emotion of pleasure or pain may carry with it the reflective idea of that emotion; and the 'knowledge of good and evil' is simply an emotional state of which we are reflectively conscious [4]. Here, then, we seem to have a remedy to check or suppress the overmastering passions. We have a reflective idea as to our good and evil which may become a true knowledge, i. e. a reflective idea of what

---

[1] E. iv. 7, and C.—On the obscurity in Spinoza's account of emotional ideas, cf. above, pp. 236 ff.
[2] E. iii. 9 S.; E. iv. deff. 1, 2.
[3] Above, pp. 132 ff.
[4] Cf. E. iv. 8, and dem. '... atque adeo boni et mali cognitio nihil aliud est, quam Laetitiae vel Tristitiae idea, quae ex ipso Laetitiae vel Tristitiae affectu necessario sequitur (*per Prop. 22. p. 2*). At haec idea eodem modo unita est affectui, ac Mens unita est Corpori (*per Prop. 21. p. 2*); hoc est (*ut in Schol. eiusdem Prop. ostensum*), haec idea ab ipso affectu, sive (*per gen. Affect. Defin.*) ab idea Corporis affectionis, revera non distinguitur, nisi solo conceptu; ergo haec cognitio boni et mali nihil est aliud, quam ipse affectus, quatenus eiusdem sumus conscii. Q. E. D.'

Spinoza is concerned to show that self-consciousness is a necessary result of consciousness:— i. e. that the 'idea ideae' requires only the first 'idea' for its explanation. He does not consider whether *actual* human consciousness is necessarily also self-consciousness. But *in God*—i. e. in the completeness of the Attribute of Thought—every idea is necessarily turned upon itself. The mind of man, *so far as it is a self-contained thought of God*, is necessarily self-conscious. Cf. above, pp. 132 ff., below, p. 302.

is really good and bad for us. And this knowledge is on one side of itself an emotional state, and therefore capable of fighting against the passive emotions.

But the value of this 'knowledge of good and evil' to a man who is struggling with the passions is not so great as at first appears. So far as it is merely a reflective emotion, it is on the same plane as the other passions, each of which in man is (or may be) an object of reflective consciousness. Inasmuch, indeed, as the reflective knowledge which it involves is adequate, it is an emotional state directed to our true good. The actions, which follow from it, are *our* actions; and in carrying out the desires based upon it[1], we are *free*. But its power to control our lives does not depend in the least upon its truth or reflective character: its strength in the conflict with the other competing *affectus* is measured solely by its emotional intensity[2]. And its emotional strength is merely that of one amongst an indefinite number of emotional forces, which, under the circumstances of our imaginative life, are for many reasons liable to overcome it.

For (i) the desires, which are based upon the passive emotions, draw their strength from the external causes to which they owe (in part) their origin: whilst the desire based upon the 'true knowledge of good and evil' derives its emotional intensity solely from our own essential being. Its force, therefore, is measured by the limitations of human nature[3]. (ii) The constant changes and chances of the present are always rousing passive emotions in us. As felt at what is present and actual, these are more intense and occupy our attention more than any emotion connected with a future occurrence. The *quality* of the emotions, it is true[4], remains unaltered, whether they are presented under the form of

---

[1] For from it, as from every *affectus*, there necessarily arises a *cupiditas*; cf. E. iv. 15 dem.

[2] E. iv. 14, and dem.

[3] E. iv. 15, and dem.

[4] Cf. above, p. 214.

present, past, or future time: but their *intensity* is greatly affected[1]. An emotion felt towards an object, which is pictured as past or future, is *ceteris paribus* weaker than an emotion felt towards an object actually present; and its intensity fades directly in proportion to the remoteness in time of the object. The only qualification of this rule is that, when a certain degree of remoteness in time is passed, all objects beyond are pictured as equally distant, and all emotions connected with them become indistinguishably and equally faint[2].

It follows that the desire for our true good, which is based upon adequate knowledge, so far as it has reference to a future state or occurrence, is proportionally fainter than our desires for things which appeal to us immediately as pleasant[3].

And (iii) an emotion towards a thing which we picture as necessary is *ceteris paribus* more intense than an emotion towards a thing which we picture as 'possible' or 'contingent'—i.e. a thing, which we do not know to be necessarily existent or necessarily non-existent, whether we consider the external causes which determine its existence or its own essential nature[4]. And an emotion towards a thing which we know not to be actual, but which we picture as possible, is *ceteris paribus* more intense than an emotion towards a thing which we know not to be actual, but picture as contingent[5]. *A fortiori* an emotion towards an object pictured as present is much stronger than an emotion towards an object which we know not to be present, but picture (not as possible, but merely) as contingent[6]. Indeed an emotion towards a contingent object is the weakest of all; weaker even than an emotion towards a past event[7].

[1] E. iv. 9 S.
[2] E. iv. 10, and S.; iv. def. 6, note.
[3] E. iv. 16.
[4] E. iv. 11; iv. deff. 3, 4.
[5] E. iv. 12.
[6] E. iv. 12 C.
[7] E. iv. 13. Things are 'con-

Book III.   So far, therefore, as our desire which is based on the 'true knowledge of our good and evil' has reference to objects pictured as merely contingent, it is most easily repressed by any chance desire excited in us by objects presented as actual [1].

We can now understand why the 'true knowledge of good and evil,' though it has an emotional basis, influences us so little in our actual life. True knowledge is unaffected by time, and if we were living a purely intelligent life, we should have a just appreciation of the relative significance of all its events. Their existence and duration would be adequately apprehended: and the imaginative distinctions of 'past,' 'present,' and 'future' would not deceive us in our judgements of the intrinsic qualities of our experiences. The 'knowledge of our true good' would exercise an emotional power corresponding to its truth.

But in our actual lives we are influenced by things which we apprehend imaginatively and not intelligently. For such an imaginative apprehension it makes all the difference whether the object which excites emotion is pictured as past, present, or future. These temporal differences are the forms in which our imaginative consciousness confusedly apprehends the duration or existence of things [2], and the intensity of our emotional states depends largely upon them. Hence the 'true

---

tingent,' 'possible,' and 'actual' (as contrasted with necessary) only for the imaginative consciousness. A thing is 'contingent' for us, so far as we know merely that there is no inherent impossibility in its conception: 'possible,' so far as *in addition* the causes, which determine its existence, are not known to be actually determined to produce it, or again to exclude its existence. The degree of ignorance, which is involved in the conception of a thing as 'contingent,' is thus greater than that involved in the conception of a thing as 'possible.' Cf. above, p. 60, note 5.

[1] E. iv. 17.
[2] Cf. above, p. 168.

knowledge of good and evil' does not penetrate below
the surface of our actual lives. It remains an abstract,
universal, scientific truth, which is not realized or felt by
us in the details of our emotional struggles. We desire
our true good and are reflectively aware of this desire.
We formulate this as a general principle: but it remains
a *mere* general principle, a 'pious wish.' Hence it has
but little influence on the actions of our everyday life.
For we picture our true good as future and merely
contingent: and the emotional force of this idea is over-
whelmed by the more intense emotions excited by the
objects, which we picture as present [1].

It would seem, therefore, that such knowledge is useless
where it is most required. It cannot check the passions
of the moment; for it does not teach us to weigh proba-
bilities and to sacrifice the momentary pleasure to the
more permanent satisfaction, which we can picture only
as contingent. And where the knowledge is powerful—
i. e. when it is the reflective consciousness of our desire
for a *present* good—the desire itself does all the work,
the reflective idea is (for practical purposes) a mere otiose
accompaniment. The 'true knowledge of good and evil,'
indeed, not only often succumbs to all the forms of lust;
it actually increases our trouble and pain, by stirring up
unprofitable conflict in our souls; a conflict in which it,
as an emotional state, is too weak to win the victory [2].

### § 2. THE LIFE OF MAN AS INTELLECTUALLY AND MORALLY IN BONDAGE.

Imaginative experience is characterized by its arbitrariness. So far as we are confined to imaginative
apprehension, our views of things are formed *in us* and
not *by us*, and formed with a personal and peculiar

---

[1] Cf. E. iv. 62 and S.   [2] Cf. E. iv. 17 S.

Book III. colouring which depends in the main upon our past circumstances and present environment. The imaginative consciousness is in fact a consciousness without principles of synthesis or order of its own. Its contents are incoherent, or at least their coherence is—so far as the subject is concerned—arbitrary and contingent. And the world, as it exists for such a mind, is correspondingly unintelligible, arbitrarily coherent, devoid of rational order and law. In imaginative experience each man lives in his own personal world, which has been constructed for him by chance conjunctions and on principles of which he is in no sense the originator and which he cannot grasp. He lives in a world centred—if *for him* it is centred at all—round his personal prejudices, his likes and dislikes. The distinctive advance of the scientific consciousness lies in the substitution of universal, necessary, objective principles of construction for these subjective, arbitrary, and personal rules of synthesis; in the conception of a Reality one and the same for all thinking beings, and in the attempt to grasp the principles of its interrelation and necessary coherence [1]. Now the 'life of passion' is the practical side of imaginative experience, the intellectual aspect of which Spinoza has described in Part II of the Ethics. In the 'life of passion' the same characteristics, which marked the imaginative apprehension, reveal themselves. So far as men are controlled by the passive emotions, they live in (possible and probable) isolation. Each is driven by the influences which happen to affect him; and there is nothing to guarantee harmony and agreement in their lives. On the contrary, there is every chance, not only that they will come into hostility one with another—for many of the passions are directed to objects, the joint enjoyment of which is impossible—but also that they will live in constant conflict with themselves [2]. They

[1] Cf. above, pp. 170 ff.     [2] E. iv. 32–4.

## THE LIFE OF PASSION

have, in fact, no real 'self,' no genuinely unified personality. They are 'individuals' and 'one' through an aggregation and coherence of their elements, which is brought about by the chance pressure of their environment, rather than through any inner principle of union. For they do not control their own lives by the rational and adequate knowledge of their true good; they are the victims of every fresh desire, as it arises from the feelings of pleasure or pain which the influences of the moment excite in them[1].

It is this want of personality, this nightmare-like subjection to any and every chance influence, which makes the 'life of passion' so unsatisfactory. There is a want of reality in us, a want of consistency and unity in our being, and a complete absence of conscious control of our lives. We are slaves of innumerable and constantly-changing masters. Add to this, that we are driven as much by pain in all its forms as by pleasure (our desires are based on emotions of *tristitia* as much as on those of *laetitia*), and the picture is nearly complete. Nearly; but not quite. For there is a yet more miserable form of the life of passion, in which all humanity seems to be lost.

It sometimes happens that one passion becomes overmastering. A man becomes ridden by e. g. lust of money, lust of power, or sexual lust, just as a madman becomes possessed by a fixed idea. In such a case the victim is really insane. 'Avarice, ambition, lust, &c. are forms of madness, although they are not commonly counted amongst the diseases[2].'

---

[1] The pleasure which they feel is as a rule the increased vitality of some part of their body and mind at the expense of the whole: *titillatio* as distinguished from *hilaritas*, the term which Spinoza employs to express the *laetitia* of the man who lives the rational life. Cf. E. iv. 42, 43.

[2] E. iv. 44 S.

# CHAPTER III

## THE MORAL LIFE AS THE LIFE OF REASON

### § 1. INDIVIDUALITY IN THE GRADE OF 'RATIO.'

BOOK III. REALITY for the scientific consciousness is an objective system of necessary laws. Distinctions of time and place, and the uniqueness of being in the parts of the Whole which these distinctions indicate, have vanished. And the mind of the man of science has undergone a corresponding change. It is no longer the associated complex of unique feelings and opinions—the accidentally-coloured aggregate of reminiscences—which constituted the loose 'personality' of the stage of imagination. All the feelings and ideas which were uniquely 'ours'—which were due to the unique set of conditions in which each of us had lived and developed—have been purified away as such. Our mind, in the stage of 'ratio,' is an organized system of coherent truths, the principle of their coherence being the common principle of all legitimate deductive reasoning. 'We,' so far as our mind is concerned, are simply and solely the 'intellectus': i.e. the necessarily-interconnected logical system of adequate ideas. And (since our corporeal being *is* that of which our mental being is the idea) 'we,' body and mind, are resolved into the Attributes of Extension and Thought: our body and our mind are modes of Extension and Thought conceived in their necessary modal dependence, as 'essences.' Our mind, or our 'self,' is that common permanent being, which characterizes all intelligences in their essential nature: our body is that common extended nature, of which all human intelligences are as such the apprehension[1].

Our 'self' therefore (as the 'self' of 'ratio') is the reality, of which the 'self' of imagination was the partly-illusory appearance. We have gained reality and permanence: but we have also gained universality. *What we are* is now identical with what every one, so far as he is in the stage of 'ratio,' is. The 'element' of 'ratio' is common to all rational beings, and their essential being is one and indistinguishable. Their intellectual life is one and the same, and their practical life exhibits a corresponding identity. Imaginative individuality, which separated man from man, was constituted by peculiarities ultimately due to differences of time and place. These have revealed themselves as not real—as mere negations—and have therefore vanished. And it seems as if they have carried with them all individuality: as if, when once the illusory barriers have fallen, nothing remains but the all-complete Thought and Extension of God. Or at least it seems as if human nature *in the abstract*, human intelligence *as such*, the human body *in general* alone are left to constitute man's 'individuality.'

Now, if 'individuality' means that which separates from everything else, it is certainly true that, so far as man lives in the stage of 'ratio,' he has lost his individuality. The more man is what he is for science, the more he reveals his identity with all other men, and the more his being is (for himself and for others) the 'humanity' common to all men.

And further, it is true that *for science* this 'humanity' remains to a great extent an abstraction. The essential nature of the mind and the essential nature of the body are—so far as the scientific consciousness can carry us—

[1] Above, pp. 175 ff.

Book III. universals which have not revealed their concreteness. If, in the stage of 'ratio,' man becomes *one* with all men; if, in his scientific intelligence, he becomes *one* with God's Thought, and in his corporeal being *one* with God's Extension, this 'oneness' is the unity of mere absorption. Man's 'being' is merged in the nature of things: and the nature of things, so to speak, does not give him anything back. Man's 'self' is swallowed up in that abyss of abstract identity which, as some critics would have us believe, Spinoza calls God.

But these difficulties disappear on a more careful consideration of Spinoza's conception of 'ratio.' Science is the first attempt to think clearly: and the universe of science is the first intelligible reality; i. e. reality as it first emerges for a consciousness which has begun to think, to construct a consistent experience. Hence, as we saw [1], the scientific consciousness, though true so far as it goes, goes a very small way in understanding the nature of things. Science is 'abstract': not, indeed, in the sense that its universals are mere abstractions (like the 'notiones universales' of imagination), but in the sense that their concrete content remains for it implicit. Thus e. g., 'the essential nature of man' or 'humanity' is not for science a mere picture-universal: it is not obtained by superimposing the 'images' of this, that, and the other man, omitting the differences of the fringe, and emphasizing the central portion in which the pictures coalesce. It is a genuine universal conception, constructed by deduction from the laws of Thought and Extension: a synthesis (on logical principles) of the simpler ideas, the 'common properties' of minds and bodies. But science cannot articulate this universal into the concrete system of 'essential natures,' which would explicitly express its content. Such an articulation would reveal the intimate individuality of each man as an essential

[1] Above, pp. 175 ff.

character, which contributed its distinctive share in the formation and maintenance of the common medium of all men's being—'the essential nature of man' or 'humanity'[1].

So again, for science the essential nature of the human mind remains adequate thinking, the intelligence as such. Science cannot articulate this universal. It cannot show how the adequate thinking, which constitutes this and that mind, contributes its own significance to the totality of true thought; how this, its distinctive significance, together with all other distinctive intelligences, constitutes the complete content of God's complete understanding[2]. It is *scientia intuitiva*—the complete knowledge of the 'philosophic' consciousness—which fulfils the work of science by the intelligible reconstruction of the universe in some such way as this. And we shall see that in the stage of *scientia intuitiva* man is real with a permanent and genuine individuality[3].

Hence, the scientific consciousness is a half-way stage in the emergence of perfect understanding; and the life of reason is a half-way realization of ideal human nature. The scientific thinker or rational agent has not, as such, realized his complete and permanent being. He has not attained to the 'individuality' with which he consciously fulfils the unity of God, and, in so doing, grows to his full stature, his distinct (though not separate or isolated) 'self.' On the other hand, he has not shaken himself entirely free from his imaginative individuality which separates him from other men. His scientific thinking and his reasonable or moral conduct take place on an 'imaginative' or 'passional'

---

[1] The 'essentia' of a thing is exactly coextensive with it (E. ii. def. 2). The 'common notions' of science 'nullius rei singularis essentiam explicant' (E. ii. 44 C.

[2] dem.). Cf. also above, pp. 177 ff.

[2] Cf. E. v. 40 S.

[3] Cf. below, ch. 4.

background. In the Fourth Part of the Ethics, Spinoza is describing the knowledge and life of man at a stage in which adequate ideas control his conduct, but do not fill his whole consciousness: at a stage in which he has neither left imaginative experience completely behind him, nor passed beyond the 'abstract' truth of science to the concrete truth of *scientia intuitiva*.

### § 2. GENERAL PRINCIPLES OF THE LIFE OF 'REASON,' 'VIRTUE,' OR 'FREEDOM.'

*The rational is the moral or free life.*

(1) It is the essential nature of everything to strive for its own maintenance. In asserting itself, it exhibits its power: and its power is its virtue [1]. The ultimate and unique basis of all virtue in man is therefore the *conatus sese conservandi*: on the natural and inevitable tendency to self-affirmation is grounded the whole moral life of man. If we desire *to be happy*, we must first desire *to be*. And this desire *to be*—to secure our own advantage, to maintain our life and health—is the inevitable expression of our nature. We show our power (and therefore our virtue) in this endeavour and its success [2].

But in so far as what we do follows from inadequate ideas in us, it is in part the expression of what is not ourselves. It manifests, therefore, not our power or virtue, but the power of external causes. Man exhibits his true nature, power or virtue, only in so far as his actions follow from his intelligence or reason—from his adequate ideas. The life of virtue is thus for Spinoza the life of reason: the moral life is the practical aspect

---

[1] E. iv. def. 8: 'Per virtutem et potentiam idem intelligo; hoc est (*per Prop. 7. p. 3*), virtus, quatenus ad hominem refertur, est ipsa hominis essentia seu natura, quatenus potestatem habet quaedam efficiendi, quae per solas ipsius naturae leges possunt intelligi.'

[2] E. iv. 20, 21, 22 and C.

of the scientific apprehension. And it exhibits a corresponding independence in the agent. The scientific thinker constructs his world for himself in accordance with the laws of his own (and all) intelligence. The morally-good agent lives the life of freedom, i.e. the life which is controlled by the laws of intelligence or reason. The moral life is that in which *our* mind controls all that we do [1]. And *our* mind is our intelligence, for it is *ours* in so far as its ideas are adequate. For when we think adequately (and only then), God is thinking in us *in so far as he constitutes the essential nature of our mind* [2].

In living the life of reason, therefore, we are manifesting our power and our virtue, our freedom and our agency: we are realizing and asserting our own nature. And, since reason (which *is* our self) can demand nothing contrary to nature [3], in following the guidance of reason we are inevitably seeking and securing our true advantage. Hence Spinoza can say, 'Ex virtute absolute agere nihil aliud in nobis est, quam ex ductu Rationis agere, vivere, suum esse conservare (haec tria idem significant) ex fundamento proprium utile quaerendi [4].' And hence we have a perfect right—an absolute 'natural right'—to remove what we judge to be 'bad' (i.e. a hindrance to our true expediency, the rational life), and to secure and use what we judge to be 'good' (i.e. useful to maintain our being and our enjoyment of the rational life) [5].

---

[1] Cf. above, pp. 199 ff.; 218 ff.; E. iv. 73; Tr. P. 2, § 11 'Atque adeo hominem eatenus liberum omnino voco, quatenus Ratione ducitur, quia eatenus ex causis, quae per solam eius naturam possunt adaequate intelligi, ad agendum determinatur; tametsi ex iis necessario ad agendum determinetur. Nam libertas ... agendi necessitatem non tollit, sed ponit.'

[2] Cf. above, p. 130, and E. ii. 11 C.

[3] E. iv. 18 S.

[4] E. iv. 24.

[5] E. iv. App. cap. 8.

BOOK III.
The end of the free man is to know and love God.

(2) The 'end,' which a man sets himself, is the content or 'what' of his desire: and his desire is the expression of his nature. The nature of the 'free man' is intelligence. His desire is the expression of his intelligence or adequate ideas. His 'end,' therefore, is the maintenance and development of his intelligence.

For man *that* is truly advantageous, which tends to promote his 'enjoyment of the life of his mind': i.e. which serves to advance his power of true thinking, to maintain and expand his intelligence. 'The ultimate end of the man who is guided by reason (i.e. the supreme desire by which he studies to control all his other desires) is to conceive adequately himself and all things which can fall under his intelligence[1].'

But adequate knowledge implies knowledge of God: for without God nothing can be or be conceived. 'The supreme good of the mind, therefore, is the knowledge of God, and its supreme virtue is knowing God[2].' Hence the ultimate end of the free man is to know God.

Further, in the consciousness of his own intelligence, man is conscious of his own power, i.e. of his own increasing vitality. This consciousness is an active emotion of pleasure. In it he realizes that 'peace of mind' which arises from clear knowledge and is the highest form of self-satisfaction, the supreme happiness which man can enjoy[3]. And, since the perfection of the free man's intelligence involves the knowledge of God as the ground of all things, in the increase of his intelligence his love of God increases. For, the more he knows, the more he enjoys his own power and the more

[1] E. iv. App. capp. 4, 5; iv. 26, and dem.; iv. 27.
[2] E. iv. 28, and dem.
[3] E. iv. 52: 'Acquiescentia in se ipso ex Ratione oriri potest, et ea sola acquiescentia, quae ex Ratione oritur, summa est, quae potest dari.' Ib. iv. 52 S.: 'Est revera acquiescentia in se ipso summum, quod sperare possumus.'

he knows God as the source of that power, i.e. the more **Chap. III.** his mind is filled with the love of God[1].

Thus, the 'end' of the free man is the 'knowledge of God,' 'the adequate knowledge of himself and of all things which can come under his intelligence,' or 'the knowledge of the union which his mind has with the whole of nature[2].' In the attainment of this end, he enjoys the highest and most permanent happiness of which human nature is capable, the most perfect 'peace of mind' for which we can hope; and he is filled with the love of God as the author of that happiness.

(3) This ideal is one in which all men can share. It is, indeed, an essential feature of the free man's end that all other men should, so far as may be, attain to the same level of being as himself. The knowledge of God is a 'good,' which all men, so far as they are men, can enjoy: for 'it belongs to the essence of the human mind to have an adequate knowledge of the eternal and infinite essence of God[3].' The good, which the free or rational man desires, is good for human nature *as such*. Hence, so far as men are guided by reason, they necessarily agree in their natures. There is nothing in the nature of things more serviceable to man than his fellow men, so far as all are controlled by reason; and the more each seeks his own good, the more all forward one another's true interests[4]. The shallow misanthropy of the pessimists, the empty ridicule of the satirists, and the other-worldliness of the priests, all are refuted by the facts. A sane judgement of life bears irrefutable witness to the need of men for one another, and to the value of human society for the realization of the ideal[5].

*The end of the free man is common to all men*

---

[1] Cf. E. iv. App. cap. 4 (which refers to the 'intuitive knowledge' which is the completion of 'ratio'); v. 15-20, and 20 S. Cf. also below, ch. 4.

[2] Cf. above, p. 4.

[3] E. iv. 36 and S.; above, p. 4 (VVIL. i. pp. 5, 6).

[4] E. iv. 35, with C. 1 and 2.

[5] E. iv. 35 S.; App. cap. 7.

Book III. It is the passions which isolate men and bring them into conflict. It is finite goods which arouse jealousy and anxieties [1]. The knowledge and love of God unite all men in their pursuit. So far as any man lives the life of reason, power, virtue or freedom, and sets knowledge before him as his 'good,' he must—by the nature of the case—endeavour to further the attainment of the same good in other men; and the more, the more he himself has attained [2].

From this point of view, certain terms acquire a definite meaning. We are said to be *religious*, so far as our desires and actions originate from the knowledge of God. We are said to manifest a *love of duty* (*pietas*), so far as reason governs our endeavours to benefit our fellow men [3]. The desire which impels a man, who lives by the guidance of reason, to win the friendship of others is called a *sense of honour*[4]. *Honourable* means that which men, who live by the guidance of reason, approve: *disgraceful* or *base* that which conflicts with the friendly relations of such men [5].

The basis and motives of the rational life are emotions of pleasure.

(4) If we feel sorrow or pain, our vitality or power is being diminished. If we feel pleasure or joy, our vitality is being increased: we are more real, more ourselves, or have a greater share in the divine nature [6]. All pleasure (provided it indicates an increased vitality of our whole being, and not merely of a part at the expense of the rest) is good. The rational life is the

---

[1] E. iv. 37 S. 1, and VVlL. i. p. 5.

[2] E. iv. 37: 'Bonum, quod unusquisque, qui sectatur virtutem, sibi appetit, reliquis hominibus etiam cupiet, et eo magis, quo maiorem Dei habuerit cognitionem.'

[3] A form of 'pietas' is *modestia*: cf. above, p. 219, note 2;

and E. iv. 37 S. 1, App. cap. 25. 'Patriotism' covers a part of the meaning of *pietas*: but there is no satisfactory English equivalent.

[4] 'Honestas'—the impulse of fairness or honourable dealing, which wins respect.

[5] E. iv. 37 S. 1.

[6] Cf. e. g. E. iv. App. cap. 31.

life of freedom or action. It presupposes, therefore, as its condition increased vitality in the agent, and as its motive the agent's consciousness of his increasing vitality, i. e. active emotions of pleasure.

Hence the motive and basis of all actions of the rational life is the positive desire for good, and not the negative avoidance of evil. For, so far as our motive is the avoidance of evil, we are influenced by feelings of pain; i. e. we are not 'active,' not manifesting our power or virtue, but controlled by passive emotions, exhibiting want of power, depression of vitality[1]. It is the sick man who eats from fear of death: the healthy man enjoys his food. So it is the diseased moral nature that does good from fear of evil. The free man acts from the joy of acting. His 'wisdom is a meditation of life, and not of death[2].'

It is superstition (not true religion) that advocates self-abasement, that regards this world as a place of sin and sorrow, and that frowns on the pleasures of life. The free man will endeavour, so far as in him lies, 'bene agere et laetari[3].'

## § 3. APPLICATION OF THE ABOVE PRINCIPLES.

The rational life is the life of intelligence, i. e. the life in which all man's desires and actions are based on his adequate ideas, or follow from his own essential nature as a thinking being. Everything of which man is, in this sense, the efficient cause, is necessarily 'good' for him; for it is the expression of his own self-assertive force, the explication of his essential being. No harm or evil can befall a man, except from 'external' things, i. e. from the conflict of the other parts of nature with his

---

[1] Cf. above, p. 218.
[2] E. iv. 67; iv. 63 and S. 1 (with the C.) and S. 2.
[3] E. iv. 50 S.; 73 S.; App. capp. 22, 24, and 31.

BOOK III. own self-assertive force. If we were purely intelligent beings, we should be completely 'active' or 'free': no longer at the mercy of 'external causes,' but self-sufficient. Our whole life would be a sense of increasing vitality, continuous pleasure. We should 'suffer' nothing; and 'good' and 'bad' would have no meaning for us. For knowledge of good implies knowledge of evil; and knowledge of evil is the reflective consciousness of a diminished vitality, i.e. an inadequate idea, which, as such, could not enter into the mind of a purely intelligent being.

Hence the parable of Genesis embodies a philosophical truth. 'To know good and evil' implies a lapse from the ideal state of freedom: a lapse, however, which is not historical, since men never were (and never could have been) perfectly self-sufficient, 'intelligent,' 'active,' or 'free'[1].

We are, and necessarily remain, subordinate and dependent parts in the complex of causes and effects which Spinoza calls 'the common order of nature.' To some extent, therefore, we are at the mercy of 'external' things, i.e. things governed by laws which have no regard to our convenience. We are obliged to accommodate ourselves to this 'order,' and the rational life involves a constant intelligent subservience to it. Keeping our ideal in view, we can trace the maxims of this intelligent accommodation.

The free man's attitude to his non-human environment.

1. There is nothing in nature (except our fellow men) whose converse and society can forward our intellectual life. We have no need, therefore, to preserve the things and creatures of our environment. Our expediency requires that we should employ them to serve our purposes. We have a perfect right (since reason demands it) to make such use of animals, plants and natural

[1] E. iv. 64 and C.; 68 and S.; App. capp. 5, 6.

objects generally, as will best further our own development[1].

In the first place, then, we (not only may, but) ought to exploit our environment for the study of the nature of things and of ourselves. Observation and experiment are indispensable for the acquisition of the crafts and arts, and these are necessary to the rational life; for, without them, self-knowledge and knowledge of things would be impossible to us[2].

And, secondly, we have a right to use animals for food. It is a mere superstition, and no sound principle of reason, which would forbid the slaughter of animals. Everything is, as we know, be-souled[3]. Animals are not—as the Cartesians supposed[4]—mere machines without feeling. But, none the less, we have a right to treat them as serves our true convenience. Now, the attainment of our ideal involves the perfect development of our body. For a mind which is powerful to think *is* a body which is powerful to move and act. But the human body is a complex individual, compounded of many and diverse complex individuals. The being of each of the subordinate complexes (or organs) has to be maintained: their constitutive proportion (that between the movements of their component corpuscles) has to be preserved; and the constitutive proportion of the whole body (that between the movements of all the subordinate complexes) has to be kept unaltered. All this requires constant care of our body, constant nourishment of the most various kinds, constant restoration and substitution of the component corpuscles[5].

The care of the body is a necessary means to the free

---

[1] E. iv. 18 S.; 37 S. 1; App. capp. 26, 27.
[2] Cf. e.g. E. iv. App. cap. 27.
[3] E. ii. 13 S.
[4] Cf. Descartes, Letter 113 (in the edition of Charles Adam and Paul Tannery, Paris, 1898).
[5] Cf. e.g. E. iv. 38, 39; App. cap. 27.

Book III. man's end, and it gives a value to certain other human pursuits. Thus, e.g., it explains the need of mechanics and medical science, it justifies the pursuit of money up to a certain point, and it renders it right and necessary for the wise man to enjoy the pleasures of life—good food and drink, beautiful scenery, exercise, theatres, &c. —provided he does no injury to his fellows[1]. It is superstition to suppose there is any merit in mortifying the flesh. Cheerfulness is good as a necessary condition of the higher life.

The life of the rational man, in his relations to his non-human environment, is determined through and through by his desire, as an intelligent being, to maintain and develop his intelligence. Everything is good, useful or expedient, so far as it subserves this end: and, so far as it subserves this end, everything is, and ought to be, done by the free man. The moral law is no arbitrary code, ordaining this and forbidding that. It is the law which reason makes for itself to express its own innermost being. The passions are excluded only so far as they involve *either* a diminution of our total being, and therefore of our intelligence, *or* a sacrifice of our general vitality to that of a part, and so again a hindrance of our intelligent activity. The rational life is a 'free' life; for it is the life of an intelligence moulding its environment into an expression of itself. It is reason shaping itself in an order foreign to it, converting the external 'order of nature' into the living revelation of our innermost self.

The free man's attitude to his fellows.

2. There is no single thing with which our nature 'agrees' so intimately as with our fellow men. From them we can derive most furtherance or hindrance[2] in the ideal life. 'Union is strength': the union of two individuals of the same nature doubles the power of

[1] E. iv. 45 S. 2; App. capp. 28–31; VVlL. i. pp. 6 and 7.
[2] Cf. E. iv. App. cap. 10.

each¹. And, so far as men are guided by reason, their interests are identical, their natures are the same. Only in the common life of a society of free men, living for the common ideal of reason according to laws which the society has framed in the interests of all, can we attain to complete freedom. Under such conditions we are more free than if we were to live in a desert with nobody to humour but ourselves².

It is true, indeed, that for the most part men are not guided by reason, but governed by passions: and, so far as this is the case, their interests tend to diverge and to bring them into hostility with one another. Yet even then they remain *men*: and are, as such, able to help and comfort one another in their needs as nothing else in the world can³.

Clearly, therefore, if we are to live the rational life, we must endeavour to win the friendship of our fellow men by every means in our power. Above all, we must try to lead them to live the rational life themselves, in order that we may be strengthened by common pursuit of our true good⁴.

The maintenance of outer concord and peace depends upon the state, and so far as we obey the ordinances of the state and respect its decrees, we contribute to preserve union—from whatever motives our actions may proceed. But, in order to lead our fellow men to live the rational life, we must win their love. And for this purpose, the most essential requirements are that we should live a life of 'religion' and 'duty'⁵: i.e. our fulfilment of the law of the state, and our treatment of our fellows, must spring from motives of reason, or be

[1] E. iv. 18 S.
[2] E. iv. 35 C. 1 and 2, and S.; iv. 73; App. capp. 7, 9, 26.
[3] E. iv. 70 S.; App. cap. 14.
[4] E. iv. App. capp. 9, 12. Hence the superlative merit of the true educator.
[5] E. iv. App. cap. 15. See above, p. 272.

BOOK III. based on true knowledge of the value and significance of human existence[1].

Condemnation of the passions.

3. As a general principle, all forms of *laetitia*, since they indicate heightened vitality, are 'good'; and all forms of *tristitia*, since they indicate diminished vitality, are 'bad.' This condemnation of the forms of *tristitia* remains almost unqualified. But the approval of *laetitia* is very much restricted. For a 'pleasure' may indicate heightened vitality of a part only of our being, and may involve diminished vitality in the rest of our body and mind; or, again, a present enjoyment may lead to a greater subsequent depression. All such pleasures are hindrances to the ideal, and, so far, 'bad.' They are said to 'admit of excess': i. e. *per se*, as pleasures, it is a gain to experience them, but we 'can have too much' of them in relation to the proportions of the rational life. As Spinoza expresses it, they, on their corporeal side, may violate the constituent balance between the motion and rest of the parts of the body. And as remedies for these 'partial' or 'excessive' pleasures, 'partial' pains may be 'good': 'good,' i.e., as correcting a disturbance, restoring the balance[2]. The general sense of well-being or vitality, which Spinoza calls 'cheerfulness' (*hilaritas*), alone, of all the forms of *laetitia*, is always without qualification

---

[1] For an excellent account of Spinoza's political philosophy, see Pollock, ch. 10. Spinoza's theory of the state is sketched very lightly in E. iv. 37 S. 2. The only point, with which we are here concerned, is Spinoza's contention that the state has come into existence to promote and maintain concord; and that, with this object, it overrides the diverse passions which govern man in a 'state of nature' by the more powerful and uniform passions of hope of reward and fear of punishment. The majority of citizens respect the law and keep the peace, because they believe that the violation of the state's ordinances would on the whole be to their detriment. The 'free man,' of course, respects the law from intelligent motives; i. e. because he realizes that the order, which the state maintains, is the indispensable basis of the ideal life.

[2] Cf. the Aristotelian doctrine, *Nicom. Ethics*, Bk. VII.

'good'; and the general sense of depression, which he calls *melancholia*, is always without qualification 'bad'[1].

Further, most of the forms of *tristitia* (and of the *cupiditates* based on them) are always 'bad'[2]. And, lastly, all those emotions—whether they are forms of *laetitia* or *tristitia*—which depend upon ignorance of ourselves and of things, are always 'bad'[3].

4. A hasty reading of Spinoza's account of the rational life is apt to leave a negative impression. It seems as if, in condemning the majority of the emotions, he has left the mere skeleton of a life for the free man: a formal reasonableness without concrete filling. But this is erroneous. For the passions, which have been swept away, we must substitute the motives which really actuate the free man. We must not conceive the reason of the free man as an abstract principle, but as a living knowledge which expands and grows in him to meet the concrete demands of life. 'We can be determined by reason apart from passion to do all those actions, to which we are determined by passion[4].' Spinoza's condemnation of the passions excludes from the free man's life only those acts, which are not *his* actions at all, but reactions to *stimuli* in which he plays the part of a patient. Thus, e.g., 'pity' is condemned as 'bad' or 'useless' for the rational life. All that is valuable in 'pity' is the generous help of which it is the source. But the free man will give the same generous help—and

---

[1] E. iv. 42; cf. iv. 41 and 43.
[2] e.g. Odium (E. iv. 45), Invidia, Irrisio, Contemptus, Ira, Vindicta, and the other passions which arise from Odium (E. iv. 45 C. 1), Poenitentia (E. iv. 54), Indignatio (E. iv. 51 S.), Humilitas (E. iv. 53), Commiseratio (E. iv. 50). An additional reason for the 'badness' of Commiseratio is that it involves ignorance of things. For the Cupiditates, cf. E. iv. 58 S. and 60.
[3] e.g. Existimatio and Despectus (E. iv. 48), Superbia and Abiectio (E. iv. 55 and 56).
[4] E. iv. 59.

Book III. will give it more effectively—from motives dependent upon clear knowledge [1].

The free man's whole being is interpenetrated with the love of God which arises from the clear knowledge of himself and of all things. He realizes his place in the scheme of things, and his mind is filled with the peace that comes of this understanding. Fully conscious of the supreme value of this peace of mind and of the intelligence which it implies, he endeavours, without passion and without prejudice, to fulfil it in himself and in all men. His life is an unswerving effort towards this end: he does not adopt inconsistent means—however plausible they may seem [2]—to attain it. He is not misled by the pleasure or pain of the moment to underestimate or overvalue a future 'good' or 'evil.' For his whole activity is the expression of clear knowledge; and for clear knowledge or science what is true once is true always. Hence he sees things as they are—in their eternal necessity, their intrinsic value—not as they illusorily appear in the shifting lights of temporal contrast. And inasmuch as his whole being is filled with the joy of realization, the consciousness of doing his utmost for an ideal which he knows to be the true one, he is untouched by remorse, or by shame. He neither frets nor fears, but is at peace.

### § 4. THE POWER OF REASON.

We have spoken of the ideal as the rational or free life, and we have followed Spinoza in his condemnation of the passive emotions, and his demand that self-control (i.e. the control of reason or intelligence) shall be substituted for the motive power of the passions.

---

[1] E. iv. 50 S.
[2] Thus, e.g., he does not try to win men's friendship by deceit (E. iv. 72), flattery (iv. App. cap. 21), or giving of doles (App. cap. 17).

But how is this possible? In what sense, and by what means, can the intelligence conquer the passions and control our conduct?

It belongs to a treatise on medical science to explain how the body is to be developed to its best state of health, and to a treatise on logic (or method) to indicate how to emend and perfect the intelligence. But it is part of our task to show how—granted a healthy body and a sane intellect—the mind has power over the passions. For we have rejected the current opinions. We have denied any absolute power of the mind over the passions; we have proved that the will is not free. And with this rejection, we must also reject the acute (but untenable) hypothesis of Descartes as to the way in which our volitions are communicated to our nerves and muscles. We cannot originate volitions *ex nihilo*, nor, given a volition, can we transfer it to determine our bodily movements in the way Descartes supposed. He imagined that the soul, though united to the whole body, has its *special* seat of operations in the pineal gland[1]. On this gland, the soul—he thought—acts immediately, producing changes in its position by bare volition. And, through such changes of position, the soul can modify and control the motions of the 'animal spirits,' and their action on the muscles; and so bare mind can determine bare body[2].

Now, we have shown that the 'power' of the mind is identical with its intelligence: that the mind is 'powerful' in so far as it thinks clearly. And it is a matter of common experience that we can—in some sense—control our passions. It remains for us to show how this possibility of control follows necessarily from the

---

[1] Descartes, *Passiones*, i. §§ 30, 31.
[2] Cf. E. v. Praef., with its clear criticism of the theory of Descartes.

BOOK III. nature of our mind; i.e. from its 'power,' 'essence,' or 'virtue,' viz. its adequate knowledge.

1. A passion is a 'confused idea.' It is the immediate consciousness of a change in our bodily being, which is at the same time *eo ipso* a change in our psychical being. We are conscious of the two-sided change; but only as an occurrence, an isolated something which happens in us. In reality, it is due to an infinity of bodily and psychical conditions, which determine and constitute its 'why' and its 'what'; but we are aware of it solely as a change in or of us, without apprehending its causes or recognizing that it had any causes. We have a confused or inadequate apprehension of it: we merely 'suffer' it as a passive emotion [1].

This is true even of those passions which refer to an external object. The causal connexion, which we recognize in their case, falls within the passion: we do not recognize the passion itself as the effect of its necessary conditions. Thus, e. g., we love or hate a person, because our increased or diminished vitality is—in the total confused state of mind, which is our passion—associated for us with the idea of that person as its cause. Our love or hate is the confused consciousness of this causal connexion, and is *at best* a partial (and therefore, inadequate) apprehension of the conditions of the change of vitality which we are experiencing. Z, e. g., is the object of our love; in our confused emotional state, the idea of Z is 'associated' with our heightened tone of being as its cause. But Z is no isolated, originative centre of activity. What Z does, is really done *through* Z by the infinite chains of causes and effects which constitute the 'order of nature.' If our emotional state were to clarify, if we were to get an adequate apprehension of our feeling of increased vitality, we should shake ourselves free from the 'asso-

[1] Cf. above, pp. 201 ff.

ciation' of the idea of Z. We should refer the change of our vitality to its complete totality of conditions; i.e. we should, in feeling the pleasure, refer it to God as its cause. We should love God. But then our love would no longer be a 'passive emotion': it would depend upon clear and adequate knowledge in us, and would therefore be the necessary expression of our nature *quâ* intelligence. Our 'love' would be an 'active' emotion, the clear outcome of the activity of our very self.

Hence we can say, generally, that 'any passion ceases to be a passion' (and becomes an active emotion) 'the moment we form a clear and distinct idea of it[1].' The moment we cease to have experiences formed in us, the moment we are clearly conscious of our own experiences, we have 'taken our life firmly into our hands': we have begun to live ourselves, to act, and have ceased to be the passive theatre in which the forces of our environment sustain the persons of the drama. In proportion as we understand the changes of our vitality, we have freed ourselves from imaginative experience, and are moving in the world of science. Error (or inadequate ideas) and passion have clarified to truth (or adequate ideas) and action. Hence 'an emotion is more in our power, and our mind is less passive in regard to it, the more we know it[2].'

As regards love and hate and their derivatives, clear thinking of this kind dissociates the changes of vitality from the imaginative idea of their external cause, and connects them with their full and complete conditions. And this means that love and hate as such—towards this or that particular person, e. g.—and the anxieties and doubts which arise from them, will vanish. If our pleasure and our pain are clearly apprehended as due (not to Z, but) to the eternal and necessary order, in which Z is a dependent and determined link, we can no

---

[1] E. v. 3.  [2] E. v. 3 C.

longer love or hate Z, nor feel anxiety or doubt as to his behaviour [1].

But every passion without exception may be transformed—at least in part—into an active emotion, by the clarification of confused into complete knowledge. For every passion is, on its corporeal side, a modification of our body. And our body, as a mode of Extension, shares the common properties of all extended things. At least, therefore, to this extent we can form an adequate idea of every passion [2]. We can, that is, apprehend our passions from the point of view of science, as resultants—on their corporeal side—of the universal and necessary laws of Extension, motion and rest. And so far at least we can attain to an objective view of our passions: so far at least they cease to be *passions*.

No doubt, a scientific knowledge of this kind remains abstract: it does not exhaust the whole content of the passions. They are not wholly transformed for us, but remain in part unclarified, not the objects of intelligence, mere personal experiences. Yet, *to some extent*, we are no longer the playthings of external forces: *to some extent* we have taken a firm grip of our own experiences. We are less the victims of what is not ourself, we are less dominated by passions.

And what is true of pleasure and pain and their derivatives, is true also of desire. The desire, which draws its material from our pleasures, will be a desire which results in action (and not in passion), in proportion as those pleasures are dependent on adequate (and no longer on inadequate) ideas [3]. For in so far as a desire is rooted in clear knowledge, it and its results are explicable as the effect of ourselves alone: we are its adequate cause, or we are 'agents' and 'free' in respect to it. Thus e. g. the desire to make others live after our humour, if based on inadequate ideas in us, is a passive emotion, which is

[1] E. v. 2.  [2] E. v. 4 C. and S.  [3] Cf. E. iv. 59.

called 'ambition' and is a form of pride. But, if based on adequate ideas, it becomes the desire to lead others to live the rational life, and is a form of nobleness of mind —'pietas[1].'

2. 'To know' means to apprehend things in their eternal or timeless necessity. If, therefore, we form a clear idea of an emotion of pleasure, we cannot refer it to a series of temporal and local conditions: still less can we regard a single object, pictured in isolation as merely 'there,' as its cause. We must take the passion in our thought out of the imaginative series, and conceive it in its necessary and timeless determination. Or, if we remain within the imaginative series, we must at any rate carry the causal reference indefinitely back along the infinite chain of causes and effects. But this means that we cannot regard the things or persons, to whom we attribute the origin of our emotions, as *free* or *responsible*; i. e. we cannot love or hate *them*, at least not with the same intensity as before[2]. And, generally, in proportion as we apprehend the necessity of things, we acquiesce in the changes of our experience. Our pains and our pleasures become *for us* what they really are—part of the eternal order of nature—and we cease to fret over what we understand. The intensity and the bitterness of a passion depend for the most part upon the erroneous idea that 'all might have been otherwise.' Knowledge brings with it the full understanding of the conditions of our pain or pleasure. We know that what is, must be. The useless regrets of imagination give place to the endeavours to make the best of what is, which result from reason[3].

---

[1] E. v. 4 S.; cf. above, pp. 215, 219, 272.
[2] E. v. 5 dem.; and cf. above, pp. 282, 283.
[3] E. v. 6 and S. It is very difficult to express this thought of Spinoza without making him appear inconsistent. In reality and for knowledge what is, must be: the endeavour 'to make the

Book III.   3. The emotions which depend upon adequate ideas in us, so far as they are contrary to the passive emotions, cannot coexist with the latter in our minds. One or other set of contrary emotions must give way, or change until they no longer conflict[1]. Now the adequate ideas in us are the ideas of the common properties of things: ideas, therefore, whose objects are always and everywhere present. So far as we 'picture' these common properties, we picture them always the same and always with equal vividness[2]. On the other hand, the passions depend upon inadequate ideas: ideas, whose objects vary with the constantly-shifting environment. We cannot always 'picture' these objects (for they are not always present), nor always with the same vividness. In the conflict, therefore, the 'active' emotions have to this extent the advantage. The issue is more likely to modify the passions into conformity with them, than vice versa—especially when the objects of the passions are no longer actually present[3].

Further, the active emotions are referred to more causes than the passions. For the objects of the adequate ideas, on which the active emotions depend, form the interconnected whole of Extension and of Thought: whilst the objects of the inadequate ideas, on which the passions depend, are bodies and ideas torn from their context and pictured as isolated, independent things and persons. Hence the active emotions—as having for the consciousness which experiences them a wider reference,

best of what is,' is itself a part of what is and must be. And the confused pictures of contingency, with the vain regrets which they engender, are themselves—for the knowledge of science—necessary elements in what is and must be. The scientific consciousness recognizes this, and in its recognition it is 'freed' from the bondage of the passions. The imaginative consciousness is without this recognition, and in its privation it is the victim of error and passion.

[1] E. v. Ax. 1.
[2] E. v. 7 dem.
[3] E. v. 7.

# THE POWER OF REASON

and as depending for it upon more causes—tend to maintain their power and freshness more than any passions, and are more easily excited than the latter. In the conflict, therefore, the active or rational emotions are more likely than the passions to predominate. They tend 'to occupy our minds more [1].'

Lastly, we can give to the rational emotions the strength which comes of systematic interconnexion. They will thus occupy our mind more and more, and (as it were) crowd out the passions.

For the order of our thoughts is the ideal expression of the order of our bodily modifications [2]. Now, as intelligences, we can form adequate ideas and deduce other adequate ideas from them, thus constituting an intelligible system of truth, which is the expression of the nature of the intellect [3]. So long as we are not the sport of 'external' impulses—not 'buffeted by emotions contrary to our nature'—we can think clearly and connectedly. And this is at the same time the production of a sequence of bodily modifications according to the same order, viz. the order of the intellect. (Thus when we think confusedly, or 'picture,' our bodily modifications succeed one another in the order of the—*to us*—arbitrary connexion of external causes. And, speaking inaccurately, we say 'our environment acts on our body, and

---

[1] E. v. 8; 11; 20 S. A passion tends — more than an active emotion—to restrict our thought. It ties our mind down to the contemplation of a single cause, whilst an active emotion stimulates our thought to apprehend the interconnexion of things. A passion is thus a hindrance to thought. And, conversely, so far as an emotion is referred to one or a few causes only, it is more pernicious or is more of the nature of a passion, than is an equally intense emotion, which refers to a greater number of causes (E. v. 9).

[2] E. v. 1. 'Prout cogitationes, rerumque ideae, ordinantur et concatenantur in Mente, ita Corporis affectiones, seu rerum imagines, ad amussim ordinantur et concatenantur in Corpore.' This is the exact converse of E. ii. 7, so far as the doctrine applies to man.

[3] Cf. above, pp. 171 ff.

BOOK III. calls up changes in its being which are also changes in our mental being, or 'we suffer passions.' But, when we think clearly, our intelligence forms thoughts in its own order—the order of every intelligence—and our bodily modifications succeed one another in exactly the same order. And, speaking inaccurately, we may say 'we control our thoughts, and thus control our bodily affections,' or 'we experience active emotions.')

In the 'calm intervals' of our life, therefore, we can, by clear and connected reflection, increase and strengthen the active emotions, thus forming a consolidated bulwark against the assaults of passion [1]. Spinoza draws a practical corollary from this: whilst we are still striving after complete knowledge of our passions, our best course is to learn a certain rule of life, or certain practical maxims. If we constantly repeat such maxims, reflect on them, and apply them to actual or imaginary situations in our lives, we shall give them a greater influence over our imaginative consciousness. They will become familiar to us, and ready to our hand when occasion arises. Such a maxim, e.g., is 'Do not repay hate with hate, but conquer it with love or nobleness of mind [2].'

If, in our calm moments, we constantly reflect on wrongs and insults, and consider how a noble generosity or love overcomes them, we shall render this abstract maxim highly concrete. The 'picture' of an insult will, for us, become associated with the 'picture' of this maxim: and when we are insulted, we shall straightway act according to the maxim. But Spinoza adds a warning. In reflections of this kind, we should dwell on the *good* side of all these experiences, not on the evil. For this will increase our consciousness of power, our joy, and so our active emotions: whilst meditation on the evils of life, as such, will lessen our power and produce a fictitious

---

[1] E. v. 10 and S.          [2] E. iv. 46 and S.

self-control. A man, e. g., who has been ill-treated by his mistress, is apt to console himself with thoughts of the proverbial fickleness of woman, &c., &c. But the moment his mistress smiles on him again, he forgets his 'philosophy,' and is again the slave of his passion. He has never won true liberty: for liberty means full knowledge of our own power, or 'virtue,' whilst he has but prided himself on his experience of the vices and weaknesses of human nature.

As our intelligence grows in power by constant reflection, our knowledge of things becomes more and more complete and coherent. As regards the passions, this means that we get a more and more adequate scientific understanding of them and their conditions. And this is the same as to say, that we refer all the corporeal modifications, which the passions involve, to the idea of God as an extended Substance: we understand all that occurs in us as the inevitable consequence of the complete nature of things[1]. The emotional aspect of this knowledge is an active emotion of joy accompanied by the idea of God as its cause:—i. e. our emotional state will be love of God[2]. Thus, the increase of scientific knowledge is the increase of our love of the intelligible order which we apprehend. And, since this love is associated with all the corporeal modifications which we experience, it will fill our mind to the exclusion of all other emotions, and will persist and expand in us *so long as our body exists*[3]. If it cannot absolutely destroy all the passions, at least it will occupy the greatest part of our mind, and reduce the passive emotions to the least part of consciousness[4].

Nor is it infected with the evils which attach to other forms of love. Love towards a finite and changeable

---

[1] E. v. 14.
[2] E. v. 15.
[3] E. v. 16, 20 S.
[4] E. v. 20 S.

Book III. object is the source of jealousy, envy, and all forms of anxiety. But love towards God is untouched by these troubles. For God is not liable to passion, nor to any form of emotion, since passion implies inadequate ideas, and even active emotion means a transition from a less to a greater vitality[1]. God, therefore, cannot love or hate any one[2]. And he who loves God cannot endeavour to win God's love in return[3]: cannot, therefore, feel anxiety or disappointment in his love. And since this love of God is the supreme 'good' of reason, it is a 'good' which we desire all men to share: hence we can neither envy, nor feel jealousy of, others in regard to it[4]. Finally, since God cannot be conceived inadequately, in conceiving God we are active, i.e. feel joy. We cannot, therefore, hate God; for we cannot associate the idea of God with our own depression of vitality. Hence the love of God can never turn to hatred[5]. God indeed, as the cause of all things, is conceived as the cause of pain and sorrow: but in the apprehension of the causes of pain, we cease to suffer. The confused experience, which was our pain, clarifies into the clear understanding which is a consciousness of power, or joy[6].

The love of God fills our minds, in proportion as we completely understand. But complete understanding is more than the scientific consciousness: more, indeed, than any human mind can reach. In all human minds there persist inadequate ideas and therefore passions. Yet as we advance in science—still more if we attain to the intuitive knowledge which is philosophy—the greater part of our mind is constituted by adequate ideas: we are, therefore, less and less the victims of passion. And this growth in knowledge is, as we shall see, an increase in our vitality. For the self, which

[1] E. v. 17.
[2] E. v. 17 C.
[3] E. v. 19.
[4] E. v. 20 and dem.
[5] E. v. 18 and C.
[6] E. v. 18 S.

knows more, contains within its individuality a greater amount of the real: i.e. 'possesses more and more the character of Reality¹.'

¹ Cf. E. v. 40 S.; and below, ch. 4. Bradley, *Appearance and Reality* (2nd edition), p. 365.

# CHAPTER IV

## THE IDEAL LIFE AS CONSCIOUS UNION WITH GOD

### § 1. INTRODUCTION.

Book III.   With the account of the moral life as the life of reason, the main task of the Ethics is in a sense completed. Spinoza has applied his general metaphysical theory to the nature of man, and has shown how the emotional and cognitive sides of that nature are interdependent and necessary consequents of the order of things. He has established the ideal of reason as based on the self-realization of the mind: he has shown how man, in living the life of 'religion' and 'duty'—in manifesting 'nobleness and strength of mind'—is fulfilling his truest self, and is therefore 'free.' Morality is not an irksome burden, which we must bear for the sake of reward. The only bondage is subjection to the passions: and the freedom of morality liberates us from them. The life of virtue is the life of power. To live it, is to be or become ourselves. To live the life of passion is to merge ourselves in the alien forces of the 'common order of nature,' to cease to be anything which has a character of its own[1].

These conclusions are independent of what follows. They remain unshaken, whatever our view as to the temporal existence of man. They would still be true, even though the 'self' which we win were so dependent upon local and temporal conditions that 'we' are 'real'

[1] Cf. E. v. 41 and S.

in no other sense than that in which the 'things' of Chap. IV. imaginative experience are 'real.' If, apart from our existence as members of the common order of nature, 'we' are nothing; and if, before birth, 'we' in no sense were—if, after death, 'we' in no sense shall be—still, during this our life, the positions which Spinoza has established remain firm. During life, we can and must endeavour to realize our most essential self: and, in this endeavour, 'we'—since we are following the inevitable tendency of our nature—are becoming as 'real' as we have it in us to be: even though that 'reality' should remain a mere imaginative reality, i.e. the reality of things, whose 'individuality' is to occur at a particular place and time, and to last through a definite period.

Spinoza, indeed, has established more than this. In our scientific knowledge we are moving in the region of truth; and, so far, 'we' are 'eternal' or independent of temporal conditions. But science remains abstract, and the 'we' of science is—for all Spinoza has shown— a mind-body merged in the general nature of Thought and Extension, or at least no further individualized than is the *infima species*, 'man.' The free man or moral agent *may*—for all we know—remain, as regards his individual being, outside the world of truth or eternal reality. He may owe his being as *this* person to the imaginative barriers, from which he cannot completely free himself. He may, so to speak, live the rational life by a borrowed permanent reality and eternity, without himself being 'real' or 'eternal'[1].

In the concluding section of the Ethics[2], Spinoza endeavours to carry his conception of the human ideal to completion. He tries to show that there is a grade of man's self-realization, in which the mind is itself eternal or fully real: that, in the highest to which we

[1] Cf. above, pp. 265 ff.      [2] E. v. 21-40.

BOOK III. attain, we are actually enjoying in our own selves the fullness of being, which is the mark of complete reality.

In outline, Spinoza's position is this:—in the most complete thinking of which we, as intelligences, are capable, our thought is God's thought; and God's thought is God thinking so far as he constitutes the essence of *our* mind, i. e. God's thought is *our* thinking. That oneness of our intelligent being with God merges us in the divine thought, and *eo ipso* most fully characterizes us, or gives us our 'self.' And in that transfusion of our thinking being by God's being, we are 'real' with the divine reality, or God is real in, *and as*, us: i. e. we are 'eternal.' In the glow of that self-realization—which is *at once* the identity of all selves with God, *and* the most fully characterized distinction of all selves from God and from one another—our mind unites or fuses in itself our whole being. There is no longer an *emotional* in distinction from a *cognitive* consciousness. The cognitive consciousness is emotional, and the emotional is cognitive, or rather our consciousness is both transformed. Hence, we can say *either* 'our thinking is God's thinking and God's thinking is our very self': *or* 'our consciousness of our felicity, or our love—which flows from the understanding of that felicity and its cause—is God's love of himself and of us; and God's love of himself is our love of God.'

## § 2. THE CONCEPTION OF ETERNITY.

'Duration.'

Spinoza is not quite consistent in his use of the term 'duration'[1]. He is anxious to avoid the misunderstanding which confuses 'eternity' with 'indefinite length of time': and therefore frequently refuses to

---

[1] This inconsistency seems to be due to the partial survival in Spinoza (especially in his earlier writings) of the contemporary scholastic use of the word; cf. Grzymisch, pp. 42, 45.

predicate 'duration' of that which is eternal[1]. When that is so, he identifies 'duration' with 'persistence in time.'

On the other hand, 'time' is, for Spinoza, the result of a limitation of duration: the conception of 'time' is an imaginative aid to enable us to picture persistence or permanent existence. 'Time' cuts 'duration' into lengths, thus destroying its completeness or continuity, and giving it a beginning, an end, and stages. When this is the case, 'duration' is the general term, of which eternal existence and temporal existence are forms—not exactly 'species,' for the former is duration adequately or intelligently apprehended, whereas the latter is the confused, partial or imaginative 'picture' of it [2].

It is necessary to remark on this inconsistency, because, in E. v. 20 S., Spinoza speaks of the 'duration of the mind without relation to the body,' where he means the *eternity* of the mind: whilst elsewhere (e.g. E. v. 23 S.) he identifies 'duration' and 'time,' and therefore excludes both from the conception of the mind's 'eternity.'

Spinoza *once* uses the expression 'immortal' (deathless) of the mind as equivalent to 'eternal'[3]. That he does so only once is probably due (as Pollock suggests) to his anxiety to avoid the misleading associations of the word. For, of one thing there can be no doubt: Spinoza did *not* mean to establish for the human soul an infinitely-prolonged after-life in another world[4]. This popular travesty of the philosophic conception of 'eternity' is so alien to Spinoza's whole thought that we cannot for a moment attribute it to him. It hangs together with the very conceptions against which

'Immortality.'

---

[1] Cf. e.g. E. i. def. 8 Expl.
[2] Above, p. 31.
[3] E. v. 41 S.
[4] Cf. Pollock, p. 270; and the excellent article by A. E. Taylor in *Mind* (N. S. v. No. 18), to which Pollock refers.

Book III. Spinoza's whole work is an unhesitating protest—the conceptions of God as a lawgiver and judge, and of felicity as the 'reward' of virtue. In one place, it is true, Spinoza has used an expression which is extremely misleading. 'Herewith,' he says [1], 'I have completed my account of all that concerns this present life.' But, even if we forget that 'this present life' would naturally mean for Spinoza *our life so far as we are 'imaginative,'* and implies as its antithesis (*not* a future life of the same kind, but) an actual life of a different kind, viz. our life so far as we are 'intelligent,' we cannot lay any stress on this passage. In view of what Spinoza says about the mind's 'eternity' [2], we must regard this utterance as a momentary slip: if, that is, we persist in interpreting it to imply a 'future life' in the sense that here and now we are mortal, but elsewhere and afterwards 'put on immortality.'

Eternity.  In spite of an occasional lapse into the wider use of 'duration' [3], Spinoza had already, in the *Cogitata Metaphysica*, clearly distinguished between eternity and indefinite lasting, and fixed his terminology to mark that distinction.

He starts with the division between 'being whose essence involves existence' (i. e. substantial Reality) and 'being whose essence involves only the possibility of existence' (i. e. modal Reality, or, from the point of view of the *Cogitata Metaphysica*, 'created' being [4]).

Created things, so far as their possible existence is actually being realized, are said to 'endure' or 'last.' The comparison of their 'duration' with that of things

---

[1] E. v. 20 S.
[2] i.e. *in the Ethics*. For, in the K. V., Spinoza has not completely freed himself from the popular confusions which he attacks. For the development of Spinoza's conception of 'eternity,' see Grzymisch, especially pp. 7–9, 16, and pp. 41 ff.
[3] Cf. e.g. Ep. 12 (above, p. 31), and E. v. 20 S.
[4] C. M. i. 4; ii. 1 and 10.

## THE CONCEPTION OF ETERNITY 297

which have a definite and determinate movement, results in 'time': the *ens rationis* or *modus cogitandi* (i. e. *modus imaginationis*), which measures duration. Duration is really identical with the total existence—in distinction from the essence—of a created thing: lessen or increase its duration, and you lessen or increase its existence. It is only a logical distinction which separates the two [1].

When we talk of things having existed 'from all eternity' (*ab aeterno*), we are misusing the term ' eternity.' We are confounding eternity with an indefinite duration: a duration without beginning. Eternity cannot be expressed in terms of duration, even though it be an 'infinite' duration, i. e. one without beginning or end [2].

But God is rightly said to be 'eternal.' For God's essence is one with his existence: and therefore God cannot be said to have 'duration,' since duration is existence conceived apart from essence. If God had duration, his duration would increase from day to day. He would become more real as time goes on: he would be, so to say, continually creating himself. But God's being—his essence or existence—is infinite, i. e. complete actually now and always. The 'eternity' of God, then, means simply his infinite completeness. It is his existence, which is his essence, and is wholly and absolutely actual; not partly real now, and partly about to be. We mean the same thing when we speak of the essential nature of a triangle as an *eternal* truth. It is what it is fully and completely, and does not come to be. It is not more real now than it was in the days of Adam: nor has it lasted for a longer time now than then.

Hence 'eternity' is the very essence of God, so far as that involves necessary existence [3]. Eternity ex-

[1] C. M. i. 4, § 2. '... durationem a tota alicuius rei existentia non nisi Ratione distingui.'
[2] Cf. E. i. def. 8 Expl.
[3] E. v. 30 dem.

BOOK III. presses timeless necessity of being, and has nothing to do with lasting through an 'infinitely long' time. 'There is no *when*, no *before* and *after*, in eternity[1].'

From the point of view of the Ethics, all things are 'eternal' so far as their existence is the necessary consequence of God's essence. As conceived in God, all things are eternal and infinite modes; are 'actually real' with the timeless necessity of God's eternal being[2]. Things are said to be 'actual' *either* so far as they exist at a definite time in a definite place, and then their existence is their 'duration': *or* so far as we conceive them to be contained in God, and to follow from the necessity of the divine nature. In this latter sense, things are 'real' or 'true,' so far as we conceive them 'under the form of eternity,' and so far as their ideas involve the eternal and infinite essence of God[3].

In the concluding section of the Fifth Part of the Ethics, Spinoza is immediately concerned with the eternity of the *human mind*. But, though the human mind differs in essential nature and in degree of reality from other modes, and though therefore its 'eternity' differs from theirs; none the less, *all modes*, in so far as they are conceived in their necessary dependence on God, are timelessly actual or 'eternal'[4].

### § 3. THE ETERNITY OF THE HUMAN MIND.

All modes, as modes of *natura*    Every mode, in its necessary sequence from the nature of God, has its actuality dependent upon God's

[1] E. i. 33 S. 2.
[2] Cf. E. v. 30 dem.; Ep. 12 (above, pp. 27 ff.); and above, pp. 76 ff.
[3] E. v. 29 S.
[4] Contrast Pollock, pp. 275 ff. His arguments seem to me to fall to the ground, when we recollect (i) that Spinoza confessedly confines himself in the later books of the Ethics to the human mind; cf. e.g. E. ii. Praef. and E. v. Praef.: (ii) that, for Spinoza, there are differences of degree and of kind in the reality of modes; cf. above, pp. 73 ff.

# THE ETERNITY OF THE HUMAN MIND 299

essence, or is 'eternal.' Every mode—we may perhaps Chap. IV.
express it—is real in so far as the Whole lives and moves *naturata,*
in it: and what is 'real' is *necessarily* actual, i. e. is eternal.
itself fully and unalterably, without development or
degradation, or process of any kind. Now the degree
or kind of such actuality (the nature of the 'eternity'),
which any mode enjoys, depends entirely upon the degree or kind of reality of the mode in question. The
problem is—*How* does the Whole live and move in *this*
mode? *How much* of reality does it contain? *To what
degree* and *in what sense* does it participate in the divine
nature?

To be able to answer these questions implies what
Spinoza calls *scientia intuitiva*[1]. And the possession of
this knowledge *in respect to our own modal being* is the
enjoyment of our supreme felicity. For it is that
'cognitio unionis, quam mens cum tota natura habet,'
in which Spinoza finds the complete self-realization
of man[2].

Let us see how Spinoza develops this conception. The unity
The category of whole and parts is, as we know, in- modes in
adequate to express the nature of things[3]. The modes God is
are not 'parts' of Substance. The oneness of the modes dividu-
in God is more intimate than the oneness of parts in ality.
a whole. Nor is Substance a whole of modes. The
modes can neither be nor be conceived apart from God.
God is not merely *implied* in the modes, as a whole is
implied in its parts. God *is* the modes, and the modes
are nothing except in so far as they are expressions of
God. It is the separation of the modes from God (as if
they were 'parts' of a whole) which causes the inadequate
understanding of the imaginative consciousness, for which
Reality becomes a world of finite things.

We have, then, to remember that the reality of all

[1] Above, pp. 180 ff.  [2] Above, p. 4, note 1.
[3] Above, pp. 42 and 43, 89 ff.

300        THE ETHICS OF SPINOZA

BOOK III. modes is God. It is God's thinking which is our mind, God's extension which is our body, God's eternal self-affirmation or 'power' which is our actual being.

At the same time, God's completeness, his absolute oneness, is not abstract, but concrete. The modes, which express his being, express it in all ways: his complete oneness reveals itself in complete multiplicity. In the absolute unity of all things in God, all things are most fully characterized, distinguished, or individual. It is the task of 'philosophy'—the ideal knowledge which Spinoza calls *scientia intuitiva*—to attain to the clear vision of the intimate individuality or characteristic essence of all things in God. This vision is the consummation of that clear thinking which begins in science. And it is the result of an inference 'which starts with the adequate idea of the real essence of some of God's Attributes, and proceeds to the adequate knowledge of the essence of things [1].'

Spinoza claims to have accomplished this task as regards the human mind, i.e. to have shown 'how our mind follows in its essence and existence from the divine nature, and is in unbroken dependence on God [2].' He claims, therefore, to have shown in the Ethics, *in what* the characteristic individuality of the human mind consists, or what is the degree and kind of its reality and eternity.

All men are eternal, in various degrees.

Our mind, it will be remembered, was regarded as a complex of ideas, the ideal side of a complex of extended corpuscles [3]. What we call 'our mind' at any time is a compound of adequate and inadequate ideas: i.e. is partly our 'self,' and partly the borrowed and mutilated ideas, which are complete in God's thought, but *in God's thought* constitute other 'selves' together with our own. These 'confused' ideas are—*quâ* con-

[1] Above, pp. 180 ff.   [2] E. v. 36 S.
[3] Cf. above, p. 131.

## THE ETERNITY OF THE HUMAN MIND 301

fused—not really 'ours.' They do not constitute the essential nature of our mind; they constitute our-mind-in-its-environment. And they indicate not so much what we are, as what we are not; they reveal our limits, the 'torn edges' which make us finite[1]. They are the signs of our powerlessness or inability to stand by ourselves, our dependence upon the 'common order of nature'—the context which sustains our temporal or imaginative existence. If we could shake ourselves free from 'external' influence, our mind would come to itself as adequate ideas: as God's thought, in so far as that thought constitutes the essence of our mind and nothing else. At death we are 'shaken free.' For, with the dissolution of our body, the interaction of external bodies with ours must cease; and the consequent confused ideas (which are the ideal side of this interaction) must vanish. We can neither 'imagine' nor 'remember' (we are not subject to the influence of 'association'), except whilst our body 'endures,' i. e. exists in time and space[2]. But death is only one way in which we thus 'come to ourselves.' The essential condition is that we should think clearly and adequately, and think *only* clearly and adequately. In other words, the essential nature of our mind is intelligence; we are really and completely 'ourselves,' in proportion as 'we' are entirely clear consciousness.

For Spinoza, therefore, the essence of the human mind is intelligence; it is fully itself, 'quatenus intelligit'—so far as it understands, or thinks adequately. But when we think adequately, God is thinking in us so far as he constitutes our mind alone. In our essential being, therefore, we realize our oneness with God, or God is expressing himself in us. And this means that in our clear and adequate consciousness we are eternal: we

[1] Cf. e.g. E. iii. 3 S. [2] E. v. 21.

have attained to the kind of eternity, which characterizes human nature. In this sense, our mind—as an adequate, significant thought in the context of God's thinking— is part of the complete intelligence of God [1].

But more is needed to complete Spinoza's conception. The mind, as a mode of Thought, is the ideal expression of a mode of Extension; and is so *for itself*, since every mode of Thought is, *as such*, turned upon itself [2].

In our temporal existence, our mind is the ideal expression of our actually (i. e. temporally) existent body, and our self-consciousness is the feeling of ourselves as *this* animate piece of Extension. But in our essential or real existence, our mind is the adequate knowledge of our body, and our self-consciousness is the adequate apprehension of ourselves as an eternal mode of God: i. e. the adequate idea, which is the essence of our mind, is the ideal expression of our body in its true or essential nature, viz. as an eternal mode of Extension [3]. And the idea of this idea is the reflective consciousness of this our true 'self.'

We have already seen that scientific knowledge implies as its centre or basis 'a self, which is constituted by the permanent and necessary properties common to all modes of Extension and of Thought [4].' Philosophic knowledge—*scientia intuitiva*—implies a 'self,' which is at once permanent and necessary, and individual. 'We,' as subjects of philosophic knowledge, are a mind which apprehends itself as the idea of the essential nature of *our* body. In other words, the 'self' of complete knowledge is an individuality, which has universal, necessary and permanent being in its oneness with God, but is yet concrete and uniquely characterized. *Because* we are one with God, *because* God expresses

---

[1] Above, pp. 92, 93; E. v. 40 S.; ii. 11 C.
[2] Above, pp. 132 ff., p. 257, note 4.
[3] Cf. E. v. 22.   [4] Above, p. 178.

# THE ETERNITY OF THE HUMAN MIND

himself in us, we are not lost in the abstract universality of the objects of science, but have come to a rich and real personality. *Because* we are fully ourselves, we are full participants in the divine nature. *Because* 'we' are nothing but God's adequate knowledge of the essential nature of our body, we fully realize our 'self,' or enjoy our individual character in its fullness [1].

Since 'there is necessarily given in God an idea, which expresses the essence of *this* and *that* human body under the form of eternity [2],' it follows that *to some extent* every man is eternal. 'The human mind cannot be absolutely destroyed with the body, but something of it, which is eternal, remains [3].' This proposition puts the matter as survival after death, and as if the 'eternal part' of the mind were a disembodied spirit. But it follows from Spinoza's position (as we have seen) that every man is 'eternal' *to some extent* in the strict Spinozistic sense of 'eternal.'

Every man in some—perhaps an infinitesimal—degree shares in the clear consciousness of himself and of all things, which is his eternity. For this is the characteristic of humanity [4]. And the essential nature of every man's body is an eternal mode of God's Extension; and is therefore the 'ideatum' of an eternal 'idea' of God's Thought, which is the essential nature of that man's mind. But there are infinite grades in the reality of different men, infinite grades in the fullness of the 'essence' of their body; infinite grades, therefore, in the eternal being of different men's minds.

What is the nature of that gradation? The general principle of the gradation.

---

[1] Cf. above, pp. 243 ff.
[2] E. v. 22 (the italics are mine); cf. ii. 8 C. and S.
[3] E. v. 23.
[4] The passage in Ep. 19 (above, p. 245) must not be unduly pressed. Even the criminal, 'who serves God unwittingly and is consumed in the service,' is not absolutely and entirely without clear knowledge of himself and his function. Otherwise he would not be human at all.

principle is that a thing is at its best (or perfect) in proportion as it asserts and maintains itself. A thing is more real, in fact, the more there is of it. The ideal ('best' or 'most blessed') man is he, the *greatest part* of whose mind is adequate knowledge, or is 'eternal'[1]. For the 'eternal' part of our mind is its 'best' part: since we are 'active' in so far as we understand, and the more a thing is active (and the less a thing is passive) the more perfection it has[2]. Consequently, in proportion as we attain to scientific and philosophic knowledge, we are less subject to harmful emotions; and we are less afraid of death[3]. And, since the degree of our mental reality is the ideal expression of our corporeal perfection, 'he who has a body capable of very many activities has a mind, of which the greatest part is eternal[4].'

We can to some extent fill in these indications from the general teaching of the Ethics. Our 'self' is clear knowledge and all that depends upon, or is involved in, that. Our 'self,' therefore, will be much or little, our 'individuality' worth owning or valueless, our 'eternity' full or empty, according as 'we'—body and mind—are developed and disciplined 'after the order of the intelligence,' or undeveloped and undisciplined, at the mercy of the 'common order of nature.' As regards the development of the body, the Ethics is almost silent: the subject falls outside its scope. But, as regards the development of the mind, we have full materials in the sketch of the 'free man,' and in the account of the three grades of knowledge. There is no need to repeat Spinoza's teaching: but we may attempt to sum up his main contention. The man, whose self is most real, whose eternal individuality is most concrete and valuable, is he whose life is one unswerving effort towards clear knowledge—not the

[1] Cf. e.g. E. v. 31 S., 38 S.
[2] E. v. 40 and C.
[3] E. v. 38.
[4] E. v. 39.

# THE ETERNITY OF THE HUMAN MIND

knowledge of mere theory, but the knowledge which informs and vitalizes conduct: the 'knowledge,' which to Socrates and Plato was identical with goodness. It is no life of visionary idleness, of mystic contemplation. It is a life of intense activity filled with the duties and pleasures of a many-sided existence: the life of every day, but not lived with an 'everyday' spirit. For the activity of such a life is not the restless passing from interest to interest, but the untroubled expression of a single purpose. The consciousness of the significance of that purpose is the spirit that animates the free man's conduct: and in the knowledge of its fulfilment, he is in perfect possession of himself.

In the realization of ourselves as intelligences, our emotional nature has been absorbed. So far as we 'understand,' we *are* real: we are no longer in transition, and therefore no longer emotional beings. But, though we have no consciousness of increasing (still less of diminishing) vitality, we are intensely conscious of actual vitality. To this consciousness Spinoza gives the name of 'felicity'—*beatitudo*—the consummation of *laetitia*[1]. And, in our consciousness of our felicity, we are necessarily also conscious of God as its cause: i.e. we necessarily love God, in so far as we understand his eternal being. This 'love,' since it rests on intelligence and not on imaginative apprehension, may be called the 'intellectual love of God'[2].

*Amor Intellectualis Dei*

We may express the state, in which we attain to our fullest being, in terms of this 'love of God.' What was true of our perfect self-realization as complete 'knowledge,' is true of it as 'love' of God. We love God with a love which is eternal, because our love of God is God loving himself in us[3]: just as we know God under the form of eternity, because our understanding of God is God thinking himself in (or as) us. The mind, in its

---
[1] E. v. 33 S.   [2] E. v. 32 C.   [3] E. v. 36.

Book III. knowledge of God, is a part of God's complete knowledge of himself. And the mind, in its love of God, is a part of the complete love of God for himself[1].

This 'constant and eternal love of God, which is God's love of men,' is our 'salvation,' 'felicity,' or 'freedom.' It is the 'peace of mind,' which the Scriptures have rightly called 'The Glory of God'[2].

§ 4. REVIEW.

If our interpretation of Spinoza is right, what exactly has he proved of man?

The so-called 'individuality' of imaginative experience has shown itself as illusory, and has vanished. Our 'self' is not the unique set of feelings bound up in the unique association of corpuscles, which appear together here and now as the resultant of the causality of the indefinite complex of finite things. 'Things' in this sense of the word—(particular objects of sensitive experience; and the subjects of such experience, themselves the objects of other sensitive experience)—have no reality as such, are not what they profess to be. Their self-dependence, uniqueness, distinction from one another are illusory. They pass over into one another, and the limits which seem to mark them off are the products of confused thinking. There are no real barriers: and the 'things' constituted by the 'barriers' of time and place have no more real subsistence than the imaginative barriers which constitute them. The first result of clear thinking is to dissolve these imaginative barriers: to show that the independence and isolation of 'things' is not ultimately real, and, if taken for ultimate, is the source of error. Science—the first stage of intelligence—reveals the beginning of the truth, when it reconstructs the world as a system of common properties, or (as we should

[1] E. v. 36.  [2] E. v. 36 S.

express it) of universal laws. It substitutes for the world of 'things' a world which coheres necessarily through the interconnexion of content according to universal laws, or principles of synthesis, which are themselves the articulation of the scientific intelligence. Instead of 'this' and 'that' body, we now have the general nature or essence of body: body, conceived as a mode of Extension, an instance of the laws of mathematics, mechanics, and physics. Instead of 'this' and 'that' mind, we have mind as such: the essence of mind as a mode of Thought, an instance of the universal laws of psychology and logic. And in place of 'this' and 'that' man we have man as such: man as the essential nature, which is the 'humanity' of *Peter* and *Paul*; i. e. man as a mode of Substance, an instance of the laws of Extension and Thought.

Our 'self' at this stage is that which characterizes all men as such, our 'humanity.' We have a common interest and ideal, a common love of knowledge; and live a common or social life as the means to satisfy that love. We can, at this stage, justify the duties and rights which constitute the moral ideal, when it is identified with the rational or social life. The fulfilment of these duties, and the satisfaction of these rights, is 'good' for us, because it is required by our reason for the realization of itself. Life in accordance with social morality is the life of our 'selves': our 'freedom' and our 'activity.' It is, so to say, the only wholesome nourishment for our selves: and it would be folly to reject it for the life of passion, just as it would be folly to eat and drink poison [1].

In this rational life, then, human nature is realizing itself, human intelligence is coming to itself. But 'human nature' and 'human intelligence' are not to be understood as the abstract universals of imagination.

[1] E. v. 41 S.

Book III. They are concrete realities. And as real they are (in our experience) 'embodied' in 'this' and 'that' man, 'this' and 'that' mind. 'Human nature' is the nature of *Peter* and *Paul*, so far as they attain to their best: 'human intelligence' is the thinking of 'this' and 'that' man of science or philosopher, so far as it is true. And yet the essential nature and the true thought of *Peter* and *Paul*, though characterized and individualized in them, are one and the same through and in their differences. *Peter* and *Paul* win personality for themselves, according as they share in the common humanity or intelligence; and that common humanity or intelligence is the unity of *Peter* and *Paul*, not the abstraction from their differences.

*Peter* and *Paul* remain distinct from one another with the illusory distinctions of the imaginative consciousness. They are born, live, and die under different local and temporal conditions. To some extent they must remain at the mercy of the common order of nature—the sport of passions, which lead them into conflict, or at least into divergence. Yet, in so far as they share in the realization of their common nature, they have entered into the inheritance of a different kind of being, and a different level of individuality.

For the mind, which thinks truly, is one with the reality which it thinks. What is true, is true independently of time: and the mind, which *is* true thinking, is free from temporal and local conditions or is itself an 'eternal' mode. Man in the stage of science ('so far as he understands') is an 'eternal' mode: *Peter* and *Paul*, in attaining to common 'humanity,' are so far no longer 'single things,' but show themselves in their necessary being as 'eternal' modes of God. And this 'eternity,' which belongs to all 'things'—so far, that is, as a 'thing' means an object of science, an essential nature, a law, a truth—belongs to the human mind in a fuller sense. For the human mind not only is eternal, but is so *for itself*: it has, and retains, the unity of self-consciousness. A self-conscious mind at any rate—whatever may be the case with other modes—is a unity, which does not dissolve into general properties before the analysis of science, but comprehends within itself (and for itself) in a necessary and living union all the multiplicity which science reveals in it. A mind which is clearly conscious of this its individuality—which knows itself *at once* as a necessary consequent of God's Thought *and* as a necessary element in that Thought—is a mind which has attained to intuitive knowledge of itself: and in that knowledge it is 'eternal' with the fullest 'eternity' of which man is capable. For God is actual in it, not merely as God is actual in all minds—but in it, *as this mind*. Yet, it is *this* mind as being an essential constituent of human mind as such: its 'individuality' comes to it, not as a character which separates it from other minds or thoughts of God, but as a character which unites it with them all. It is a thought which has unique significance: but its unique significance is given to it by, and in, the context of God's thinking. It and all intelligences by their individual significance together constitute the complete intelligence of God [1].

[1] E. v. 40 S.

# INDEX

Abiectio, 212, 279 n.3.
Acquiescentia in se ipso (Philautia), 211, 216 n.2, 270 n.3.
Action, X Passion, 199-200, 203; and Desire, 228-34.
Actual existence, 119-22: cf. 177-9.
Actuality, two senses of, 77: cf. 225-6.
Admiratio, 217.
Aemulatio, 215.
Aeternae veritates: see Eternal.
Aeternitas = necessitas existentiae, 75 n.2: and see Eternity.
Affectio, 201.
Affectus ('Emotions'), how related to Ideae, 201-3, 205-6, 236-7; 'active,' 218-9; 'passive' = 'confused ideas,' 114, 204: cf. 282-5; three primary 'passive,' 203-5; complex or derivative, 208-18; infinite variety of, 206-8; 'association' of, 212-4; 'imitation' of, 215-6; condemnation of, 278-80.
Alphabet of Reality, 150 n.3.
Ambitio, 215, 216, 263, 284-5.
Amor, 209: cf. 282-4; Dei, 96-7, 244-8, 270-1, 289-91; intellectualis Dei, 2, 181, 233 n.1, 305-6.
'Animal Spirits,' 157, 281.
Animi Fluctuatio, 213.
Animositas, 219.
Antipathia seu Aversio, 213.

Appetitus, 193, 198 n.3, 227 ff.
Aristotle, his doctrine of pleasure, cf. 278 n.2; κίνησις and ἠρεμία, 84; κοινὰ ἀξιώματα, 173; 'propria,' 174; ἄτομον εἶδος, 179: cf. 293.
Association: see Memoria.
'Asylum ignorantiae,' 61.
Atomism: see Spinoza.
Attribute, Spinoza's definition of, 18; =the 'what' of Substance, 17-27; 'extra intellectum'? 17-27 (see especially 26); infinite (complete) in suo genere, 23-5; of Extension, 67-9, 82-8; of Thought, 70-2, 93-7; of Thought, its relation to other Attributes, 134-8; change in Spinoza's terminology, 18-21.
Attributes, parallelism (coextensiveness) of, 25, 126, 136-8: cf. 287-8; cannot be 'deduced,' 67, 102-7; infinite number of, 39 n.5, 41, 69-70, 134-5; = 'Lines of Force,' 65-7; X 'Propria,' 41 n.2.
Audacia, 217 n.1.
Auxilia imaginationis (Time, Measure, Number), 31-5: cf. 121.
Avaritia, 216, 263.

Bacon, Francis, 80 n.2, 164 n.1.
Beatitudo (=mentis libertas), 4 n.2: cf. 181, 305.
Benevolentia, 210.

Blyenbergh, Gulielmus de, Spinoza's correspondence with, 63 *n.*, 244-8.
Body and Mind, no causal connexion between, 153-4; the human, part of Extension and Thought, 92-3, 125-30, 177-9.
Boxel, Hugo, Spinoza's letter to, 39 *n.*5.
Bradley, F. H., 102 *n.*1, 162 *n.*1, 291 *n.*1.

*Castitas*, 216.
*Causa = ratio*, 53 *n.*1 : cf. 230 *n.*5 ; *sui*, 5, 28, 53 *n.*1; *transiens*, 58 *n.*5, 64 *n. a.*
Causality of God: *see* God.
Chasdai Creskas (Rab Chasdai), 41 *n.*2, 51 *n.*1.
*Clementia*, 219.
*Cogitatio*, 21 *n.* 3, 22, 24-5 ; *and see* Attribute of Thought.
*Cognitio, reflexiva = idea ideae*, 5-7; *boni et mali*, 256-61 ; *intuitiva* : see *Scientia intuitiva*.
*Commiseratio*, 210, 211, 279 *n.*2.
*Communes notiones* : see *Notiones*.
*Communis ordo naturae*, 79, 112-113, 119-22 : cf. 252, 255 ff. : see also *Natura naturata*.
Composite bodies, 83 *n.*1, 85-8.
*Conatus*, 77-8, 87 *n.*1, 191-3, 225 ff., 256 ; involves no *determinate* time, 192 *n.*4, 225-7 ; is the basis of all the Emotions, 206-8; and of all 'Virtue,' 268.
*Conscientiae Morsus* ('Disappointment'), 214.
*Consternatio*, 217-8.
*Contemptus*, 217, 279 *n.*2.
Contingency, and Finiteness, 52-5 : cf. 121, 168 : of Modes, 29-35, 47-50.
Contingent X Possible, 60 *n.*5, 259 *n.*7.

*Corpora simplicissima* ('elementary corpuscles'), 83 *n.*1.
Creation X Generation, 68 *n.*6.
*Crudelitas seu Saevitia*, 210 *n.*1.
*Cupiditas*, 193, 205-6, 227-36.

*Decretum Mentis = Determinatio Corporis*, 197-9.
*Dedignatio*, 218.
Degrees of perfection or reality, 73-4, 109-11 : cf. 298 *n.*4.
*Dei infinita idea*, 94-7, 114-5, 127, 148: cf. 223-5; *amor*: see *Amor*.
*Denominatio extrinseca*, 147 *n.*3.
Descartes, orthodoxy of, 61 *n.*3 ; his conception of Animals as Machines, 275 ; 'Animal Spirits,' 157, 281 ; 'Corporeal Matter,' 9, 30 *n.*1, 31 *n.*1, 85 *n.*1; Error, Sin, and Free-Will, 132 *n.*4, 194-9; Passions as 'confused ideas,' 204 *n.*1 ; Science and the Geometrical Method, 9-11 ; Substance, 21 *n.*1 ; the 'Seat of the Soul,' 281.
*Desiderium*, 213-4.
Desire : see *Cupiditas*.
*Despectus*, 212, 279 *n.*3.
*Desperatio*, 214.
*Deus* : see God.
*Deus sive natura*, 14 : cf. 36 *n.*2.
Devil, the, 248 *n.*1.
*Devotio*, 218.
Duration and Eternity, 29 ff., 121, 226-7, 294-8.

*Ebrietas*, 216.
Emotion : see *Affectus*.
Error (and Evil), 165-70, 238-54 : cf. 63 *n.*, 108 *n.*2, 121.
*Esse obiectivum* ( X *formale*) *ideae*, 6, 7, 71 *n.*1.
Essence and Existence, 95 *n.*1, 119-22, 221-5.
*Essentia*, defined, 26 *n.*1, 191 *n.*4 ;

## INDEX

*Dei actuosa=potentia*, 78; *formalis* × *obiectiva*, 6, 7; of things, an 'eternal truth'? 77 *n.*1, 120.
Eternal, an 'eternal truth,' 29, 57 *n.*2, 77 *n.*1, 120: cf. 297.
Eternity, =Self-dependence= Immanent Necessity, 57 *n.*2; and Duration: *see* Duration.
*Ethics*, early draft of the beginning of the, 18 *n.*5.
Existence, of Substance × that of Modes, 28 ff., 47-50; and Essence: *see* Essence.
*Existimatio*, 212, 279 *n.*3.
*Experientia vaga*, 163-5.
*Extensio*, 21 *n.*3, 22-4, 30-5: *and see* Attribute of Extension.

*Facies totius universi*, 87-8, 114.
Faculties = 'mere abstractions,' 132.
Fate, 59.
*Favor*, 210.
Final Causes: *see* Teleology.
Finite, the, = the contingent, 52-5; = that which is limited by another thing of the same kind, 23-5; is partly not-real, 79 *n.*2: cf. 251-4; paradox of, 143; *and see* Contingency.
*Fortitudo*, 219.
Free, the 'free man': cf. 268-80.
Freedom, an 'imaginative' idea, 169, 199; Spinoza's conception of, 141-4, 193-200, 227-34, 268 ff.

*Gaudium*, 214.
*Generositas*, 219.
Geometrical Method, 9-13, 115-9, 187-90: cf. 230-2.
*Gloria*, 216 *n.*2; *Dei*, 306.
God = Substance, 36-8; = *ens realissimum* or *perfectissimum*, 38-9; is *causa sui*, 53 *n.*1; 'subsists of infinite Attributes,' 38-41; exists of necessity, 45-58; excludes Negation (=*ens absolutè indeterminatum*), 39, 44, 104-7; is 'one,' 'unique,' 'whole,' 42-3; is 'simple,' 'indeterminate,' concrete,' 43-5; the *proximate* cause of everything, 81 *n.*; acts 'purposively,' 232-3; 'personal'? 144; 'self-conscious'? 72, 144-5: cf. 232; causality of, 58-64, 230-3: cf. 243-8; 'Essence' of='Power,' 65-6, 78, 191; 'Essence' and 'Existence' of = 'Eternal Truths,' 57; Eternity of, 28 ff., 297-8; Freedom of, 58-63: cf. 230-4; *Propria* of, 41-5; twofold causality of, 80-1: cf. 113, 118; idea of = the basis of philosophy, 9; our knowledge of, 39 *n.*5; Spinoza's conception of, in the TdIe, 8, 9; as conceived in the *Ethics*, is self-contradictory, 104-7, 118.
Good, a relative term, 3: cf. 241 ff.
*Gratia seu Gratitudo*, 209, 210 *n.*1.

Heereboord, *Collegium Logicum*, 58 *n.*5.
*Hilaritas* × *Titillatio*, 263 *n.*1, 278.
*Honestas*, 272 *n.*4.
*Horror*, 218.
'Humanity,' realization of = the Moral Ideal, 3-4, 241-53: cf. 179-80, 264-8, 300-3, 306-9: *see also* Moral Ideal.
Hume, 61 *n.*3.
*Humilitas*, 211, 279 *n.*2.
Huxley, quoted, 90 *n.*2.
Huyghens, Spinoza's letters to, 42 *n.*1, 44 *n.*2, 55.

Idea, and *Ideatum*, 6-8, 70-2, 138-

40, 146–52; alleged ambiguity in Spinoza's use of, 131 n.3 : cf. 237 n.2; 'adequate' X 'true,' 146–52; 'clear and distinct': cf. 150; =*intellectus*=primary mode of Thought, 70, 93–4; *Mentis*=*ipsa Mens*, 140; *infinita Dei* : see *Dei*.
Idea *Ideae*, Spinoza's conception of, 132–4, 138–41 : cf. 257 n.4; infinite process involved in, 7 : cf. 140–1; =*cognitio reflexiva*, 5.
*Ideatum* : see *Idea*.
Identity, personal, 125 n.1.
*Imaginatio*, 152–70; X *Imago*, 155 n.5.
'Immortal' (=Eternal), 295–6.
*Impudentia*, 216 n.2.
Indefinite X Infinite, 27–35.
*Indignatio*, 210, 279 n.2.
Individuality, degrees of, 125–32: cf. 141–4, 264–8, 292–4, 300–9; of 'particular things,' 76–80, 96, 175–7; of man, partly illusory: cf. 130, 140 n.1, 141 n.3, 265, 300–1, 306.
*Individuum*, 82–8.
Infinite, the, 27–35; Attributes, 39 n.5, 41, 69–70, 134–5.
*Infinitum actu*, 32.
*Intellectus* = primary mode of Thought, 70, 93–4; =*voluntas*, 132 ; X *memoria*, 230 n. 5 ; *infinitus*, 94 : cf. 114 ; *Dei*, 62–3, 71 ; *infinitus Dei* sometimes= *infinita idea Dei*, 94–6, 130 n.1. See also *Ordo*.
*Invidia*, 210, 279 n.2.
*Ira*, 209, 210 n.1, 279 n.2.
*Irrisio*, 218, 279 n.2.

Kant, his refutation of the ontological proof, 54–5.
'Knowledge of good and evil,' 256–61.

*Laetitia*, 204, 236; the 'active' emotion of, 218–9.
*Laus*, 216.
*Libertas* : see Freedom *and* Will.
*Libido*, 216 n.4, 263.
*Luxuria*, 216.

Maimonides, 61 n.1.
Measure (= *imaginationis auxilium*), 31–5.
Mechanical ( X Logical and Teleological) *nexus*, 230 n.5.
*Melancholia*, 279.
*Memoria* (=Association), 157–65 : cf. 230 n.5, 301.
Mendelssohn, 186 n.1.
*Mens* : see *Idea Ideae*, Mind, *and* Body.
Method, what, 5–9; principles of the most perfect, 8, 9; geometrical : see Geometrical.
*Metus*, 214, 217 n.1.
Meyer, Spinoza's letter to, 27–35.
Mind (the human) a complex of aggregates of *ideae*, 131, 138–41; a part of the 'infinite power of thinking,' 92–3, 125–30, 309; = the idea of the body, 24 : cf. 177–80: see also *Idea Ideae* and Body.
*Misericordia*, 211.
Modal apprehension, in part illusory 113 n.3; ground of? 112–3.
Modes = the dependently-real, 15–6 ; = particular things, 75; not mere 'illusions,' 15 : cf. 110 n.1; immediate infinite and eternal, 74–5 : cf. 88 n.3 ; mediate infinite and eternal, 75 : cf. 88 n.3 : see also Contingency, Duration, Existence.
*Modestia seu Humanitas*, 215 n.4, 219 n.2; = a form of *Pietas*, 272 n.3.

*Modi imaginandi*, 168-70.
Moral Ideal, common to all men, 271-2; =to know and love God, 270-1 : see also Humanity.
Moral Standard, the, 241-50.
Motion-and-Rest, 82-8 : cf. 63, 68 *n*.2, 69, 75, 96, 114.

*Natura naturans* and *Natura naturata*, 65 *n*.1, 107-13.
*Natura naturata* and the *communis ordo naturae*, 119-22, 221-5, 252.
Negation, excluded from God, 109-11 ; X Privation, 110-1 : see also God.
Nero, 249.
*Notiones communes* (κοινὰ ἀξιώματα), 172-5 ; = *fundamenta rationis*, 175 *n*.1; apprehended intuitively, 183.
*Notiones universales*, 161-4.
Number (*imaginationis auxilium*), 31-5.

*Odium*, 209, 279 *n*.2 : cf. 282-4.
Oldenburg, 18 *n*.5, 20 *n*.1 ; correspondence with Spinoza on the Tr. Th., 63 *n*.; on Whole and Parts, 89-93.
Ontological argument, validity of, 54-5.
*Ordo intellectus, ad intellectum*, 159 *n*.1, 171 *n*.1, 175 *n*.4.
Orestes, 249.

Parallelism : see Attributes.
'Particular Things,' 75-82 ; their *essentia* is an 'eternal truth,' 77 *n*.1 : cf. 120.
Passions : see *Affectus*.
Perfect and Imperfect, 239-41.
Personal identity, 125 *n*.1 ; is God personal ? 144.
Philosophy, Spinoza's conception of, 1, 180-1.

*Pietas*, 272 *n*.3, 285.
Plato, 305.
*Poenitentia*, 211, 216 *n*.2, 279 *n*.2.
Possible : see Contingent.
*Potentia Dei = Dei actuosa essentia*, 65-6, 78, 191.
Presentation, the world of : see *Communis ordo naturae* and *Natura naturata*.
*Propria* X Attributes, 41 *n*.2 ; knowledge of, necessarily adequate, 174.
*Pudor*, 216 *n*.2.
*Pusillanimitas*, 217 *n*.1.

*Quantitas*, 31 *n*.1 : and see, under Descartes, 'Corporeal Matter.'

*Ratio* (= *cognitio secundi generis*), 170-80; apprehends things *sub specie eternitatis*, 176 : cf. 178 ; its abstractness, 176-80.
Reason, the Life of, 268-80 ; the power of (over the Passions), 280-91.
*Religio*, 272.

Schopenhauer, 53 *n*.1.
Schuller, 70 *n*.2, 72 *n*.2.
Science : see *Ratio*.
*Scientia intuitiva*, 180-5 : cf. 175 *n*.1, 251-3, 299-303, 307-9; its intuition rests on inference, 182-4.
Secondary Qualities, illusory, 168-70; reduced to Primary by Descartes and Spinoza, 68 : cf. 85-8, 96, 114.
*Securitas*, 214.
Self-Consciousness, 234-6; cf. 309: and see *Idea Ideae*.
Sensation (K.V.), 128 *n*.3.
'Series rerum fixarum aeternarumque' (TdIe), 80 *n*.2 : cf. 173 *n*.2, 182 *n*.2.

## INDEX

*Signa* (=one source of *Imaginatio*), 163, 164 *n*.1.
*Sobrietas*, 216.
Socrates, 305.
'Sons of God' (K.V.), 82 *n*.1, 88 *n*.3. Soul, and Body, 125-32; essentially apprehends the Body, 94 *n*.1, 125 ff.: see also Body and *Idea*.
*Spes*, 214.
Spinoza, 'Atomism' of: cf. 141 *n*.3, 150 *n*.3; influenced by Bacon, 80 *n*.2: cf. 164 *n*.1; not a 'Fatalist,' 59 *n*.1; not a 'Mystic': cf. 233 *n*.1; his Physics, 82-8; his Political Philosophy, 276-8; his Psychology of Conduct, 186-219: cf. 227-37; his Theory of Knowledge, 146-85; his tendency to abstraction, 96-7, 115-9, 224-7.
*Sub specie eternitatis*, 176, 178.
Substance=the self-dependently real, 14-6; indivisible, 30; =*ens absolutè indeterminatum*, 44; 'one'? 21 *n*.2; unique, 28; the object of complete knowledge, 8, 15-6; prior to its states (Modes), 16-7: cf. 107; infinity, eternity and necessary existence of, 27 ff.; its unity not relational, 108: cf. 101; Descartes' conception of, 21 *n*.1.
Substance and Attribute, 17-27, 102-7.
Substance and Mode, 14-7, 107-19.
*Superbia*, 212, 279 *n*.3.
*Sympathia seu Propensio*, 213.

Teleology, 59-63, 169-70, 187-90, 228-34.
*Temperantia*, 216, 219.
*Termini transcendentales*, 160-1.

Tetens, 186 *n*.1.
Thing, a 'single,' 124-5, 191-3: and see Individuality.
Thought, 'wider' than Extension? 134-8; infinite process within, 135-6; modal system of, 93-7: see also Attribute of Thought, *Cogitatio*, and *Idea*.
Time (= *imaginationis auxilium*), 31-2: cf. 119-22, 168 *n*.2; its effect on the Emotions, 214, 258-9; Spinoza's account of its illusoriness is unsatisfactory, 226-7.
*Timor*, 217 *n*.1.
*Titillatio* × *Hilaritas*, 263 *n*.1, 278.
'Togetherness' of Attributes in God, 102-7.
*Tristitia*, 204, 236; no 'active' emotion of, 218-9.
Truth, degrees of, 151; its own criterion, 7, 149: see also *Idea*.
Tschirnhaus, his criticism of Spinoza, 70 *n*.2, 72 *n*.2, 134-6.

Uniqueness of God, 55.

*Veneratio*, 218.
*Verecundia*, 216 *n*.2.
*Vindicta*, 210 *n*.1, 279 *n*.2.
*Virtus*=*Potentia*, 268.
*Voluntas* (*Volitio*), 193 *n*.1; =*Intellectus*, 132.
Vries, Simon de, 18 *n*.5.

Whole, and Parts, 89-93; = *ens rationis* (*imaginationis*), 89.
Will, of God, 62-3; 'indeterminate' (Descartes), 194-6: see also Freedom.
Words, 164 *n*.1.

*Zelotypia*, 213-4.